THE
NAKED
PILOT
The Human Factor in   Aircraft Accidents

by the same author

Eagles
The Blood Brothers
Call Me Captain
Cone of Silence
Electric Train
Excellency
The Gun Garden
The Heart of the Storm
Milk and Honey: Travails with a Donkey
The Proving Flight
The Siren Song
Sword of Honour
The Take Off
The Temple Tree
Village of Stars
The White Sea-Bird
The Wind off the Sea
The Stick

non-fiction
The Human Factor in Aircraft Accidents
The Water Jump: The Story of Transatlantic Flight
Strange Encounters
The Complete Skytraveller

with Betty Beaty
Wings of the Morning

THE NAKED PILOT

The Human Factor in Aircraft Accidents

DAVID BEATY

Airlife

England

For, and with, B

Copyright © 1995 by David Beaty

This edition published in the UK in 1995
by Airlife Publishing Ltd
11th impression 2000

Previously published in hardback by Methuen in 1991

British Library Cataloguing-in-Publication Data
  A catalogue record for this book
  is available from the British Library

ISBN 1 85310 482 5

Printed by Livesey Ltd, Shrewsbury, England

Airlife Publishing Ltd
101 Longden Road, Shrewsbury SY3 9EB, England
Email: airlife@airlifebooks.com
Website: www.airlifebooks.com

Contents

List of Illustrations		vi
Foreword to Paperback Edition		vii
Acknowledgements		ix
Preface		1
One	The Man in the Left-Hand Seat	7
Two	Those Daring Young Men in their Flying Machines	21
Three	The Last Great Frontier in Aviation	27
Four	Communication	32
Five	To See and Not to See	45
Six	Deadly 'Set'	55
Seven	On Being Deceived	68
Eight	The Male Ego	75
Nine	Decision-Making	93
Ten	Learning and Regression	106
Eleven	The Clockwork Captain, or Deus in Machina	119
Twelve	Boredom and Absence of Mind	132
Thirteen	Conformity: the Three-Headed Hydra	148
Fourteen	Laterality: Green for Danger	170
Fifteen	Fatigue and Stress	186
Sixteen	Human Factor Education	204
Seventeen	Human Factors in Management	221
Eighteen	In the Echelons of Power	246
Nineteen	The Knock-On Effect	269
Twenty	Forward to the Last Great Frontier	280
Appendix		293
Glossary		297
Select Bibliography		299
Index		302

Illustrations

1a Balloonists' portable altimeter, c.1912 (Science Museum)

1b Airspeed indicator, 1910 (Science Museum)

2a The instrument panel of the Vimy, 1919 (Science Museum)

2b The cockpit of the Vimy (Science Museum)

3a Members of the ill-fated R101 project, 1930 (*Daily Mail*)

3b The control cabin of the R101 (*Daily Mail*)

4a A typical blind-flying panel, mid 1950s (Quadrant)

4b Comet I instrument panel, 1951 (Rediffusion Simulation)

5a Comet IV instrument panel, 1959 (Rediffusion Simulation)

5b Boeing 707 instrument panel, 1960 (Rediffusion Simulation)

6a Concorde panel, 1976 (Rediffusion Simulation)

6b Boeing 747–200, late 1970s (Rediffusion Simulation)

7a Boeing 737–300, mid 1980s (Quadrant)

7b Boeing 747–400, 1988 (Rediffusion Simulation)

8   The A-320 Airbus, 1990 (*Daily Mail*)

Foreword to the Paperback Edition

When the *Human Factor in Aircraft Accidents* first appeared in 1969, it was recognised in the Press worldwide as 'The first major attempt to pin down the human failings that caused planes to crash.'

However such human factor causes were resisted by aircraft manufacturers, airlines and the pilots themselves till the major disaster of Tenerife in 1977 when two 747s collided and 583 people perished. That caused elements of the aviation industry to begin to make tentative moves towards understanding the problem. By the time the hardback of *The Naked Pilot* was published in 1991, human factors were being researched and taught in psychology departments and airlines in Europe and America. Indeed the study and practice of aviation human factors was beginning to blossom into an industry.

Even so, there had been and still is understandable resistance to that study in that we all tend to deny making mistakes in a society that blames and demands heavy penalties from those of us who do make them, especially ones with huge financial implications such as those resulting in an aircraft accident.

Denial is a defence mechanism that is used by our society and frequently by ourselves as individuals to ensure its and our survival. It is dangerous to go against the grain of public opinion and the opinion of our masters. We might lose our jobs. We would certainly lower the esteem in which we are held. Even Darwin hesitated for years before publishing *The Origin of the Species* because of public opinion at that time, and kept a low profile on whether our similarity to the bodily characteristics of animals might in some way and to some degree be matched by a similarity to the ways animals think and feel and react.

Happily, in the last four years since *The Naked Pilot* was published, there has been significant progress. The age-old witch hunt to identify a scapegoat – usually the pilot – has begun to give way to the concept of the collective mistake. The practice of Cockpit Resource Management (CRM) has been twinned with Line Oriented Flight Training (LOFT), though even as late as 1992, only four airlines in America had integrated CRM/LOFT programmes.

Then human factor education courses have been started in some enlightened airlines. There is a human factor examination requirement in the pilot licence. Joint training of flight deck and cabin crews has started, to which one or two enterprising airlines have added despatchers, ATC and maintenance staff. In other words, the concept of all being in this together and all being responsible for the outcome has at last caught on. Hopefully management personnel will also be incorporated. ICAO has initiated a sustained campaign to increase awareness of the pervasiveness of human error in aviation amongst the middle and senior managers of the international aviation community, particularly in some regions where there is an even lower understanding of human factors than elsewhere in the world. A bomb resistant container has been designed. An explosive detector is being installed at Heathrow and Gatwick and will eventually be in place on all BAA airports. More and more glass cockpits are appearing in airliners.

What is still to be accepted is the commonality of the causes of mistakes that lead to accidents in all areas of human behaviour. Forgetting to switch the lights off before leaving a car may result in a flat battery. Forgetting a switch on an aircraft may cost dozens of lives. Airliners continue to collide both into each other and into the ground for similarly universal human factor reasons. There have been at least twelve Controlled Flight Into Terrain (CFIT) accidents with horrific loss of life since the beginning of 1992.

There is need to look at mistakes in a much wider context instead of in constrained and separated specialised enclaves with little communication between them. Too many separate individuals and organisations appear to be pursuing the same rabbit from different directions without realising it. Individual expertise in the different environments of air, sea, road, rail and ground are of course essential, but a connection between them and a cross-fertilisation of information on the pivot of a corporate understanding of human factors needs to be established and maintained if we are to progress deeper into the many different areas of human understanding. One such, which so far has been avoided, is how far personality is a factor in the making of mistakes – but this minefield eventually will have to be addressed.

That further progress is needed is self evident. The safety standards of a number of airlines, particularly in China and Russia, have sunk to unacceptable levels. Economic crises throughout the world have given rise to calls for cutting down on safety resources at a time when civil aviation is still expanding at around four per cent a year. The world's scheduled airlines lost nearly 16 billion dollars between 1990 and 1993. Aircraft manufacturers have had to cut back sharply on production. At the same time, a 1000-seater airliner (2000 seats in the military version) has begun to be planned, as has a larger replacement of the Concorde. The present high level of public confidence in air travel could suffer a severe set-back should a human factor disaster occur on a potentially greater scale than the Tenerife collision.

On the positive side, the aviation industry has now begun to realise the fundamental importance of human factor understanding. Boeing has just published *Accident Prevention Strategies* which advances the collective mistake theory. It reasseses 232 major accidents over the ten years to 1991 and identifies 37 individual links which could contribute to an accident.

Because of its intensive supervision and testing, its vast network of information exchange, its introspection and present excellent safety record, other industries such as the medical and nuclear are coming to aviation to learn about human factors.

What is needed is the establishment and maintenance of awareness in people of the potential of human factors for both triumph and disaster. Unless there is receptiveness, all instruction will fail to penetrate deaf ears.

Acknowledgements

In the writing of this book, I owe a debt to more people than there is space to name and thank – those who have talked to me, those who have helped me in other ways, and those whose books I have read.

But I would particularly wish to thank Captain Ken Beere, ex-British Airways, whose knowledge and insights have been vital for the book, and also to thank him and his wife, Bonny, for their time, skill and effort given unstintingly throughout, and finally to thank their daughter Jo for diagrams.

I would also like to thank Captain John Faulkner and Qantas for their generous help and co-operation. I am also grateful to Ronald Ashford, Group Director Safety Regulations, and Dr R. M. Barnes, Senior Medical Officer, Safety and Research, both of the CAA; Ken Smart, Deputy Chief Inspector of Air Accidents, AAIB; Captain Laurie Taylor, ex-Principal Vice-President and Executive Secretary of IFALPA; Captain Jack Nicholl, former General Manager British Airways Flight Training and ex-Principal of Oxford Flying Training School; Dr Roger Green of the Institute of Aviation Medicine; Captain Michael Stonehewer of Dan Air; Captain Alex de Silva of Singapore Airlines; Captain Heino Caesar, Lufthansa Flight Operations and Safety Pilot; Captain Edgar Klöppinger, ex-Lufthansa; Swissair; Pan American and United Airlines; the Commonwealth of Australia's Bureau of Air Safety Investigation, Captain Alan Gibson; and Bob Dignam and the *Daily Mail* who have again been generous with illustrations, as have Rediffusion Simulation.

Professor Norman Dixon, who first taught me psychology at University College, London, has continued to encourage and stimulate my interest in human factors. Professor Jim Reason of Manchester University, whose research into human error is known world-wide, has been most helpful. And I would also like to thank Professor Earl Wiener of the University of Miami, co-editor of the comprehensive *Human Factors in Aviation*, and of course my editors at Methuen, Ann Mansbridge and Alex Bennion.

I have learned a great deal from all my contacts, but I would emphasise that in this attempt to research and interpret human factors, the views, opinions, and human errors are mine alone.

Preface

On 29 September 1941, I flew one of three radar-equipped Wellingtons down the Portuguese coast to Gibraltar on the way to Malta for a tour of operations to make night interceptions of Rommel's convoys to North Africa.

On arrival at Gibraltar, we were told that a Wellington bomber ahead of us had turned right instead of left at the southern tip of Portugal and was now presumed lost over the Atlantic – apparently a by no means unique occurrence.

Why?

That was the start to my interest in human factors in aircraft accidents.

Throughout my time in Malta, aircraft coming from Gibraltar often landed in enemy Sicily. Aircraft returning from operations ran out of fuel and flopped into the sea. Extraordinary human errors were made in the planning and carrying out of war operations.

Back in England, I studied RAF intelligence reports full of little crosses where aircraft had crashed into mountains. I watched young inexperienced pilots take off 90 degrees to the runway or undershoot coming in to land. Pilots beat up the homes of their girl friends – and crashed. Pilots were continually forgetting to put down the undercarriage, ignoring the blare of the warning horn. At the height of the Battle of Britain, the head of Fighter Command, Air Marshal Dowding, goaded by the number of damaged Spitfires and Hurricanes, issued a signal to all stations that pilots who behaved in this way should be punished 'with the utmost severity'.

More aircraft were lost through accidents than by enemy action.

In BOAC after the war, I flew at first as a first officer with ex-Imperial Airways captains – many of them pleasant, some living up to their nickname of 'Barons'. Communication on the flight deck could be very strained. First officers did not contradict the captain or correct his mistakes. I had my hand smartly smacked when I leaned over the throttle box to put a captain's VHF on the correct switch after he had complained of not being able to hear anything. He would give the order, he said, when he wanted me to do anything. Otherwise I was to shut up and do nothing.

Although BOAC's safety record was good for the time, there were numerous incidents with icing and the piston engines had a tendency to fail over the Atlantic. The worldwide accident rate was ten times what it is now. Flights were long and laboured and fatigue began to be identified as a major problem. But there were other factors which I wanted to identify and study such as conformity, perception, decision-making – all factors that involved human error rather than pilot error; in other words, mistakes that are the result of our human condition rather than mistakes in piloting skill.

When I left BOAC to take up full-time writing, this then became my field of study and interest. It was about the human factors in aircraft accidents that I wrote, and the multiple causes – not just the simple 'pilot error' that was then being almost universally promulgated. Human factors cannot be *proved* as causes of accidents – but areas of possible error can be looked for, patterns perceived and action taken to prevent occurrences and recurrences.

A serious accident occurred in Prestwick when an aircraft was trying to land in bad weather. A verdict of pilot error was brought in by the Inquiry. The KLM captain wrote to me in great distress. There followed a number of letters from pilots who had been similarly blamed, including Captain Harry Foote, whose story is described in this book.

At this point, I felt the subject needed greater psychological insight, so I returned to university and took a Master of Philosophy degree at University College, London. Afterwards, I joined a joint Ministry of Aviation and RAF Institute of Aviation Medicine (IAM) team as the psychologist investigating aircrew workload. I incorporated the results of my researches in a book called *The Human Factor in Aircraft Accidents,* which was received in 1969 with great interest and, because it broke new ground, a good deal of incredulity. Never is tunnel vision seen more clearly than when you tell people they make mistakes – this, of course includes oneself.

One day, my daughter laid the table for breakfast. I noticed she had put the forks on the right and knives on the left. I expostulated to my wife. Next day, in a hurry, I set the breakfast table myself. This time it was I who put the forks on the right and the knives on the left.

I used this laterality confusion in *The Wind off the Sea* in 1962. Giles Gordon, the well known agent who was then judging for the Book Society, chose it rather than John Wain's *Strike the Father Dead.* Giles, I discovered later, had a similar laterality problem to my main character. So, I found later, had many other people. I found this laterality confusion in myself on numerous occasions. I remembered I had once put on right rudder when an instructor 'failed' the starboard engine on an asymmetric training exercise.

Now the problem of human factors in aircraft accidents – unfortunately *after* disasters – has begun to be addressed by airlines. The BBC became interested and in 1970 featured a programme on air safety on which I was invited to appear. In the usual cock-fight type of programme, opposing me was an airline captain and a BOAC doctor who had written a book on aviation medicine.

The first thing I saw when I walked into the studio was a black decapitated aircraft nose. To this monstrosity, David Dimbleby proudly introduced me with the words, 'At enormous expense, the BBC have hired this Trident cockpit, so you can sit in it and point out how easy it is to misread instruments and turn on wrong switches.'

I climbed inside. I had only been in a Trident once, but in those days aircraft instruments were pretty standard, and I wasn't particularly worried.

Then I started to look around – and was immediately horrified. I couldn't recognise a single dial, switch, lever or gauge. It was as though I was in some Wizard of Oz aeroplane with wonky numbers and crooked needles.

The cameras moved nearer. The programme was about to go on the air. I was wondering what on earth I was going to say to the watching millions, when suddenly I saw a knob on the instrument panel. Looking over my shoulder, the airline captain saw it too.

On the knob were the words 'Bomb Release'.

At once what I was looking at made sense. This was no Trident cockpit! This was a theatrical prop for some film!

Indignantly I climbed out, and the airline captain and I refused to have anything more to do with the thing.

The programme never recovered. I said pilots made various mistakes. The airline captain said they didn't. Every now and then the BOAC doctor chimed in to keep the peace.

Considerably shaken, I arrived at the hotel where I was staying the night. Room 53, the clerk said as he gave me the key. Up I went to the third floor, put the key into the door of room 35 – and couldn't turn it.

Indignant again, I went back to the clerk, who accompanied me – this time to the fifth floor, where he opened the door of room 53 without difficulty.

This confirmed what I had written about laterality in *The Human Factor in Aircraft Accidents*. But it was not just laterality errors that I found myself liable to make. I could make just about all the mistakes in the circumstances described in this book. And I am sure that many of us – if not most – are in much the same sort of boat.

Yet pilots in particular have to hide their mistakes. They think 'It's just me. I had better not let on. What would the management say?' So, not unnaturally, they deny their error liability lest the management think less of them or they lose their image of themselves.

There is no intention here of blaming individuals who make the mistakes described in this book, only of identifying areas of possible error. What I am trying to indicate is that it should be recognised that it is our human condition to make such mistakes, and that this state of affairs should be acknowledged. Some valuable way forward has certainly been made in 'owning up' to errors which are then publicised. But the pilots in these incidents still remain anonymous for fear of disciplinary action.

Until the normal human-factor aviation errors can publicly be admitted without fear of reprisals, recognised as a human condition and adequately researched, the causes cannot properly be diagnosed, nor the remedies discovered. The same sort of human-factor accidents will continue to happen, and what has been called 'the last great frontier in aviation' will remain unconquered.

One

The Man in the Left-Hand Seat

The twentieth century is the age of the machine – the most complex and ingenious of which are designed to take us off our planet earth. But at the heart of these almost unbelievably sophisticated creations is the thin-skinned perishable bag of carbon, calcium and phosphorus combined with oxygen and nitrogen, a few ounces of sulphur and chlorine, traces of iron, iodine, cobalt and molybdenum added to fat and forty litres of water – Man.

There he sits at the centre of this Aladdin's cave of scientific genius, the finger on the button, the tiny battery which will operate all this complexity. A complexity which has evolved with breathtaking swiftness in the last fifty years, into the study of which has been poured trillions of dollars, while Man has evolved with plodding slowness, and on the study of whom we grudgingly spend little, perhaps because we really don't want to know.

Whether we take the theological or the Darwinian origin of Man, or any other theory, he has come from the mists of time – the mists which one version of Genesis declares Yahweh (afterwards to be the God of Israel) used to moisten the clay to make the figure of a man, and into whose nostrils he then breathed life. Even before this Old Testament account, a Mesopotamian legend described a man formed of clay, wet with the blood of Bel.

The Darwinian theory denies Man's divine origin. Many scientists believe that we have evolved from a speck of life in the primeval swamps, though they argue about which came first; nucleic acids or proteins. And even before Darwin published his *Origin of Species* in 1859, researchers in Denmark had obtained proof that a cave-man, the contemporary of the cave-bear, had existed millennia before Bel was supposed to have mixed his blood with clay to produce that version of Man's origin.

To most people at that time, the idea of a very ancient man was absurd, and Darwin was appalled by the contumely with which his theories were greeted. Tempers ran high. In 1860 the famous duel between T. H. Huxley and Bishop Wilberforce took place, and the wife of the Bishop of Worcester is reported to have said, 'My dear, descended from the apes! Let us hope it is not true, but if it is, let us pray that it will not become generally known.'

But in spite of the protests, anthropologists now seem certain that we are cousins to the ape and the descendants of hominids who flourished over a million years ago: though from which of the several types of hominids we are sprung is open to question. Some American scientists once believed that modern Europeans were descendants of Neanderthals. Not so, say some British scientists: we came out of Africa, from a sub-Saharan Garden of Eden. Probably we are a mixture. Our genealogical tree has been described not as a straight palm bearing a proud crown which is Man, but as 'a tangled thorny and bristling bush'.

And it is an unpalatable truth that the chemical composition of our blood is the same as that of the ape, that we suffer from the same sort of illnesses and that modern Man's brain before birth is comparable to that of the ape, though Man's continues to grow in childhood until it is three times that of the ape, yet its ground plan remains essentially the same. As for another not too distant cousin, the chimpanzee, his IQ is an impressive 85. He is the only non-hominid to make tools and it is said that our possession of buttocks rather than the brain distinguishes us.

As Man and his forebears, it would seem, lived for millions of years in tundra and jungle conditions, it is natural to suppose that Nature would have endowed him to survive and prosper in those environments, and that we have inherited most of these endowments, many of them unsuitable for the technological environment we have created.

As these hominids spread further afield, they supplemented their root, berry and seed diet with meat – some of it their fellow hominids. Many of the ancient skulls that have been discovered were remnants of meals, the skulls smashed and the brains picked out. The origin, perhaps, of picking other people's brains, a practice which present-day man has enthusiastically embraced. A theory has been advanced that the swift growth of the brain in the Pleistocene era was a result of cannibalism – a selective cannibalism in which the brain was prized for its aphrodisiac qualities and which Oscar Mearth avers caused the brain to grow from a mere 400 cc to the 1,400 cc of Neanderthal man (the average *modern* man's is 1,360 cc).

In fact, Man has been defined by an eminent anthropologist as 'A primate who ate his own kind.' So, when he ate meat, Man had to learn to hunt and kill, and for that he needed not just to feel hunger but to feel aggression, and, just as importantly, to learn to control and channel that aggression. When he wasn't hunting his fellow hominids, he hunted bear, hyena, mammoth, elephant and sabre-toothed felines. Against these four-footed animals his upright carriage, an advantage in that it freed his hands, was a disadvantage in terms of speed. So he learned to sharpen flints, hurl them and make weapons, acquiring tactile skills and dexterity.

He used his voice to communicate with his fellow hunters. And although there is a theory that mankind could at one time communicate by thought transference, and that language is a retrogressive step, it is generally held that tool-making, language and our upright carriage are what distinguish us from animals. More importantly perhaps, he learned to take risks and to have swift, certain reactions when things went wrong. Nature supplied glands to secrete adrenalin and increase his heart beat and give power to his lungs and muscles instantly, and other glands to supply him with noradrenalin to help him escape or freeze into the camouflage of the landscape.

He learned to observe, to remember the habits of the game he hunted and, when he wasn't hunting, the attributes, poisonous or otherwise, of the leaves he ate. Like other animals, he soon found out that the shortest route between two points is a straight line. 'As the crow flies,' we say, treading a bold path across a manicured rectangular lawn. And while Nature made Man curious and therefore exploratory of unknown territory and new phenomena, he had to be very suspicious of novelty, of anything that was different or new.

Hunting in packs was easier and much safer than hunting alone, so gradually he began to fit into some sort of social group, to learn to be accepted by them, to form a pecking order and to defer to an authority figure like the Silverback (the group leaders) of his gorilla cousins. He learned to keep warm in caves and, perhaps most easily of all, to find a mate and propagate his own kind.

So how far have we advanced from the cave-man? Not so far, many people would say. Man's brain reached its present size more than 100,000 years ago. Strauss and Cave (the anatomists) have written of Neanderthal man: 'If he could be re-incarnated and placed in a New York subway – provided he were bathed, shaved, and dressed in modern clothing – it is doubtful if he would attract any more attention than some of its other denizens.' Similarly, could he slip on that four-gold-barred jacket without being recognised? What *should* be recognised is that characteristics inherited from him might well get inside that jacket and on to that aeroplane.

So how can modern Man deal with the aeroplane and other machine monsters he has created?

The machine, the technology, has advanced more in a hundred years than man's brain has in a hundred thousand. There is a certain terrible similarity between God breathing life into the nostrils of man, and the machine into which the tip of Man's finger breathes life. We all know what endless trouble

God had with His creation. Is it not time we studied how Man is coping with his?

For unlike the machine which has developed an even larger and more complex 'brain', Man has not been quite so fortunate. Anthropologists have developed a means of measuring the ratio of brain weight to body weight (from portions of early skeletons) and this they term the 'index of cephalisation'.

In normal healthy men, the ratio is approximately 1:50. This compares favourably with the male gorilla's ratio of 1:200. The sobering discovery, however, is that the estimates of ratio taken from prehistoric human remains shows no startling contrasts with that for modern Man. And though we know that mental capacity depends more on cortical connections than mere size, it is an interesting fact that mankind, though much better cerebrally endowed than other creatures, does not head the cerebral list.

Nevertheless, over the years that separate us from our earliest ancestors, our brains and memory stores have become larger and we have acquired more connections between nerve cells. What no one seems to know is when and how brains began to provide the ability to make errors. An early description of human error is Adam's eating of the apple in the Garden of Eden. And having committed the error, Adam, like his present-day descendants, knew he had to find a scapegoat – Eve.

But although mankind has acquired consciousness, more connections and a vast memory store, transmissions of information in and out of the brain, perhaps because of the divided lobes, remain comparatively slow – slower than is the case with some birds, who are in fact ahead of us in the cerebral league, where finches occupy first place. Perhaps Man's urge to fly is his reaching for the next step in the evolutionary process. There is an interesting diagram from Professor Langley, Secretary of the Smithsonian Institution in 1897, of the skeleton of a man and the stretched-out vertical skeleton of a bird. The similarity is remarkable

But whatever the basis of Man's urge to fly, it is Man who is the centre of the endeavour to be airborne and, like train drivers, sailors and all operators of transport, the pilot is a well-trained but ordinary human being. A human being with all the psychological endowments of his ancestry and his upbringing, with the added hazard of his need to adapt to this fast-moving up-to-date world.

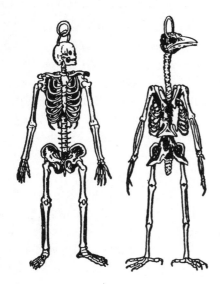

Man and Bird
*from Professor Langley's
article (1897)*

Like the rest of creation, mankind has slowly evolved biologically through changes in our genes over thousands of generations. Far faster has been mankind's cultural evolution. But now, particularly with the development of high technology like aviation, even our cultural evolution has become too slow. In our cultural evolution we have gained the ability to cause change at a hitherto undreamed-of speed, and both biological and cultural evolution are inadequate to adapt us to the environment we are creating.

Few environments can be as different from the natural world as the flight deck of an aircraft. Cut off from the earth and an earth-dweller's horizon, hurtling through another dimension, across time-zones, surrounded by machinery, monitoring dials and head-up displays, glued to his environment, moving with it (the world beyond probably muffled in cloud), the human being at the centre can alternate between long periods of boredom interspersed with the need for concentration, rapid decision-making and action.

So what is this particular human being like?

The airline advertisers, who have learned a little applied psychology, wisely portray him as a kindly, competent, grizzle-haired man (something of the Silverback of our cousins, the gorillas) and his calm friendly voice over the address system is in tune with this reassuring image. As Tom Wolfe puts it, 'the drawl of the most righteous of all the possessors of the Right Stuff'. Certainly the pilot is no longer seen as the daring young man on the flying trapeze or the dashing youngster driving his sports car to collect his latest conquest among the stewardesses. After all, he doesn't need to drive fast cars to project *his* macho image. For where is the car that can compete with the power of a big jet? The pilot would say that on the ground he is more likely to be found in the family Volvo on his way to the supermarket for the week's shopping. Today's Jumbo captain would see himself more as a James Herriot than a James Bond.

Psychologists tell us that there is an identifiable pilot personality, that he is most likely an intuitive extrovert, and that he is an active-masculine personality. Eysenck has presented pilots as above-average in stability in comparison with the rest of the population. Yet among commercial aircrew, psychiatric disorders are second only to cardiovascular disease as a cause of loss of licence.

Other writers have found pilots to be matter-of-fact, with strong needs for personal achievement and high regard for the responsibilities of family life, yet subject to excessive unconscious aggressive hostility related to frustrated achievement and the difficulty of reconciling their sense of responsibility with their need for novelty. Perhaps, in other words, coming to terms with both the family Volvo and their life on the big jets.

Aviation is still very much male-dominated, and for the purposes of this book it is the male pilot who is described, but there is no reason why women should not be just as good pilots as men. Yet men have resisted their move to the flight deck, as they have resisted every advance in women's equality.

When Amelia Earhart flew the Atlantic with Wilmer Stultz in 1928, men made snide remarks that she had simply been a piece of freight and that the Atlantic would certainly eat any woman who fought it on her own. She vowed to show them and in 1932, in a solo flight from Newfoundland to Londonderry, she did, going on to become one of the most illustrious aviators, along with Amy Johnson, Jean Batten, Beryl Markham and many other women. When the Second World War came, women did tremendous service with Air Transport Auxiliary (ATA), ferrying every sort of aircraft from Spitfires to four-engined Stirlings – only to be shut out of civil-aviation pilots' jobs when the war ended. (See Chapter 8.)

Although there is still a steady intake from the RAF, many pilots will have come in straight from school or university. They will have been educated to at least A-level standard and may well hold a degree. Few pilots will mention their desire to fly as a reason for their calculated decision. Being masculine and matter-of-fact, they would prefer to say that it was based on firm commercial calculations. Certainly, if a pilot had any illusions about the glamour of flying, these would probably be discarded within the first few weeks of flying training.

The granting of a licence is merely the first check upon his ability. Throughout his career he will be called upon to demonstrate to hard-bitten examiners his awareness of the latest regulations and his continuing ability to do his job to the highest standard. His performance during the twice-yearly simulator checks will by analysed no less critically than that of an actor playing his first Hamlet. If he survives, he prays that the doctors will pass him fit on his regular medical check. In return he will get a smart uniform, a great fillip to his self-esteem, an image in society, a good salary and the opportunity to sit up all night hunched over the aircraft controls in a cramped flight deck.

Few people meet the criteria demanded. Pilots are required to be averagely good at all things. Eliminate from the population at large all those who require spectacles, those suffering from minor medical conditions like colour blindness, young men who never went on to further education, those who couldn't steer a tram down a Roman road without hitting a tree, and the people who quite sensibly insist upon sleeping in their own bed at night, and there are precious few left to choose from.

From this group, there are few proven criteria of how to choose men and women who will remain cool and capable of making balanced judgments under trying circumstances, knowing that an instant decision taken at one hundred feet above a dark runway may well be analysed later at a four-hour meeting of desk-bound critics and found wanting. Personnel selection techniques have emphasised skills and basic intelligence. Such measures do fairly well at predicting early success in flying training, but most do no more than predict 25 per cent of variance in pilot performance at advanced stages of civil aviation training.

On the surface, the pilot is no different from most professional men and women, or from his fellow pilots. The variability of their control of any standard aircraft performance is slight. Yet, as Professor Roscoe points out, 'Giant differences among pilots are revealed as tension and confusion mount under operational stress.'

Understandably, most airline pilots want a quiet life. On the surface, a pilot might well, like Tolkien's hobbit Bilbo Baggins, say that he doesn't much care for adventures and that his ideal day is one in which he departs on time, arrives on time, and has a thoroughly routine and boring flight between the two events. After all, disruption can alter his work pattern for up to a month, causing him to miss his son's sports day or his daughter's eighteenth birthday.

If all four engines on your B-747 stop, as happened to a pilot when the power units were clogged by volcanic dust, the internal alarm stimulus is to act immediately. But Lufthansa warns its pilots 'the chance of saving the day by spontaneous reaction is extremely remote, the chance of catapulting yourself into deepest trouble is very high'. Yet immediate response to a dangerous stimulus has been inbuilt in Man through his ancestors for millions of years, and often the most difficult decision he has to make is to do nothing. As he sits at the airport, watching other aircraft depart in weather conditions he considers unsafe, he will be under enormous pressure to follow suit against his better judgment. Some of his own passengers, given the chance, would encourage him to take off. It has always been a source of wonderment to pilots that many travellers would much prefer to risk violent death than be half an hour late. The maxim 'Better be half an hour late in this world than a quarter of a century early in the next' falls on deaf ears. And yet, though the pilot wonders at it, under certain stresses he may well succumb to the very same innate, unreasonable time pressure. Accident records show all too often that under the pressure of the need to clear the runway, the need to get the aeroplane positioned somewhere else, the need to get away before the weather further closes or flight limitations ground him, the pilot takes off.

For though the routine and ordinary take place for so much of the time that few pilots now will ever see a crash, and some will complete a career without ever experiencing an engine failure, it is on the rare, stressful and dangerous occasions that the pilot reveals the presence or absence of those necessary qualities which as yet no test can predict. The important thing is what lies below the surface of the apparently good-humoured, matter-of-fact man with the four gold bars who, if you asked him what he thinks of his job, would probably answer 'It's better than working for a living.'

In other words, what does the man in the smart uniform who climbs aboard the aircraft carry in his 'luggage', as the counsellors call it – and by luggage they don't mean his overnight bag or briefcase. They mean the weight of his problems past and present, his personality, his hopes and fears and aspirations. Most of all, his psychological hang-ups and how they all relate to his biological inheritance, as he travels across time zones with a group of people he may not have met before.

Man's ancestors, the apes, are divided into chimpanzees, gibbons, gorillas and orang-utangs. Male chimpanzees are polygamous and opportunistic – they tend to mate with whichever female comes into season. Gibbons, however, establish a pair-bond relationship that often lasts for life; they are familial and mutually supportive, with brothers sometimes living together, or father and son. In a gorilla group, the Silverback, the dominant male, has his pick of the females, though he may show special favour and develop a more lasting relationship with one or maybe two. Orang-utangs are solitary, or at most a unit consisting of a female and maybe one or two children, to which group adult males pay occasional visits. Early Man formed a pair-bond relationship and, give or take periodic aberrations, mankind has followed in his footsteps. But the airline pilot leaves his wife at home and travels across the world accompanied by a bevy of pretty girls who are in a subservient role to him. In the implicit hierarchy, he is the big chief. If there is any trouble or danger big chief, or Silverback, is the one who should, and most probably will, get them out of it. This is a subtle relationship fraught with marital danger. And even if there isn't actual danger, it is also fraught with imagined. For a number of airline wives were themselves stewardesses and, stuck at home with the children, it is easy for the imagination to paint lurid pictures. The old adage of what's sauce for the gander is sauce for the goose can be the justification for what follows.

Besides which, it is genuinely difficult to unwind and sleep after flying. Too much adrenalin is circulating. The pilot is experiencing too many of our ancestors' fight or flight mechanisms. He has made the long journey but what is at the end of it? The brain and body don't just quietly switch off. If he can't knock someone down, or pursue a sabre-toothed tiger through the forest, sexual activity will reduce tension and therefore predispose towards sleep. It used to be said that after long flights the only way to get some rest was through drink, drugs or sleeping with the stewardess. Implicit in that advice is the chauvinistic attitude that the woman who travels in the male's entourage is his special perk. If the cave man took a woman on his hunting trips, he would no doubt forget the pair-bond relationship even more easily.

But sleeping is not the end of the pilot's problems or even the beginning of a marital one. Most pilots have a well-developed ego and a strong sex urge. Many pilots, especially military, subconsciously equate flying with sex. Nor is it always sub-conscious. The aircraft has a phallic shape. The bawdy songs of the RAF and the even bawdier ones of the USAF equate their aircraft with a woman, their bombs with sperm.

Flying is a sexual symbol; flying dreams are held to be about sex. Therefore it is understandable that a pilot's professional and sexual worries intertwine. Ironically, many pilots find that flying has a deleterious effect upon their sexual performance. Lord Trenchard's well-known dictum, 'Remember, gentlemen, you cannot fuck and fly', has a way of becoming too horribly true. And that is an added strain on a marriage, an additional piece of evidence to a suspicious wife and an added feeling of inadequacy and loss of personal image. What, asks the pilot, if I can't land the aeroplane *either*?

And what of all his other worries: family illness and squabbles, bereavement, thwarted ambitions, jealousies, possible divorce proceedings, custody, ageing parents? All these clamber aboard with him, some ameliorated but most exacerbated by his absence. And all these add to his stress.

Because of higher than average physical requirements for entry and regular medical checks throughout his career, the pilot should enjoy a higher than average life expectancy. Yet the results of a survey by the International Federation of Airline Pilots Association (IFALPA) on the fate of 282 Argentinian, Canadian and British pilots who retired in the last decade shows otherwise. Nearly 60 per cent had died before reaching the age of 65, and 129 of these had died between the ages of 55 and 64. The main cause was heart disease.

Since the pilot is central to the safe operation of the flight, how much has he been studied?

The reply is, in my view, 'Not enough'.

The emergence of psychology is like that 'tangled, thorny and bristling' bush used to describe the emergence of Man himself. Springing from the respected discipline of philosophy, and despite such giants as Freud and Jung and James, it has suffered a crisis of identity, a lack of self-image as disturbing as that which its proponents have discovered in the humanity it studies. Scientists of other disciplines have only reluctantly and lately acknowledged it as a science, and in an endeavour to be scientific some psychologists in the middle of this century retreated to the laboratory, confining themselves to experiments on long-suffering rats, ignoring the real world and the rich fields of study of humanity in the workplace and under the stress of the technological age.

This has changed and the change is accelerating. Throughout the world some exciting psychological studies are being carried out.

What isn't changing so quickly is distrust of psychology. And although it is acknowledged that we cannot make sense of the world until we have made some sense of ourselves, much of what psychology uncovers, though in the long run vital, can in the short term be damaging to Man's lofty image of himself – an image hedged around with defence mechanisms.

Yet never did Man so urgently need the help of psychology as in his dealings with the explosion of technology. And though warnings were given decades ago, only after a spate of disasters such as Three Mile Island, Zeebrugge, Tenerife, Chernobyl, Bhopal, King's Cross, Lockerbie, Piper Alpha and Kegworth has the urgent need to study Man's mistakes in his technical environment really been acknowledged.

Of course two world wars, like those disasters, helped to facilitate the entry of the psychologist into the workplace, and especially the aviation workplace. Both sides needed to know what made up a good pilot because they were expensive to train and aircraft were scarce. Many of the tests dreamed up were bizarre or inadequate. But beginnings were made; the problem was being addressed.

And what made psychology more popular was that money could be made out of it. Workers would produce more goods in certain environments, and advertising was more successful if it used an approach informed by psychology. It can be used to manipulate the public by touching on their insecurities – 'have I bad breath, dandruff, sweaty feet?' – to buy and buy. And it is assumed that what makes money can't be wholly wrong.

Yet what saves lives is far more vital. Many airlines are at long last acknowledging that pilot error is a misnomer and that errors are due to human factors, and by no means always in the pilot. This last they acknowledge less readily, but acknowledgement of that will eventually come as it did with human factors. The fact that the pilot is sitting in the hotseat at the apex of the operation simply makes him more vulnerable to error, his own and other people's. Airlines will also need to realise that his error, if he makes it, is probably the culminating one of a sequence, and that before airline flying is made even more safe, there is still a long way to go, much to be investigated and a number of defence mechanisms to be broken down.

For the environment in which civilized man lives has changed out of all recognition. Yet he knows very little about himself, and to the complexities of technology he still brings to bear many of the qualities better suited to his earlier environment – sometimes with disastrous results. In no other field of human endeavour can this be seen more clearly than in Man's exploration of that totally new element – the sky.

Two

Those Daring Young Men in their Flying Machines

Man's attempt to conquer the sky was greeted with the same disbelief and hostility encountered by Darwin's theory of evolution – and it took aeons longer than is generally recognised. If Lucy (*Australopithecus afarensis*), the half-complete hominid skeleton fossil discovered by Donald Johanson and his colleagues in Ethiopia, had wanted to fly with Orville Wright in the first aeroplane near Kitty Hawk, she would have had to extend her life by about 3,700,000 years before becoming *homo sapiens* and for a further 300,000 years after that. A very old lady by this time, she would have been relieved to find that she would have to wait only another eighty-five years before being able to take a flight in an Airbus A320.

Despite the fact that dreams of flying had occupied the consciousness of Man for thousands of years, despite attempts in almost every society in almost every century to become airborne, it was declared to be at best impossible, at worst a sin.

His fall when he did attempt to fly was equated with Man's fallen nature, and it was therefore a blasphemy to try to become airborne. Flying was witchcraft, a work of the devil, on occasion punishable by death. But legends of flying persisted: Daedalus and Icarus, Capnobates who travelled by smoke, and Emperor Shun who five thousand years ago escaped his captors by flying away in the feathers of an obliging bird. While Church and public mocked or menaced, for thousands of years intrepid would-be aviators jumped off cliffs, spires and roofs from China and Japan to Constantinople and Egypt, while the legendary

King Bladud, king of Britain in 863 BC, egged on by sycophantic courtiers, attempted to fly from the Temple of Apollo in what is now London with 'wings that would not have held a cherub'.

But all the birdmen exhibited a quality that every early pilot needed – the ability to take risks and discount other people's disbelief. Then came Leonardo da Vinci (1452–1519) and the real birth of aeronautics. It has been said that Leonardo's absorption with flying was 'the most tremendous, most obsessing, most tyrannical of his dreams'.

It continued to obsess many other people. In the nineteenth century there were the Montgolfier brothers with their balloons, the glider Otto Lilienthal, and Sir George Cayley who designed an aircraft with forward thrust as well as lift.

Then the twentieth century – this age of aviation – dawned. But still the sceptics said, 'Impossible'. *The Times* in a leading article in 1900 thundered that heavier-than-air flight was engineeringly impossible. The would-be airmen still continued.

And in 1903, success! The Wright brothers managed to become airborne and maintain height for a distance of 120 feet. Were the disbelievers confounded? Not at all. They didn't believe it. The news of the Wright brothers' achievement did not break on the world with the thunderclap you would now expect. Only two papers mentioned it. One was the *Daily Mail*, and that in a two-inch report at the bottom of a column headed 'Flight of a balloonless airship'. The other paper? The *Beekeeper's Journal*.

The American government refused to buy the Wright brothers' patent, so they offered it to the British government for £10,000. Our disbelieving government flatly turned the offer down.

Two years later, the French produced an aeroplane, flown sixty metres in 1906 by Santos-Dumont. They would not believe that the Wright brothers' 'real' aeroplane existed until in 1908 Wilbur brought it over to a race-track at Le Mans. French and English newspapers declared him a fake, and said that his aircraft would not get off the ground. From 8 April 1908 to 2 January 1909, Wilbur flew a hundred flights in France, one of which lasted over two hours. Even so, the disbelief continued. *The Times* offered a prize of ten million pounds to the first man to fly an aeroplane over London, in the sure belief that it would never have to pay up.

Then the American Samuel Cody burst upon the British scene. Although he could neither read nor write, in 1908 he built and piloted the first aeroplane to leave British soil. Nobody gave him the money. He earned it by staging Wild West melodramas in local theatres. All his family were the cast, his sons rode horses down the aisles on to the stage, his wife hung from stage precipices and Cody himself alternated between the villain firing pistols and the hero doing the rescuing.

He too was laughed at by the press, derided as a charlatan. But the laughter died down when King George V gave him his friendship and approval and asked him for demonstrations. Even so, official disbelief continued. As war clouds developed over Europe, the Secretary of State for War declared that the government 'do not consider that aeroplanes will be of any possible use for war purposes'.

It was individuals again who bought four aeroplanes and gave them to the Navy. They allowed officers to learn in them with the proviso: 'No flying on Sundays'.

So the Royal Naval Air Service was begun.

The year 1914 came, and the Great War. Governments began to perceive that there might after all be a military advantage in aircraft. But they were seen rather as winged horses. Indeed the ability to ride a horse was considered the primary qualification for pilot selection. A good pair of hands is still reckoned the mark of a good pilot. And during the First World War, fighting in the air was conducted more along the lines of knights jousting. But the war gave a great fillip to the progress of flying (Britain finishing up with 22,647 aeroplanes) and the Royal Flying Corps became the Royal Air Force. Flying was an acknowledged reality. The air, it seemed, had begun to be conquered.

However, the pilots in their explorations were finding that the sky was even more dangerous than anybody had supposed. It was not just that aircraft broke up and engines failed – hazards that pioneers like Pilcher, Cody and Rolls had cheerfully accepted and died in their brave researches. The sky packed all sorts of unexpected punches to which pilots through the years would be exposed, and which would be fatal to many. Yet they went on. In the pioneer Pilcher's dying words, 'sacrifices must be made'.

Cold froze the fingers of the early pilots – the electric suits designed to keep them warm burned their hands. Though parachutes existed, no pilots were issued with them lest they abandoned their aircraft too soon. Altitude caused lowering of the atmospheric pressure and of oxygen levels, lack of which would eventually cause disorientation and death. The slipstream blinded pilots' eyes, and they were poisoned by carbon monoxide from the exhausts. Unlike birds, which have the right internal instinct to stay on the ground at night or in fog, they were to find it almost impossible to judge attitude (position relative to the ground) without a horizon. Ice was an appalling danger, stopping engines, overloading fuselages, spoiling the aerodynamic qualities of wings. Certain clouds could break up aircraft. If turned or pulled up too quickly at too high a speed, the normal pull of gravity (G-force) is increased many times, resulting in injury or unconsciousness. Air sickness could be crippling. As the years went by, more and more unexpected hazards were to appear – among the latest being a microburst.

This is a very strong downdraught approaching the ground and producing an outflow of tremendous winds and downflow. Usually small in area, it lasts only a few minutes but is highly dangerous, particularly for an aircraft on take-off or landing. A large downburst lasting from five to twenty minutes is called a macroburst. Both were only identified around 1980. In 1982 153 passengers and crew were killed in a 727 taking off from New Orleans. Another fatal accident occurred to a Tristar at Dallas in 1985, when 133 people were killed or injured. Pilots are now trained in the simulator on how to deal with a microburst.

Casualties among the early pioneers had been large, but amongst the Great War pilots they were enormous. It would be nice to think that doctors and governments came forward to help pilots in their struggle to live in the sky, but the fact is that aviation medicine was born because the cost of replacing so many crashed machines was considered too expensive, and some form of selection of airmen had to be made.

The Germans were the first to establish a Medical Section to test their Air Force candidates − not only medically but (surprisingly) psychologically, giving them a test on 'attentiveness, memory, quickness and sureness of movement, capacity to withstand fatigue, timidity, orientation and discrimination'.

The British continued to select on the ability to ride a horse, and in the event of an accident made the pilot, if he survived, take to the air again, resulting too often in the man losing not his nerve but his life. Only a Royal Army Medical Corps (RAMC) corporal was attached to a squadron, and the wounded from the trenches were recruited to augment the depleted ranks. When eventually examining stations were set up under Major Flack, the principle selection tool was the 'Flack Bag', purporting to discover the ceiling to which a candidate could ascend without oxygen. The figure sought was 20,000 feet − yet everyone requires oxygen at 12,000. This test continued for years, and was one I had to pass to be selected for the RAF at the beginning of the Second World War. Unfortunately, it gave pilots not only the belief that they could fly at such heights, but that men who could not were cissies.

The French system of testing would-be pilots was almost as lunatic. They tested for 'nervous shock', firing a revolver close to a candidate's ear and examining his reactions.

American doctors concentrated on the function of the vestibular apparatus in the ear, under the belief that it orientated the flyer in the air as on the ground. One test was to place a candidate on a piano stool and spin him. If he vomited, he was rejected. It was not until after the war that they discovered that they were rejecting the normal. As with the Flack test, the myth caught on amongst airmen (and persisted for ten years after the Armistice) that a man who could not maintain attitude without a visible horizon in fog or at night was no good as a pilot – a belief that resulted in hundreds of deaths from spinning in.

The formula that guided the American aeronautical organisation was that of all flying casualties 2 per cent were caused by 'the Hun', 8 per cent by 'failures of the engine or the plane' and 90 per cent by the 'failure of the flyer himself'!

And so was born the highly convenient catch-almost-all concept – pilot error.

Three

The Last Great Frontier in Aviation

So what is pilot error?

This inaccurate and unfair verdict arose for two main reasons. First was the indecent haste we all feel to attribute an accident to something, to find an outlet for our grief and dismay, to blame somebody – in other words to find as mankind has done down the ages, a scapegoat. We want to be assured that it won't happen again and, more importantly, that it won't happen to *us*. The second reason lay in the implicit belief that flying as a skill was very difficult.

Yet very few accidents attributable to airline pilot error are as a result of errors in flying skill. With the advent of simulators and excellent training programmes, piloting errors have become rare. As aircraft became stronger and more reliable, mechanical causes of accidents fell sharply. Nearly all civil aircraft accidents are due to simple mistakes and errors which arise out of our human condition and are common to each and every one of us, in varying degrees and at varying times. So is a pilot more or less likely to make them than we who ride behind him in the passenger compartment? Certainly he is more frequently exposed to the *risk* of making such errors.

If and when the pilot does make that human error, it won't be in isolation. It will more than likely be the culminating one of a series of errors made by other people. Perhaps as small as the straw that broke the camel's back, perhaps a much larger one. But the likelihood is that there will already be errors in the system upon which his error puts the final seal. And those errors already in the aviation system of which he is the apex will be *human* ones.

Slowly, in the case at least of pilots, this is beginning to be accepted. And though the RAF still use the term and the media splash it about indiscriminately when there is an aircraft accident, pilot error in informed aviation circles is very gradually being dropped.

Now with the belated acceptance of human error, the question is: 'What human errors?' How do we sort out and identify them? And are there some to which the pilot is particularly prone?

The psychologists Billings and Reynard have termed the problem of human errors 'the last great frontier in aviation'. What seems clear is that most of the tendencies to error run into one another. Like the limbs of the human body which they are so firmly planted within, human factors are separately defined, but they are mutually supportive and difficult to separate. For the purposes of clarity, in this book human factors will be separated. And in the following chapters a number of human factors will be identified in a number of aircraft accident scenarios.

It seems clear that many of these errors arise from our biological inheritance, from the very valuable mechanisms which helped us to survive in a primitive environment, and which have now become something of a liability; and though the pilot is no more *prone* than anyone else, he is more *at risk* of making errors, because he has been catapulted ahead of the field into a more frustrating and unforgiving environment.

For most of us, the world today is by no means an ideal environment for our biological make-up. In many ways it is a strait-jacket. We possess attributes and skills we don't have an outlet for, and many more that have gradually atrophied for lack of use. The basic drives of hunger, thirst, sex, for domination and for shelter we cope with, and indeed enlarge upon. Hunger, thirst and sex have to be constantly titillated so that they can be more and more exotically and expensively satisfied, and few people would be content with a centrally-heated cave for a shelter. Advertising sees to the creation of ever new needs and the ever more expensive satisfying of them.

But we don't need to hunt and kill our food or physically capture our mates, so the aggression we needed for these activities, if not consigned to the depths of our seething sub-conscious id or canalised into sports, augments the ego and helps create the macho image. Society smiles on this. We talk of an aggressive businessman, salesman, lawyer, politician – in terms of approval. The male pilot, too, has his fair share of aggression. He is a masculine type. On a list of adjectives in which the first officers described their captains, 90 per cent of the terms related to aggression, authoritarianism or egotism. There is also a fair sprinkling of such epithets in how the captains see their first officers. So the aggression, or the perception of it, is probably two-way.

But studies of accidents have shown that another human factor is constantly observed in first officers, frequently with fatal results – that of conformity, or the desire to please. Our ancestors learned early on to band together for safety and sustenance, to rub along easily with the next hominid and to defer to the leader. We find it very difficult to slough off a habit arguably millions of years old.

If conformity is a habit, however, a healthy animal curiosity seems to be in the very marrow of our bones. It is at its best a life force, a learning device, an inducement to explore, try harder, look further, find juicier berries – and is at the heart of every invention. But it is stifled by what primitive man rarely knew, and what is probably a luxury of civilisation but a pilot's burden – long periods of inaction which induce inattention and boredom.

Curiosity attempting to alleviate boredom has caused fatal flying accidents. Boredom on its own has led to inattention, to simple slips and caused yet more fatalities.

One attribute which man's natural curiosity sharpened was a particular sort of vision. Unfortunately for pilots it was not the all-round vision possessed by birds, so a definite drawback in the sky, and one to whose severe limitations psychologists are addressing themselves. At one time it was supposed that we all saw what was in front of us. If a pilot had another aircraft in front of him for x seconds and he didn't see it, then of course it was a pilot error. But any man or woman in the street could have told the experts differently. We have all hunted around for what we have subsequently found was 'staring us in the face'. The reason why is explored in Chapter 5, on Perception, where we see how, in the unforgiving environment of the air, such momentary lack of seeing can spell disaster.

So many of these errors, safe on earth, are harmless, almost lovable failings. Most people have reversed telephone numbers or turned to the left when they should have turned right. But in an aircraft, having a laterality problem, mixing your left and right, can kill.

So too can another human factor to which we, like many animals, are prone. In the face of fatigue, or sudden danger, we tend to regress. Children under stress regress to thumb-sucking, bed-wetting and anti-social behaviour. Curling up in the foetal position is a well recognised form of regressional behaviour. In difficult circumstances we reach for a drink, chew sweets, light a cigarette – all substitutes for our mother's comforting breast. And in the sudden shock of an oncoming car, many people revert to the action they would have taken in the previous car they drove. Accidents are documented where pilots have done exactly this in aircraft.

Fatigue and sudden danger release many of the tendencies which lie beneath the conscious mind. Fatigue in pilots has been studied and written about, flight-time limitations have been introduced, and yet we seem little nearer to understanding it. We all know what it feels like to be tired. 'But is feeling tired being fatigued?' the pundits ask. The problem is as inescapable as it is intractable. What is also inescapable is that most aircraft accidents occur in the landing phase – at a time when it is likely that the pilot will be tired.

We are all creatures of a certain sort of time. Not the time on our wrist watches or on the airline timetables, but of a natural rhythm which we and the natural world share. We are part of the cycle. Our bodies are cyclical. Primitive man lived not just by night and day, but by the moon phases and the seasons and the rhythms of his own body. What effect, then, does hurtling regularly across time-zones have upon the anthropoid within? How does his mind and body react to sleep deprivation, the interruption of his diurnal rhythm, his eating patterns? Can he think and act as competently? The answer is simple. We don't know.

What we do know is that one of our oldest and arguably most abused endowments, that of communicating with one another, is of paramount importance on the flight deck. In common with the rest of the animal kingdom, we used to communicate with clarity and purpose. 'Only connect,' says E. M. Forster. The cry has been echoed down the centuries. Communicate. Yet despite, or maybe because of, all the communications media, we communicate less and less on any significant level.

We know that communication is of desperate importance on the flight deck. Courses on how crew should communicate with one another have become a thriving concern. Yet 'failure to communicate at all levels' figures in the reports on accident investigations, and cockpit voice recorders (CVRs) taping the last seconds before disaster show the pilots' chilling inability to say the words that might save them.

It is in an effort to probe the human factors involved and to communicate some of their effects that the ensuing chapters have been written.

Four

Communication

Perhaps in one respect primitive man had the edge on his pilot descendant. His ability to communicate was probably a good deal more simple, immediate and pointed. It is likely that primitive man's hearers got the message through their ears, eyes or noses, and replied with speed and clarity. There is a school of thought that language, especially nowadays, serves more to obfuscate rather than inform. The truth seems to be lost amidst palatable euphemisms for things we can't face, hesitant mono-syllables for sentiments we can't express and grunts for things we don't want to know, with a lot of technical jargon thrown in which we can't understand. Our society is rapidly losing the ability to communicate. Tongue-tied by television and com-munication automation, words literally fail us. We might well go back to the old days of having professional scribes to write our letters had we not a jolly picture card for every occasion which we can put into the hand of the recipient to express joy, sorrow, love, congratulation, commiseration in every conceivable situa-tion and relationship.

Again and again, in spite of safety communication procedures between airlines, aircraft manufacturers and aviation authorities, these have gone unheeded. Canada and KLM knew about the problems of slush on the runway (Chapter 18) and had circulated airlines, but BEA took no notice – which resulted in the 1958 Munich disaster. An Elizabethan aircraft failed to take off because of slush on the runway, hitting a house and killing many of the homebound Manchester United football team.

A month before the Washington Bridge accident in January 1982, when an ice-laden Boeing 737 ploughed into the crowded bridge on take-off (Chapter 9), a similar accident caused by ice affecting registered engine power had occurred at Gander, Newfoundland, and been reported.

Cases of the defective DC-10 door had happened and been reported before the door fell off and the floor collapsed on a Turkish DC-10 near Paris in March 1974, killing all 301 people on board (Chapter 17).

But it is not always the administrators who are at fault. The pilots themselves do not sufficiently report when they have problems. After the Beechcraft crash at Spokane in 1981, when the pilots misread the Distance Measuring Equipment (DME) so they were over four miles out of position on approach (Chapter 15), five pilots contacted the Safety Board's investigation team to say that they had been involved in similar procedural errors during the Spokane localiser-3 instrument approach using DME. They stated that they did not report the incidents because each was too embarrassed and each believed that his own was an isolated incident. These included a USAF instructor instructing an experienced pilot who made the error on a hot day at the end of a tiring flight. Many others, civil and military, expressed confusion over the procedure – but none reported it.

An Aviation Safety Reporting System (ASRS) had been introduced in 1977, requiring that all such incidents should be reported to the National Aeronautics and Space Administration (NASA) on a confidential basis. Most of the pilots were not aware of the system and did not know where and how to file ASRS reports. The CAA also introduced Mandatory Occurrence Reporting (MORs). The system was taken up by Roger Green, top psychologist at IAM, under the highly successful Confidential Human Factors Incident Reporting Programme (CHIRP). This issues regular confidential accounts of the incidents reported to them; these have had a wide circulation for the past eight years.

On the flight deck, communication does not flourish. 'Communication is our most urgent problem,' said Captain Heino

Caesar, addressing the 42nd International Air Safety Seminar in November 1989.

The two or three people meeting together within the small confines of the cockpit may never have flown with each other before. Something that has remained strong throughout our evolutionary descent has been mistrust of strangers. We are uncomfortable with them, especially if we are not allowed the sniffing-over time which our ancestors would certainly have demanded. In all walks of life we need time to get used to our workmates, a warming-up period to familiarise ourselves with people we don't know.

When the pilots do get to know each other, their personalities might well be antipathetic. There might be a generation gap, and if there isn't there is the fact of implicit hierarchy. None of this makes for easy communication. And if it takes time for the ice to be broken and to become comfortable with workmates, it takes much longer before the crew can anticipate each other's reactions, weigh their strengths and weaknesses, and assess how far they can go with them, and whether it is safe or not to criticise, disagree or offer an opinion.

But of all the human factors, communication seems to be one of the few that some airlines feel able to begin addressing. The operative words are 'some' and 'begin'. It would be difficult for any airline to deny that in many accidents over the years lack of communication has spelled disaster.

In 1980, the captain of a Dan Air B-727 was given an ATC clearance to the Foxtrot Papa outer marker for an ILS descent to Tenerife airport, no delay expected. Then suddenly he was told by the controller, 'The standard holding over Foxtrot Papa is inbound heading one five zero, turn to the left, call you back shortly.'

This holding had not been published. The clearance was non-standard and therefore more difficult to understand. The crew, aware of other traffic and interrupted in preparations to make an immediate ILS letdown and landing, had difficulty visualising it. Nevertheless, the captain immediately acknowledged with, 'Roger, Dan Air 1008.'

Fifty-six seconds later the captain reported, 'Level at six zero, taking up the hold.'

It is considered a sign of efficiency to understand and read back your clearance first time. It is also inbuilt in cultural mores that to ask people to repeat something indicates defective hearing on your part and is considered slightly rude, especially to a foreigner speaking your language. Therefore the captain simply responded parrot-fashion, not really understanding what the controller meant. Reading back a clearance means that you have understood it. To ask later for clarification is to lose face.

According to the Spanish report, after accepting the hold, the captain then asked the first officer, 'Inbound one five zero to your left?'

Again according to the report, the captain was 'rather a withdrawn character not much given to verbal expansiveness'. What he now seemed to be trying to find out was whether the first officer understood the clearance – because clearly *he* did not.

The first officer on his part appeared not to take the captain's utterance as a question but as a sign that *he* understood it. So rather than admit *his* own ignorance, he simply answered, 'Yeah.'

The captain then came out with his own doubts. 'That's an odd sort of one . . . the runway.'

At long last the first officer then came out with his doubts. 'One I'm not . . . er. Suppose it's all right.'

Instead of decreasing for the descent, the B-727's speed was increasing. South of track, they were speeding towards a mountain range with peaks soaring to 12,000 feet.

The first officer should have drawn the captain's attention to this, but from the cockpit voice-recorder it is apparent that the two pilots were too absorbed in trying to work out exactly what their clearance had been.

A fatal situation of non-communication developed. The air traffic controller was under the impression that the crew knew how they were going to enter and fly the holding pattern. The captain thought the first officer knew and the first officer thought the captain knew. Bearing in mind the unpublished hold, the controller should have made sure the crew knew exactly what to do in the holding pattern. But the pilots, at times clearly uncertain, should also have asked the controller to repeat the clearance and explain.

In the hesitation and unfinished sentences, their confusion is all too apparent.

The captain again appealed to the first officer. 'I'll just turn straight round left on to one five zero when I go overhead, then?'

'Yes,' said the first officer.

'The only thing is . . . we're hmm . . . we're going to miss it. We're too close.'

Both Automatic Direction Finders (ADFs) were tuned to the Foxtrot Papa beacon, preparatory to carrying out a hold they didn't understand.

Now the first officer became uneasy. 'Bloody strange hold, isn't it?'

'Yes,' the captain replied. 'Doesn't . . . isn't parallel to the runway or anything.'

The first officer had further doubts. 'It's that-a-way, isn't it?'

The flight engineer joined in to ask an unclear question. 'That is a three, isn't it?'

The first officer said, 'Hmm.'

The flight engineer repeated his question.

The first officer said, 'Yes, well, the hold's going to be here, isn't it?'

Now the captain asked, 'Hey, did he say it was one five zero inbound?'

The aircraft was rapidly descending to 5,000 feet into an area where the safety height was 14,250 feet.

The first officer answered him, 'Inbound, yeah.'

'That's . . .' the captain said. 'I don't like that.'

The first officer said, 'They want us to keep going round and round, don't they? They want us to . . .'

At that moment the Ground Proximity Warning (GPWS) sounded.

The captain interrupted his turn to the left in order to turn to the right, saying, 'He's taking us round to the high ground!'

By an unhappy coincidence the aircraft now flew over a valley. The GPWS stopped – a sign to the captain that his avoiding manoeuvre had worked.

The first officer then suggested 'a heading of one two two actually and er . . . take us through the overshoot, ah.'

They were now in an appalling maze of their own creation, miles out of position for an overshoot. The captain continued to turn right, telling control, 'We've had a ground proximity warning.'

At that moment, the flight engineer called 'Bank!'

The captain had overbanked his turn. Immediately afterwards, six minutes and twenty-two seconds after the controller gave the B-727 clearance to the Foxtrot Papa beacon, no delay expected, the aircraft crashed 125 feet below the 5,675-foot summit of Pico de Chinguel, killing everyone on board.

The subsequent Spanish Inquiry and report provoked an international incident since blame appeared to be concentrated on the captain. The British vigorously took up his defence, citing the unpublished hold, other non-standard practices and the air traffic controller's role in the accident. As a result, a British addendum was added to the Spanish report.

The same thing had occurred after a Pan American Jumbo collided with a KLM Jumbo, also at Tenerife, when the Dutch objected to the Spanish report and also added their own version (see Chapter 8). In that terrible accident there was also a lack of communication between the crew, particularly between the highly experienced captain and the first officer.

Again and again, accident inquiry reports spell out 'lack of teamwork between the captain and first officer', or give recommendations to an airline to 'amend crew training programmes to include additional assertiveness training to first officers'.

The first officer clearly does not weigh the risks as between getting a black mark from the captain or risking a disaster killing hundreds of people. It is as if the grim possibility cannot be admitted to his calculations. He seems to weigh only between offering advice out of turn to a senior man, and the consequences for him if that advice is wrong.

As Captain Caesar, the Flight Operations and Safety pilot of Lufthansa, wrote in 1989, 'A good preparation of the future co-pilot concerning the psychology of his position is widely missing.' For there is great reluctance in a hierarchical group to prove the head man wrong. It takes a pretty confident young ape to overthrow Silverback just like that in the midst of a group operation. And does the young ape feel himself fit and ready for the heavy task for which Silverback has just been found wanting? Furthermore, in some Eastern countries, hierarchy is even stronger and the captain cannot lose face.

This was originally the case in Western aviation. In 1952 a major airline issued a directive that first officers should *not* point out or correct captains' misakes. Old habits die hard.

The ability to caution or correct the captain is not, however, the only communication difficulty on the flight deck.

Preceding the fire which destroyed the Lockheed Tristar on the ground at Riyadh in 1980 (Chapter 9), which had landed in apparent safety, but from which none escaped, there seems to have been a total lack of communication among the crew. When the fire was discovered shortly after take-off and the captain decided to return, the crew's actions deteriorated. They no longer seemed to communicate as a crew. The captain concentrated on the flying, and after a panic to find the proper procedure in case of fire, the engineer kept saying that there was 'no problem'. The Inquiry found that the first officer failed to monitor the safety of the aircraft, and the captain seemed able neither to communicate with his crew nor to take decisions. The cabin crew were not prepared to evacuate on landing, the crew were not told to wear their oxygen masks and, once the aircraft had been brought down to a safe landing, they were all left on the ground to perish while the order to evacuate was still not given. Communication was totally paralysed.

And though some of the indecision, inaction and lack of

communication might be explained by the lacuna after surviving danger – i.e. the aircraft had been brought safely down and was within reach of firefighting help – the crew did not seem to act as a team or communicate as one.

The 'captain under God alone' concept has long since gone. Should an emergency happen on a Lufthansa aircraft, the Pilot Flying continues flying – be he the captain or first officer – while the other two crew decide what the problem is and what action to take. Only then do they call in the Pilot Flying for his opinion – and only when *unanimous* agreement has been reached is any action taken.

One of the questions that is currently being asked is how crews can best be encouraged to act and communicate as a team. Recently several studies have been conducted.

In 1979, a study was carried out into the performance of B-747 crews in a simulated flight from New York to London. Various problems were posed which required decisions; poor weather was given and a fairly constant interruption from a cabin-crew member with various queries. As a result of this study a most important finding was made. Errors were a result of breakdown in crew co-operation or poor co-ordination and *not* a result of lack of technical skill or knowledge.

The conclusion was that there was a tendency for crews who communicated less well not to perform as well. But more important than the amount of communication was the quality of the communication. Crews performed better when they were better informed, were part of the operation and, to put a popular term in a slightly different context, 'in the loop' – actively involved.

The study also highlighted what is clear from studies of accidents; the absolute necessity for precision and the importance of communication style.

A further study was carried out in 1986 at the request of the US Congress. Primarily targeted at finding out more about fatigue, it presented the pilots with highly realistic flights where many things went wrong and difficult decisions had to be taken.

The study came up with some very interesting results. The pilots were divided into two groups. One group came to the test fully rested, not having flown together. The other group had done a trip together immediately beforehand. Both groups made more or less the same number of very minor errors, but when it came to more serious errors, even potentially fatal ones, the rested group made more than twice as many. So even allowing for fatigue, the group who had flown together performed twice as well in that category.

It was also found that there was more disagreement from first officers who had previously flown with their captain, and more frustration among captains who had *not* previously flown with their first officer. The researchers suggested that increased familiarity may go some way to curing this hesitancy in first officers to question the captains. Familiarity, in fact, may breed safety.

The researchers also noted that there was more task-related conversation amongst crews who hadn't flown together, as if they were trying to get to know one another.

In the RAF, crews have usually trained as a crew and flown together as a crew, and there is a great bond and great loyalty. Crew members go to considerable lengths not to be taken off their crew for illness or any other reason because of the deleterious effect this would have on the rest of the crew.

It would obviously be very difficult, if not impossible, to have such a crew concept in civil aviation today, and flying with the same crew for the rest of a pilot's working life might well bring about worse performances. But some issues of familiarisation should be addressed. As the researchers commented, 'A collection of highly qualified individuals does not necessarily constitute an effective team.'

The Russians have tackled this problem by making flight crews report to a rest-house three days before their flying duty, the main object of which is for them to get to know each other. It might well be difficult to impose this on Western pilots, but no doubt inducements might be given.

Even if crew team communication is improved there are still problems, however. Everyday language is imprecise, and we feel more at home using imprecisions. It is when imprecision of natural language is coupled with expectancy that dangerous misinterpretations can come about.

Many years ago, Professor Bartlett conducted experiments at Cambridge University which were based on party games. One of them was similar to the one where a message is passed from one person to another in a room full of people and its subsequent distortion read out. The popular one in the 1930s was 'Send reinforcements, we're going to advance,' which became 'Send three and fourpence, we're going to a dance.'

Similar misinterpretations continue to plague aviation. A captain's encouraging remark to a first officer, 'Cheer up!' was acted upon as 'Gear up!' 'You will be cleared for a visual approach' has been interpreted as 'You *have* been cleared for a visual approach!'

Furthermore, as in the Dan Air Tenerife crash, interchange with Air Traffic Control can be difficult. Control throughout the world is variable. It is also subject to nationalistic pressures. As an example, the government of Canada has been under pressure from French citizens to make control bi- lingual. This has been resisted by the pilots as damaging to air safety, but there are more voters in the French-Canadian lobby than the air-safety one.

Language in any case makes for difficulties in the cockpit, of which the most obvious are the use of non-standard phraseology and the risk of misunderstanding by random conversations in the cockpit. And though English is supposed to be the international language of aviation, many controllers have only a limited knowledge of it. After the collision between two Jumbos at Tenerife, it was said that Captain Grubb, the commander of the Pan American Jumbo involved in the collision, was quite willing to wait until the KLM Jumbo was airborne, but it was, under the conditions then pertaining, too difficult to explain that to the Spanish controller. Experiments have shown that oral instructions are only 61 per cent understood, while less than half of written instructions are comprehended. Cambridge researchers have shown that departures from standard forms of communication have contributed to many accidents.

Clearly the essence of flight safety is standardisation, but the International Civil Aviation Organisation (ICAO) has not insisted upon it in the potentially dangerous intercommunication between ground and flight deck. English is supposed to be the standard language of aviation, but for reasons of national pride Russian, French and Spanish are allowed locally.

The controller had been speaking and continued to speak to a Spanish aircraft in Spanish just ahead of Dan Air 1008. This is off-putting, but it also denies possibly vital information to an English-speaking captain. In 1976, a British Trident and a Yugoslav DC-9 collided at 33,000 feet over the beacon at Zagreb. The controller was speaking a Croatian dialect to the DC-9. Had the British captain understood the conversation, he might well have realised that they were at the same height. All on board both aircraft were killed.

In 1975, a Transworld Airlines Boeing 727 hit a mountain range near Washington because of confusion in the cockpit over the approach clearance. On the CVR the captain said, 'You know, according to this dumb sheet it says thirty four hundred to Round Hill is our minimum altitude.'

He was referring to the approach chart showing the standard procedure for an approach to Dulles runway. But after discussion, the pilots concluded that the rules allowed an immediate descent to 1,800 feet because the air traffic controller had radioed that the aircraft was cleared for its approach.

An aircraft proceeding from Colombia to Seattle received this descent clearance at 00.47: 'Nectar one six nine three Metro, you are cleared to cross Hobart at 8,000, Seattle at or above 4,000. Maintain 4,000. No delay expected. Contact Seattle Approach Control over Hobart for further clearance, over.'

The captain, who was experienced on the route, replied, 'Roger, this uh nine three Metro is cleared to – uh – Hobart – to cross there 4,000 or above – the Range Station at 4,000, and we are to report to you at – uh – Hobart, over.'

Control replied, 'Negative. Report Hobart to Seattle Approach Control,' correcting the last and *least important* of the two mistakes in the repeat-back.

Although the original clearance had said Hobart at 8,000, the aircraft mistakenly descended to 4,000 and crashed into a mountain.

In 1990, an Avianca aircraft was being held with many people on the aircraft over a foggy New York. The South American pilot reported being short of fuel, but did not use standard R/T phraseology and did not declare an emergency. Eventually cleared he missed his approach, went round again, ran out of fuel and crashed, killing many of his passengers.

Non-standard procedures and the use of different languages are obvious mantraps in aviation communications. In 1974, a B-747 was approaching Nairobi in the middle of the night. The crew were tired. The first officer was ill. The controller cleared the aircraft to 'seven zero zero zero' feet. The first officer repeated back 'five zero zero zero'. The controller should have corrected the mistake, but it was allowed to continue. Fortunately the captain saw the ground through intermittent cloud and carried out an overshoot.

QFE – (the altimeter setting which shows the height above the airfield) and QNH (which shows height above sea level) still lead to confusion. So does the use of 'left' and 'right' or 'port' and 'starboard'. Altimeter setting errors have caused a number of accidents. An aircraft coming into Calcutta was given a setting of 992 millibars. It was assumed that this was a clipped 29.92 inches of mercury and set on the altimeter. That made it read 600 feet too high and the aircraft crashed in mist.

Some strands of the web that were to enmesh the Dan-Air 727 existed as a result of non-standardisation as it began descending towards mountainous terrain in Tenerife.

The difficulties and limitations of human communication in and from the cockpit continue. The trouble is that aircraft have been getting faster and more complicated and the human tongue seemingly slower and more reluctant.

Such was the case in the cockpit of a Pacific South-West Airlines Boeing 727 which collided with a Cessna near Lindbergh Field in 1978 when communication difficulties combined with perceptual ones.

Five

To See and Not to See

Shortly before nine on the morning of 25 September 1978, Pacific South-West Airlines Flight 182, a Boeing 727 on a scheduled flight from Sacramento, was approaching Lindbergh Field, San Diego, with 128 passengers on board. The first officer was at the controls while the captain conducted the air-to-ground communications. There was also a dead-heading pilot (i.e., flying as a passenger) in the forward observer seat. The weather was fine, the winds calm, and visibility was ten miles.

A little earlier, a Cessna had left nearby Montgomery Field flying south to Lindbergh for practice ILS approaches. These would involve, for much of the time, the pilots being under the hood (that is to say, screens are put up so that the pilot cannot see anything but the instruments, while the instructor beside him retains full vision). Lindbergh Field lay below the SAN Terminal Control Radar Service Area (TCRSA), whose floor was at 4,000 feet. Aircraft in this area received radar sequencing and advisory service (Stage II radar service) but not separation. They could obtain a full Stage III TCRSA from Miramar Naval Air Station which was close by.

After the second practice approach, the Cessna departed north-east with instructions from Lindbergh Field to contact Approach Control at Miramar. They complied and were cleared to maintain Visual Flight Rules (VFR) to climb on heading 070 and not exceed 3,500 feet.

Boeing Flight 182, meanwhile, was reporting its descent to 7,000 feet with the airfield in sight. Approach Control cleared it for a visual approach to Runway 27. With this clearance Air Traffic Control authorises an Instrument Flight Rules (IFR) flight to proceed as if it were a VFR flight, turning and descending at the pilot's discretion rather than with directions from ATC. It has been said that this is to reduce workload, but in fact it probably puts *extra* workload on the pilots if they are to maintain the required visual scanning.

A few seconds later, as the Cessna climbed out of its final ILS approach, the controller warned Flight 182, 'Traffic at twelve o'clock, one mile northbound,' and Flight 182 answered, 'We're looking.'

Within four seconds, the second warning came. 'Additional traffic's twelve o'clock, three miles, just north of the field, north-east bound, a Cessna one seven two VFR out of one thousand four hundred.'

To this, Flight 182 replied, 'OK. We've got that other twelve.'

Meanwhile, clearance was given to the Cessna, and a second later the third warning to Flight 182, 'Traffic's at twelve o'clock, three miles out of one thousand seven hundred.'

To this Flight 182 responded, 'Traffic's in sight.'

This transmission was crucial. It reassured the controller that 182 had the Cessna in view. Flight 182 was told to maintain visual separation and contact Lindbergh Tower, and the controller informed the Cessna that 182 had him in sight. Under the visual clearance, it was 182's responsibility to keep the smaller aircraft in view, and to inform the controller if they had lost sight.

But Flight 182 was rapidly closing on the Cessna and the crew could no longer see it.

Four seconds after 182's transmission that it was on the downwind leg, the controller gave them their last warning about the Cessna. 'Traffic's twelve o'clock, one mile, a Cessna 8.'

The first officer was busy calling for 5 degrees flap, and the captain asked him, 'Is that the one we're looking at?'

He answered, 'Yeah. But I don't see him now.'

Then 182 transmitted to the controller, 'OK, we had it there a minute ago,' and six seconds later, 'I think he's passed off to our right.'

The crew continued to discuss the Cessna, along with the landing. The tower cleared them to land, but the first officer was still asking, 'Are we clear of the Cessna?'

'Supposed to be,' said the engineer.

'I guess,' said the captain.

'I hope!' said the dead-heading pilot on the jump seat.

That fatal dialogue said it all. The captain added further reassurance. 'Oh yeah, before we turned downwind, I saw him about one o'clock, probably behind us now.'

Seventeen seconds later, just after the conflict alert warning had begun to sound in San Diego Approach Control Facility, the first officer was pointing out, 'There's one underneath. I was looking at that inbound there.'

Yet its proximity and threat didn't seem to register in his mind. Or in anyone else's. No one said anything. Flight 182 was descending and overtaking the Cessna. Another human factor had entered in. The crew were in a 'set' (see Chapter 6), encapsulated in a small mental world of their own. A mental 'set' is a readiness for a particular thought process to the exclusion of others, resulting in fixation. Next on the CVR were only exclamations and the sound of impact.

The collision took place exactly at the time the controller had transmitted to the Cessna that 182 had him in sight.

The National Transportation Safety Board determined that the probable cause was the failure of the flight crew of 182 to comply with the regulations of a maintain-visual-separation clearance, including the requirement to inform the controller when they no longer had the other aircraft in sight. It is a conclusion that has been pronounced many times with terrifying regularity before this accident and since.

So why did the flight crew of 182 not see the Cessna, and why did they not report the fact that they had lost sight of him? The answer to the question of why the crew of 182 did not see the Cessna is a complex one of various human factors.

A considerable amount of perception is *learned*. To every young child, the world is a kaleidoscope of stimuli which mean very little. Gradually, through experience, these stimuli become meaningful: a horizontal and vertical framework is built up, and depth perception, perceptual constancy, ability to recognise an object at different angles and at different distances, the capacity to focus and judge, and orientation in space are introduced. We can then recognise something – what it is, where it is, what it is doing – from a few cues. A cartoonist draws a circle, four dots and a couple of lines and we recognise a famous politician or a film star. Not only do we learn to perceive – we also learn *not* to perceive, and to perceive *selectively*. Otherwise we would be overwhelmed by the millions of different stimuli that are bombarding us every waking minute.

In one psychological experiment, the same series of shapes were shown to two groups of subjects, but were verbally identified differently. The two groups were then asked to reproduce the shapes from memory. These were some of the results:

First Group's Reproduction	Verbal Identification	Figure Shown	Verbal Identification	Second Group's Reproduction
	Eye glasses		Dumb bells	
	Crescent moon		Letter C	
	Curtains in a window		Diamond in a rectangle	
	Bottle		Stirrup	

Once a perceptual experience has been named, then, we appear to be satisfied with that interpretation. We think we have identified the object adequately, even if in fact there are many aspects of it which we have missed.

We all look and don't see. It is a phenomenon of daily living. We don't see the bunch of keys or the pen or the book that is right in front of us. Especially we do not see if we are concentrating on something else. Furthermore, we tend to see what we want to see, like a familiar face in a crowd. At the other extreme, we don't see what we don't want to see. Especially under stress.

With regard to the psychological mechanism of attention, concentration has now been focused on the reticular formation in the brain stem. Its principal function would appear to be arousal – not only into wakefulness, but also in responding to stimuli in waking life under the control of the cortex.

The reticular formation would appear either to enhance the effect made on the brain by certain sensory impulses, or to inhibit stimuli to which there is no need to attend. Its role therefore with regard to a pilot flying an aircraft and scanning at the same time seems considerable, especially in the landing phase, when he may be feeling tired at the end of a journey.

Visual Flight Rules assume that if the pilot regularly scans the sky he is bound to see another aircraft – and avoid it. The rules, like so much in civil aviation, are inherited from the rules of the sea and waterways, even to the extent of incorporating such laws as that two vessels approaching head on always turn to the right, and the responsibility of avoidance lying with the vessel which has the other on the starboard.

These rules may be adequate for ships proceeding at from five to thirty knots, with watchmen posted whose only duty is to keep a look-out (though with recent tragedies their adequacy is in question even then). But it is doubtful whether they should have ever been applied to aircraft, whose pilots are not only watchmen (often with a large percentage of their vision blocked) but are also frequently preoccupied with other intricate duties.

Aircraft are comparatively small, and changing skies and changing background terrain provide excellent camouflage. There are not two but three dimensions. And aircraft speeds, always fast, are now approaching the velocity of bullets.

The idea that airmen should be able to see something that may possibly have been presented in front of their eyes for a few seconds is derived from the old structuralist idea of perception, long since discarded in psychology. As a British psychologist, Vernon, has pointed out, 'A rough generalisation may be made that the total amount which may be attended to at any one moment is constant. If attention is concentrated in a small part of the field, little will be perceived in other parts: if attention is diffused over a larger area, no part will be very clearly and accurately perceived.'

In any case, eye movements have been shown to differ with different fields, objects and lights – and it is clear that the field is not evenly scanned, and parts of it may be covered more effectively than others. There is in fact a blind spot where the optic nerve leaves the eye, yet what we see does not have a piece missing because perception consists of two processes. First, the image on the retina is passed up the sensory chain to the visual cortex. And there the second process takes place – it is adjusted and interpreted by what we know, by our experience, and our interpretation of the world.

Our perception can also be impaired by another factor – what we expect to see. The pilots of Flight 182 expected the Cessna to have passed behind them. The psychologist Russell Davis made a study of train-drivers who had gone through the signals at red. A significant number, he found, had gone through because they expected it to be green. There have been terrible rail accidents – the Moorgate tube-train disaster; Clapham Junction; Purley, where the train driver was convicted of manslaughter. Drivers have been charged and punished, but the underlying causes hardly studied at all.

After the San Diego crash of Flight 182, cockpit visibility studies were carried out. The photographs taken for these from the captain's and first officer's seats showed that the Cessna would have been almost centred on their windshields for 170 to 90 seconds before collision.

During the critical phase just before collision, however, the Cessna would have been positioned at the bottom of both the captain's and the first officer's windshields. The Cessna was virtually on the same course as 182, and the apparent motion of the target would have been lost. There would have been foreshortening of the Cessna fuselage, making it smaller and more difficult to see, and the Cessna would have been viewed against the bright multi-colours of the residential area below.

The eye mainly relies on movement to attract the focal system (the conscious interrogation of the world). This is not discernible in colliding aircraft, as colliding aircraft maintain a constant relative bearing to each other. Unless the pilot had previously experienced a collision (which is unlikely) he has *no learned interpretation*.

The pilot's eye position is very important to what he sees. Three years before the accident the Federal Aviation Agency (FAA) had stressed the need for action to be taken to ensure that pilots sat in the proper position for scanning.

Decades ago, doubts about the see-and-be-seen formula had begun to creep into accident Inquiries. By 1958, when a National Guard T-33 (descending to Baltimore) collided with a Viscount, there were considerable doubts about 'exposure time' – how long the aircraft could have seen each other. The accident was blamed on the T-33 pilot, who, it was calculated, had the Viscount in possible view ahead of him for sixty seconds. The Viscount pilots, who might have seen the T-33 for only twenty-six seconds, were not blamed.

Collision accidents continued, however, and in most of them the pilots were blamed. Significantly, 36 of the 44 major accidents between 1948 and 1960 occurred close to the airport where one or both were taking off or approaching to land, and 29 involved an airliner and a small aircraft – either a light aircraft or a fighter. Since 1960, *all* collisions have occurred in the vicinity of an airport, most of which have involved an airliner and a light aircraft.

In a collision between a Caravelle and a light aircraft over Orly, Paris, in a visibility of thirty kilometres, members of the Inquiry showed a physiological and psychological awareness of human factors. They figured out that since the closing speed was 150 metres a second, five seconds before the crash the image of the light aircraft measured only 0.7 centimetre. The Inquiry allowed five seconds for identification, estimation of heading and collision risk, pilot decision and reaction time of the aircraft, and decided that this was insufficient.

But in later mid-air collisions too numerous to mention the old formula was back: 'The failure of both pilots to see and avoid each other's aircraft.'

What should be learned from the disaster to Flight 182 is that the pilot's visual separation of aircraft should never be used where there is the capability of providing – as there was in this instance – lateral or vertical separation by ATC for either aircraft.

The further findings of the Inquiry confirmed this. Amongst its recommendations were that:

The FAA should implement a Terminal Control Radar Service Area at Lindbergh Airport.

The FAA should review procedure at all airports which are used regularly by air carriers and general aviation aircraft to determine which other areas require either a Terminal Control Area (TCA) or a Terminal Control Radar Service Area (TCRSA) and establish the appropriate one.

Visual separation in Terminal Control Areas should be used only when a pilot requests it, except for sequencing in the final approach with radar monitoring.

The FAA should re-evaluate its policy with regard to the use of visual separation in other Terminal Areas.

This accident and the Inquiry recommendations caused a considerable furore.

There had been a mid-air collision only a few months before

between a Cessna and a Falcon jet over Memphis, so public concern was, at least for a while, considerable. The presence of small aircraft around an airport has always been a hazard. But the prospect of more TCRSAs and TCAs caused angry protests from general aviation pilots, manufacturers and their associations. Arguments concerning economic factors and controller workload were advanced, and there were objections to the curtailment of general aviation flight freedom.

For over twenty years the NTSB had bombarded the FAA with collision studies and recommendations, but the collisions continued. In September 1986 another mid-air collision occurred near Los Angeles when a Piper aircraft strayed unnoticed into the Los Angeles Terminal Control Area and collided with an Aeromexico DC-9, killing all on board and fifteen people on the ground.

And while collisions naturally cause public alarm, the number of near misses cannot be ignored. In the past there was some reluctance on the part of pilots to report such near misses. They may have realised that they were not where air traffic control had ordered them to be, or were at the wrong holding altitude over a beacon.

As with all other incidents, pilots must feel able to report near misses without fear of reprisal. Occasionally, near misses grab the headlines. In 1987, an Alitalia Airbus climbing out of London bound for Milan came within a hundred feet of striking a British Airways Jumbo awaiting clearance to land at Heathrow. Luckily, the sky was clear. The Alitalia pilot caught a glimpse of the Jumbo, frantically hauled back on the controls and passed only feet under the Jumbo's belly. Concorde has had a number of near misses; so, to screaming headlines, have aircraft carrying members of the Royal Family. There are others all over the world which do not make the headlines.

In America, when further results of the National Transport Safety Board's investigations were made known in mid-July 1987, among other conclusions the Board found that there are severe limitations to the see-and-avoid concept of air separation.

One wonders how often and over how many decades this conclusion has to be repeated.

Perhaps another type of visual impairment should be added – there are none so blind as those who won't see.

Six

Deadly Set

There is a further aspect of the collision between Flight 182 and the Cessna. As was mentioned in the previous chapter, shortly before the crash occurred the crew of Flight 182 had not only had perceptual difficulties in seeing the Cessna, but had also developed a 'set' of *not* seeing it. They convinced each other that the Cessna had passed behind them. They reinforced each other's belief. Their vision became tunnelled. This is particularly easy with three or four people encapsulated in close proximity on a flight deck.

'Set' is another of the survival characteristics we have inherited. The human brain evolved to help individuals live and survive circumstances very different from our own. It predisposes us to select our focus on that part of the picture paramount at the time – a vision often so totally focused that it ignores the rest of the environment. The pattern of selectivity programmed into humans by the ancient world is totally obsolete in the present day, where a flexible scanning through-out the visual environment is required. The human beings in the cockpit have to steer a difficult course between too many and too few visual stimuli.

German psychologists have always been conscious of the particular dangers of rigid thinking. Men like Duncker, Wertheimer and Köhler are known as Gestalt psychologists – after the German word meaning 'pattern'. Their emphasis has been on the need to avoid what they call 'functional fixity'. But with all of us, if we are given a lead to see things in a certain way that is probably the way we will see them, ignoring other interpretations.

An experiment was performed to test the effect of prior 'set' in identifying this picture. The first group were shown this picture:

First Group

and the second group were shown this one:

Second Group

Then both groups were shown the ambiguous picture, and asked to say what they saw. Of the first group, 100 per cent saw the young girl, and 95 per cent of the second group saw the old woman. Each group had been given a 'set' to see the picture in a certain way. Similarly, the crew of Flight 182 had got themselves into a 'set' that the Cessna was safely away.

Flying training recognises both the advantages and dangers of 'set'. A pilot has to learn a series of 'sets' in flying manoeuvres varying from normal take-offs and landings to engine failure, fire and other emergencies. But to combat 'set' and to stop a pilot so concentrating on his landing that he forgets to put his wheels down a number of devices have been invented, such as lights and horns. In spite of these precautions, because of the blinding effect of a 'set' pilots still forget to put the undercarriage down.

The crew of a DC-8 forgot to do so for a landing at Orlando,

Third Group

Florida. The crew's attention had been diverted to reported 'other traffic' in the vicinity. This was particularly relevant to the pilots as they had cancelled IFR and would have been looking out to avoid collisions. They completed their checks and initiated descent by throttling back the engines. This reduction of power started off the landing-gear horn, warning them that the undercarriage was not down. In order to preserve their concentration, they silenced it and continued the approach.

As the Accident Inquiry Report puts it, 'Thereafter the crew members became engrossed in their respective duties and the landing gear forgotten.'

They crash-landed on the runway with the wheels up, doing considerable damage to the aircraft.

Over millions of years Man has become less dependent on predestined behaviour patterns made up purely of instinct and reflex, and has learned to adapt his behaviour in the light of past experience. According to D. H. Hubel, Man's brain now has a capacity to store more items of information than there are particles in the universe. The difficulty is that Man was not intended to hurtle through the air at the speed of a bullet and take vital decisions *en route*.

The captain of an airliner touched down at Washington Airport only to find that there was no braking effect as a result of a very wet runway. He advised the first officer, advanced the throttles to take-off power and started a go-around. The aircraft became airborne, and as it passed the end of the runway at twenty-five feet, the captain called, 'Gear up.' Instead of retracting the undercarriage, the first officer pulled both throttles back to the closed position, thus cutting off all power at the vital moment. The aircraft then crashed.

The first officer testified that he did not hear advice on the go-around, and the order for gear up was the only thing said by the captain. In accounting for his action he said, 'At the time the command was given *I was expecting an order to reduce power*, and inasmuch as it looked like a crash was inevitable – when the order came, I moved them by spontaneous action.'

This bears out research which has shown that internally generated thought can block the simultaneous taking up of externally generated information, i.e. that from the outside world. Originally, our ability to blank out too many unwanted stimuli was a survival advantage. But we get nothing for nothing.

The natural adaptations that in past times helped us to survive may now in the technological age be one of our greatest threats. A capacity for conscious representation had survival value for those creatures possessing it, but to achieve its time-saving purposes, conscious experience had to be of very limited capacity.

According to Professor Dixon, formerly Professor of Psychology at University College, London, 'Conscious awareness is a small flawed barred window on the great tide of information which flows unceasingly into, around and out of the four hundred thousand million neurones and hundred billion synapses which comprise the human nervous system.' And under stress – the stress of landing, the stress of take-off – awareness narrows and the window becomes a tunnel. As it did for the captain of a DC-8 coming to the end of an uneventful flight westwards across America from J. F. Kennedy Airport, New York, via Denver, to Portland, Oregon.

The date was 28 December 1978, and darkness was approaching. Portland approach control gave him a clearance to maintain his heading for a visual approach to Runway 28.

'Roger, Portland,' he replied. 'Runway 28. We have the field in sight.'

Like numerous pilots over the years who reported seeing the runway, this one was similarly destined not to land on it. But this time it was nothing to do with actual visual perception, for the weather was practically CAVU (Ceiling and Visibility Unlimited).

'United 173, descend and maintain 8,000.'

'Am leaving ten.'

The first officer, who was flying the aircraft, called for flaps, then the gear. As the captain put the wheels down, there was a *thump* and a yaw to the right. Only the nose-gear light illuminated green. No green lights came on for the main wheels.

At 17.12, Portland requested the flight to contact the tower for landing.

'Negative,' came the reply. 'We'll stay with you at five. We got a gear problem. We'll let you know.'

'OK. We'll just orbit you out there till you get your problem.'

With a calculated 13,334 lbs of fuel on board, United 173 began orbiting with 15 degrees of flap and gear down. At that configuration, the aircraft would be using 200 lbs a minute. Therefore the aircraft would expect to run out of fuel at 18.14.

Until 17.38, the flight crew tried all the emergency routines to assure themselves that all the wheels were down and locked. During that time, the captain discussed the situation with the first flight attendant, telling her that he would let her know what he intended to do. He seemed particularly concerned to allow time for passengers to assume the right position for a crash landing. That the engineer was concerned about the time this was taking vis-à-vis the fuel situation is clear on the CVR. Also on the CVR, the co-pilot made several oblique references to the readings on the fuel gauges, which the captain also ignored.

Instructions in the United Airlines DC-8 flight manual stated that if the landing gear was apparently not conclusively down the aircraft should get the tower to have a visual check. *If* there was a reasonable indication that the gear was down, the landing could be made on the assumption that the wheels were down.

Ground school and flight training, proficiency and recurrent training direct the crew to determine the position of both main and nose landing indicators on top of the wing. The engineer officer had checked those indicators and both main landing wheels showed down and locked. The nose-wheel light remained green. In that case, the United manual stated that a landing could be made '*at the captain's discretion*'.

Once something is identified, however, it takes on a reality of its own and sticks in the mind like a burr which is difficult to dislodge. As he circled while the crew still struggled to get three green lights, the captain could see the lights of his destination at the end of a long trip beckoning him down.

Clearly he would feel frustration, as well as fatigue. In addition, the final period of any flight is also noteworthy for the degree of arousal in the captain. A glance at the illustration opposite of a captain's heart rate during a flight from London to New York shows that it soared to 165 a minute at the landing phase – with no particular problems involved.

High arousal contributes to 'set'. The mind becomes tunnelled on a particular course of action. Add to that the ingredient of fatigue and it is not difficult to see that a 'set' as hard as concrete can result. Furthermore, 'set', particularly in the captain, is infectious. There is a follow-my-leader syndrome. So it is easy to see why most aircraft accidents are caused by 'silly' mistakes in the approach and landing phase.

The captain of Flight 173 appeared to have a 'set' that the gear would collapse on landing. From the Accident Report, it appears that he did not try for a visual tower check, but instead, at 17.38, contacted United Airlines Systems Maintenance Control Centre at San Francisco, and reported the problem. He told them what had been done, saying that there was now 7,000 lbs of fuel and he would hold for another fifteen or twenty minutes while the flight attendants prepared the passengers for emergency evacuation.

At 17.44 the Control Centre called, 'United 173, you estimate that you'll make a landing about five minutes past the hour. Is that OK?'

Heart rate of North Atlantic Captain taking off London, landing New York

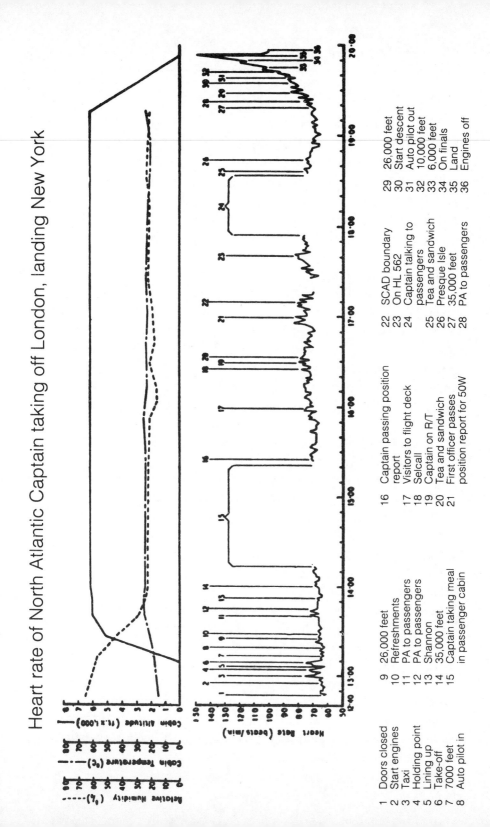

1	Doors closed	9	26,000 feet
2	Start engines	10	Refreshments
3	Taxi	11	PA to passengers
4	Holding point	12	PA to passengers
5	Lining up	13	Shannon
6	Take-off	14	35,000 feet
7	7000 feet	15	Captain taking meal
8	Auto pilot in		in passenger cabin

16	Captain passing position	22	SCAD boundary
	report	23	On HL 562
17	Visitors to flight deck	24	Captain talking to
18	Selcall		passengers
19	Captain on R/T	25	Tea and sandwich
20	Tea and sandwich	26	Presque Isle
21	First officer passes	27	35,000 feet
	position report for 50W	28	PA to passengers

29	26,000 feet
30	Start descent
31	Auto pilot out
32	10,000 feet
33	6,000 feet
34	On finals
35	Land
36	Engines off

The captain replied 'Yes, that's good ball park. I'm not gonna hurry the girls. We got about 165 people on board and we mean . . . we wanna take our time and get everybody ready and will go.' As though to encourage himself and the others, he called, 'It's clear as a bell and no problem.'

No problem? What with the gear, the fuel state, the probable crash landing and the aircraft evacuation, he didn't know which to tackle first.

The 'set' tightened.

From 17.44 to 17.44:33, the captain and the first flight attendant discussed passenger preparations for a crash landing and evacuation procedure. Donning coats was discussed for protection from fire and for identification, as if the captain's mind was fixated on a wheels-up landing. Despite the fuel situation, there was no indication that a time limit was given, and the captain did not ask how long it would take to prepare the cabin.

At 17.41:52, the first officer asked for the fuel state.

The flight engineer replied, 'Five thousand.'

Now came an interrupton. An aircraft was reported in this vicinity. The first officer scanned the sky and said he had it in sight. He then asked again, this time of the captain, 'What's the fuel show now?'

The captain answered, 'Five.'

The fuel pumps started to blink. The captain's comment was, 'That's about right.'

According to the book, total usable fuel when the fuel pumps start to blink is 5,000 lbs. So in twenty-five minutes the aircraft would have run completely out of fuel.

That time would be 18.11:45.

The crew continued to talk about the gear – with interruptions on the R/T about bearing changes and traffic advisory.

Still set on his landing problems, the captain asked the flight engineer, 'Give us a current card on weight. Give another fifteen minutes.'

The first officer interrupted, '*Fifteen* minutes?'

The captain refused to be concerned. 'Yeah, give us three or four thousand pounds on top of zero fuel landing weight.' The captain was demanding to be told the fuel he wanted to have, not the actual amount in the tanks.

The flight engineer demurred. 'Not enough! Fifteen minutes is gonna – really run us low on fuel here.'

At 17.50:47 the flight engineer gave the zero fuel landing weights plus 3,200 lbs for landing. In this he was perfectly accurate.

But at 17.51:35 the captain told the flight engineer to contact the flight representative at Portland, saying that they would land with *about 4,000 lbs*. That is, adding about 800 lbs to the fuel quantity the flight engineer had given him.

Between 17.52 and 17.53:30, the flight engineer was talking to Portland about fuel state, persons on board and emergency landing procedures. Troutdale, a small field *en route*, was mentioned as a possible landing place, even the highway.

At 17.53:30 the captain told the flight engineer to relay to the company that they would be landing at 18.05.

At 17.55:04 the flight engineer reported, 'Approach descent check complete.'

At 17.57:21 the captain sent the flight engineer to the cabin to 'kinda see how things are going'.

From 17.57 to 18.00 the captain and the first officer discussed giving the flight attendants ample time to prepare for the emergency – cockpit procedures in the event of an evacuation after landing, whether the brakes would give anti-skid protection after landing, and the procedures the captain would be using for the approach and landing.

The flight engineer then returned to the flight deck to report that the cabin would be ready 'in another two or three minutes'.

The time to total fuel exhaustion was now only ten minutes and eleven seconds.

At 18.02:22 the flight engineer advised, 'We've got about three on the fuel and that's it!'

'OK.' The captain was still 'set' on his crash landing. 'On

touchdown, if the gear folds or something really jumps the tractor, get those boost pumps off so that . . . you might even get the valves open.'

At 18.02:44 Portland asked for a status report.

The first officer replied, 'Yeah, we have indication our green is abnormal. It'll be our intention in about five minutes to land on 28 Left. We would like the equipment standing by. Our indications are the gear is down and locked. We've got our people prepared for an evacuation in the event it should become necessary.'

Eight minutes before fuel exhaustion, Portland asked when the approach would begin.

At 18.03:23 Portland asked for the number of persons on board and the amount of fuel remaining.

The captain replied, 'About five thousand . . . well, make it three thousand pounds of fuel . . . and you can add to the 172 plus six laps – infants!'

At 18.03:38 the flight crew discussed checking the landing-gear warning horn as evidence that the landing-gear was down and locked, and whether the automatic spoilers would operate with landing-gear circuit-breakers out.

At 18.05:19, the chief flight attendant came on to the flight deck.

The captain asked, 'How you doing?'

'Well, I think we're all ready.'

The captain said, 'OK, we're going to go in now. We shall be landing in about five minutes.'

The first officer interrupted. 'I think you lost number four.'

At 18.06:46 he said, 'We're going to lose an engine.'

Bearing in mind all the worry about the fuel, the captain asked a most extraordinary question.

'Why?'

It can only be explained by the assumption that he was so deep in his 'set' on the possible crash landing that he could think of nothing else.

The first officer repeated, 'We're going to lose an engine.'

Again the captain asked, "*Why?*'

The first officer's reply was brief. 'Fuel!'

For the next fourteen seconds there was a conflicting discussion between the crew on fuel state, ending with the first officer saying, 'It's flamed out.'

The captain reported approaching Runway 28 Left.

The aircraft was now nineteen miles south of the airport.

At 18.07:27, the first officer said, 'We're going to lose number three in a minute, too! It's showing zero!'

The captain called, 'You got a thousand pounds! You got to!'

The first officer replied 'Five thousand in there . . . but we lost it.'

The flight engineer asked the first officer, 'Are you getting it back?'

'No number four? You got the crossfeed open?'

'No, I haven't got it open. Which one?'

The captain called, 'Open 'em both! Get some fuel in there!' Adding, 'You *gotta* keep them running!'

The first officer replied, 'Yes, sir' and then exhorted 'Get this . . . on the ground!'

The engineer officer agreed. 'Yeah, it's showing not very much more fuel.' At 18.09:16 he reported, 'We're down to one on the totaliser. Number two is coughing.'

At 18.09:21, Portland Approach cleared the flight for a visual approach to Runway 28 Left.

But it was on the undercarriage that the captain's mind was still set. He told the flight engineer to 'Reset the circuit breakers. See if we get gear lights.'

The flight engineer did so. By now the captain was inquiring distance from the airport.

Portland replied, 'I'd call it eighteen flying miles.'

Two minutes later, the captain again called for distance. Now it was twelve miles and the flight was cleared to the tower.

At 18.13:21, the flight engineer called, 'We've lost two engines, guys!'

Seventeen seconds later, the captain said, 'They're all going! We can't make Troutdale!'

'We can't make anything!' the first-officer added.

'OK!' said the captain. 'OK! Declare a Mayday!'

Immediately the first officer called the tower, 'United one seventy-three heavy, Mayday! We're – the engines are flaming out! We're going down! We're not going to be able to make the airport!'

The DC-8 descended through the darkness, and at 18.15 crashed into a wooded section of suburban Portland, six miles east-south-east of the airport. Fortunately it did not catch fire.

The flight engineer, a flight attendant and eight passengers were killed. Twenty-three other passengers were seriously injured. The fault in the undercarriage was found to be due to a burned-out light bulb.

The Safety Board examined exhaustively all possible causes of the accident. The company's operating manuals certainly covered the gear problem, the preparations for evacuation and the cabin inspection meticulously. They stated categorically that if the visual down-lock indicators indicated that the gear was down a landing could be made at the captain's discretion. They did indicate it down. The only damage was to the landing-gear position-indicating-system switch, and the Board believed that the captain could have landed safely within thirty or so seconds after the landing-gear malfunction.

The captain and to a lesser extent the crew had developed a 'set' in which all their attention was concentrated on the landing gear, irrespective of all other considerations, including the far more important fuel state. Though both the first officer and the flight engineer made comments on the low fuel, they were *too half-hearted to make any impact on the captain.*

In a well-known psychological experiment, electrodes were fitted to the cochlear nucleus of a cat. A loud clicking apparatus was positioned close to the cat's ear and, as expected, the noise caused a marked response. The animal was 'hearing it'. Now a mouse was put in front of the cat. Although the clicking apparatus was still making just as much noise, the neural response was either greatly reduced or completely absent.

Instead of the mouse, the captain of the DC-8 saw the spectre of the apparently unserviceable landing gear and, like the cat, his concentration narrowed to that one stimulus. Some kind of 'censoring' process was preventing the signals being registered. And as with so many accidents, this was a precedent from which lessons could subsequently have been learned.

'Set' has been a factor in many aircraft accidents. Six years earlier, a similar problem arose over Florida when the crew of a Tristar were not sure that their undercarriage was down. The accident sequence was again begun *by a burned-out light bulb* in the system which is designed to show that the undercarriage is down and locked. Once again, the crew examined every possibility of finding the trouble. The flight engineer crawled down into the nose, while the captain and the first officer tried every combination of switches and circuit-breakers.

Just as obsessed as the crew of Flight 173 over Portland, the three members of the crew did not notice that the autopilot had become disengaged and the aircraft was sinking lower and lower, eventually crashing into the Everglades.

Because they had become preoccupied with an unsafe landing-gear indication, they failed to monitor the critical altimeter readings. Ironically, the air traffic controller noticed on his radar display that the aircraft was losing height, but instead of pointing this out simply asked diplomatically 'How are things coming along out there?'

The crew, still obsessed with their landing-gear problem, assuming he referred to that, for they could think of nothing else, replied seconds before the crash, 'Everything is all right!'

Seven

On Being Deceived

Everything is quite all right – that is something we all try to tell ourselves. Man is an optimist who rejects the bad news and shoots the messenger. And when the outside world is hostile, his defence mechanisms help him to rewrite the scenario. We have already seen that at the best of times his perceptions are limited, but he is also easily deceived.

Try reading every word out on this design.
You may well find you have read it as
Paris in the Spring.
Try looking at these two lines.

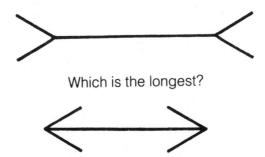

Which is the longest?

You may well say the top one is longer. In fact they are both exactly the same length.

There are many illusions which cause our perceptions to 'lie'. At first sight the figure below appears to be ordinary steps. Stared at, it suddenly becomes an overhanging cornice. Then it reverts to steps again.

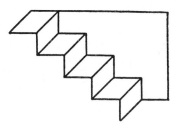

Stairs? – or cornice?

No one knows the cause of illusions, but there have been a number of aircraft accidents in which one of the factors might have been an illusion or similar phenomenon.

A curious example occurred in a light aircraft over Hollywood. The owner had a rotating light fitted on the nose. Taking off on a dark night, he proceeded to fly on what appeared to be a drunken track, going round in circles and spirals until finally he crashed, apparently out of control. No reason could be found until an investigator fitted an identical rotating light in the nose of a similar aircraft and took off on a similar night. While the aircraft remained out of cloud, no difficulty was experienced. But once in cloud, the rotating light induced an intense hypnotic effect that made the pilot feel dizzy. The vertigo was so severe that instrument flying was altogether too difficult, but as soon as he emerged from cloud the effect wore off. Thus was explained the out-of-control circles, punctuated by normal straight and level flying, that had characterised the track of the light aircraft.

Road-rescue drivers have recently reported that the drivers of vehicles being towed behind them have become disorientated by their rotating light.

A DC-6 took off from Minneapolis in the middle of the night.

Normal take-off was established by visual observations and reference to the rate-of-climb indicator.

The co-pilot called V2. The captain eased back on the stick. The aircraft left the ground.

Suddenly the captain's outside vision was obscured by the reflection of the landing lights against low cloud. He looked back into the cockpit and noted that his climb was normal. He then turned off the landing lights.

The next moment, the co-pilot called, 'Pull it up', and heaved back on the stick. But the aircraft had already struck the ground. It skidded along for another 500 yards, shedding its wings and engines, and came to rest on its left side, seriously injuring a number of passengers.

There was nothing the matter with the aircraft. The crew was highly experienced. The Board of Inquiry looked into the phenomena of pilots' sensory illusions as a possible factor – especially the conclusions of Dr John Lane, the then Superintendent of Aviation Medicine of the Australian Department of Civil Aviation. Dr Lane said that:

> the forward acceleration of the aircraft after take-off causes
> a sensation of nose-up tilt because the pilot cannot
> distinguish between the direction of gravity and the
> resultant of gravity and aircraft acceleration. If the pilot is
> not fully on instruments, this can cause him to lower the
> nose, and the acceleration in the resulting dive perpetuates
> the illusion. The aircraft can enter a shallow dive, with or
> without turning, and the pilot will still experience a
> sensation of steady climb . . . if it is also very dark and the
> direction of take-off is away from a built-up lighted area,
> there is nothing to be seen which can give a horizon
> reference and the pilot is now very likely to get this false
> impression of the attitude of the aircraft in pitch.

While accepting that this might have happened, the Board considered the probable cause of the accident to be 'pilot's inattention to flight instruments during take-off in conditions of reduced visibility.'

Yet in certain critical situations, many of his most important instruments can easily be misread. The pilot can easily make mistakes over switches and printed figures, particularly if they are not highlighted or are poorly differentiated, and are in similar and thus confusing rows. This pertains even in some of the most modern and sophisticated aircraft, where pilots can easily be deceived by the design and positioning of levers and instruments. Frequently the flaps used to be raised in mistake for the under-carriage, and vice-versa, being often very close to each other. Now the flap lever is designed to look like flap and the undercarriage lever to look like a wheel, and they are usually well separated.

The most notorious deceiver of all aircraft instruments was the three-pointed altimeter. There were three pointers on the same dial, the largest indicating hundreds, a smaller one indicating thousands, and the smallest indicating tens of thousands of feet. Pilots were continually being deceived by this altimeter, which was for many years almost universal through-out the world. They would misread, usually by 10,000 feet, and numerous accidents resulted. These altimeters are still being manufactured and used in some countries, though the CAA banned their use in most aircraft types many years ago.

The counter-pointer altimeter, with one pointer and a numerical read-out, is now more usually fitted. The ways in which different-shaped dials and different-length pointers can be read and understood on instruments has very recently been the subject of research. Speed and accuracy of interpretation has been shown to differ widely.

There are other illusions and deceptions in flying. A DC-6 crashed in San Franciso Bay in conditions where the pilot might have been subjected to what is called the 'Cocquyt' effect. This occurs if a pilot tries to maintain visual flight in an overshoot following a missed approach. He may well not know the attitude of his aircraft and therefore be unable to interpret the position of lights or landmarks that he can see. The nose-up attitude of an aircraft taking off causes a light ahead to appear lower (and the aircraft higher) than it actually is. And on descent, with the nose down, the reverse applies.

A Convair, circling Springfield, Missouri to make an approach to the runway, struck the ground one and a quarter miles north-north-west of the airport. The Inquiry stated that the crew were not aware the aircraft was so low and was descending. The pilots were probably devoting their attention outside the cockpit towards distant airport lights while flying over sparsely lighted, flat terrain in restricted visibility. The Inquiry stated:

> An important psychological factor enters into an approach under these conditions and has been credited as a factor in other accidents or near accidents. The effect of such conditions has given flight crews an erroneous impression of altitude and/or the illusion that the aircraft is flying horizontally with respect of a distant light or group of lights, when in reality the nose attitude of the aircraft is up or down.

The pilot is subject to other illusions coming in to land. The normal approach to an aerodrome is made at about 3 degrees, and if the runway slopes upwards 1 degree, the illusion will be given that he is coming down too steeply. If the runway slopes downward 1 degree, the illusion is that the approach is too flat.

In rain, reflection on the windscreen adds its own illusion by indicating a false horizon below the true, which can be as great as 5 degrees. So, coming in to land at a distance of one mile, the runway appears 200 feet lower than it actually is.

Lighting too may well distort perception of distance. Bright lights can appear closer and dim lights more distant. This is especially relevant when there are no other lights in the vicinity – approaching an airfield at night over the jungle, or in from the sea. What is known as a black-hole effect pertains, creating an illusion of height.

In January 1974, a Boeing 707 approaching the runway at Pago Pago in heavy rain and strong wind crashed, killing ninety-six people. Though weather played a part, the black-hole phenomenon was suspected.

One of the most dangerous illusions, however, is when the pilot deludes himself that he can see. If cloud suddenly blocks his vision, he may convince himself that it is only temporary or only thin – and he may either continue in the cloud or dive his aircraft to shake himself free of the stuff. If he is on a VFR flight plan, he maintains it even though he is in cloud. If he has made an instrument approach to an aerodrome, misses the runway and overshoots, rather than follow the complicated and tiring procedure, he may try to hug the ground under the low overcast as he does another circuit, deluding himself that the cloud base and visibility will remain uniform and that he can see adequately.

As a result, accidents occur. Such an accident occurred near Montana. Descending to Butte airport, the pilot reported vertical visibility as 10,000 feet – that is no cloud below – which was the last message he sent. The aircraft crashed at 8,250 feet. The report says: 'It is believed that the final few miles prior to the crash were flown visually under conditions of intermittent and alternating instrument and visual flight.'

An aircraft entered a narrow pass in Alaska and crashed into a mountain. The report stated: 'It must have been apparent to the pilot that the pass could not be negotiated VFR at 3,000 feet, since the clouds were lower than that altitude.'

A C-47 crashed into a mountain range in Ecuador. The Inquiry stated: 'It is difficult to imagine this pilot attempting to pass over an 8,100-foot peak at 7,500 feet.'

When an American DC-6 crashed, the report stated:

> It was considered that the pilots did not maintain VFR during the approach. Since they were operating on a VFR flight plan, they were obligated to conduct the flight in VFR conditions. In order to continue the flight into an area of instrument weather, the pilot was required to change to an IFR plan. In this instance to do this would have involved a delay as the flight would have to maintain VFR conditions while the IFR request was being processed. The reason the route into the area in the restricted visibility was chosen was reflected in the pilot-in-command's testimony when he stated that the weather, as given, indicated that a landing on runway 36 was very feasible and it was to the advantage of the company and himself to continue straight in.

In August 1989 the pilot of a Short 330 of Olympic Airways was attempting to fly in bad visibility by visual flight rules, with his radar switched off, when conditions demanded IFR. The aircraft crashed into a hill on the island of Samos, killing thirty-four people.

There are numerous instances of such accidents, when the pilot deludes himself that he can proceed when he quite clearly cannot. Just as perceptual illusions probably have physiological causes, so the belief that it is safe to cut a corner has psychological ones. The American psychologist Woodworth says that an animal 'prefers to follow his nose, look at the goal and go where he is looking'. The nearer the goal, the stronger the pull. The nearer the airport, the more hypnotic the drive to continue.

In 1974 a device called the Ground Proximity Warning System was introduced which gave an aural 'pull up, pull up' warning to the pilot when he was approaching high ground. Unfortunately it was introduced too early, and five years later on was still producing more false warnings than true ones. Now, fortunately, considerable improvements have been made which have resulted in a sharp reduction in Controlled Flight into Terrain (CFIT) accidents.

As a result of such pressures, we can easily be deceived and deceive ourselves. We all tend to live in, and often rely on, an environment of illusion, as is so clearly demonstrated in a belief almost amounting to worship of film stars and charismatic leaders. A B-747 was reportedly approaching London Airport. On board was Errol Flynn, who was busy chatting up a pretty stewardess. On the descent, fog suddenly blotted out the airport, and the captain announced over the PA that he would have to divert. Among the disappointed passengers was an old lady who called over the Cabin Services Manager and said, 'But couldn't we still go on to London and ask Mr Flynn to do the landing?'

We deceive ourselves, and others are deceived by our own self-deception. We are sure we can do it, so in we plunge – sometimes without thinking. No other human factor is quite so powerful or so pressing on us to have a go than the male ego.

Eight

The Male Ego

The Inquiry into the world's worst aircraft disaster, the collision of two Jumbos at Tenerife in 1977 stated that the circumstances could have induced the co-pilot not to ask questions and 'to assume that the captain was always right'.

What it does not mention is that the captain in question probably also assumed that he was always right. In other words he was possessed of that double-edged sword, male egotism. Jack Enders, President of the Flight Safety Foundation, wrote recently of 'the many myths of machoism that have plagued safety in aviation since its beginning'.

An important part of anyone's identity is how he regards himself, his place in society and his attainments – the recognition of himself as a valuable individual. Mankind needs to have, as Robbie Burns wrote, 'a guid conceit of himself'. 'Guid' in this sense meaning just and accurate.

Freud identified the three parts of men's psyche: the id or subconscious, to which many of our inherited drives are consigned; the ego, which is supposedly the conscious rational mediator between these drives; and the superego, which houses our conscience and the constraints of society. In some people, especially those in authority, the ego becomes a dangerously over-developed fellow. Unfortunately, such people are often achievers and land important jobs with power over others, where subordinates' attitudes reinforce that already inflated ego.

While such authoritarian attitudes may or may not be valuable administratively, they can be disastrous on the flight deck of an aircraft. We have moved on from the days of the Flying Barons, the airline captains of the 1930s and '40s, when a captain was known to turn back because his favourite brand of milk was not on board, and another refused to leave the ramp until his smoked salmon sandwiches were produced. Authoritarianism still makes its appearance on the flight deck, however.

The RAF Institute of Aviation Medicine has stated that the following terms have been used by pilots to describe other crew members:

Captains describing co-pilots	*Co-pilots describing captains*
Competitive	Over-confident
Over-confident	Arrogant
Strong personality	Abrasive
Obstructive	Bad tempered
Obnoxious	Unpleasant
Bolshie	Sarcastic
Difficult	Over-critical
Unco-operative	Not easy to get on with
Bored	Intransigent
Lazy	Pig-headed
Number-chaser	Unpredictable
No sense of humour	Aggressive
Minimiser	Disagreeable
Complainer	Martinet
Lethargic	Tyrannical
Resentful	Autocratic
Bullying	Authoritarian
Talkative	Incompetent
	Overbearing

Flying is considered 'macho'. There is psychological evidence (Farmer 1984, Fry and Reinhardt 1969) that pilots exhibit 'active–masculine' personalities. Supporting these findings, Novello and Youssef (1974) showed a similar profile in women pilots who resembled the average male more than the average female. But in so far as women are biophilous, interested in preserving life, while men are necrophilous, concerned with the inanimate and destroying life, women pilots should be safer to fly with. Concern for safety is considered by some men as a female attribute.

A few years ago, Professor Cragh of Lund University devised a test to eliminate young men whose subconscious motive in joining the Air Force was to prove their manhood and who would therefore take greater risks and cause accidents. The test, known as the Defence Mechanism Test, was this – candidates were briefly shown the picture of a boy, holding in his hand what the Swedes call 'an attribute', which may be a violin, a gun, or a toy.

There is a catch to the test. In the top left-hand corner there flashes a subliminal face – that of a threatening male. When the candidates are asked to draw the picture of the boy and his 'attribute' much is revealed. Some of them are unable to reproduce the picture of him and the 'attribute' without certain characteristic distortions. Some draw him as a girl or a doll. Other candidates draw a protective line across the page as if to protect the boy from the threat – interpreted by psychiatrists to be of castration. The boy desires an Oedipus Complex relationship with his mother and fears retaliation from his father. Therefore he feels strong pressure to prove his manhood.

Professor Norman Dixon reports that the Swedish Air Force followed all candidates who took this Defence Mechanism Test and found it predicted accurately those men who might take undue risks. As a result of the test the number of flying fatalities dropped to near zero. The RAF spent £40,000 evaluating this test, but have since rejected it.

Airlines even resisted having women as cabin staff. Now there are at last an increasing number of women captains flying the world's air routes very successfully. But it was not until February 1990 that the RAF accepted them. And then the first two women officers to undergo jet training at Linton-on-Ouse were nicknamed 'Jim' and 'Syd'.

In both men and women, a responsible job reinforces his or

her concept of himself or herself as a valuable person. However, the need to preserve that concept can combine with other human factors like time pressure, conformity and the desire to please to produce a lethal situation. For all the human factors are more deadly in combination.

There can seldom have been an accident where so many human factors were present, when the steady, relentless psychological deterioration of aircrew could be so clearly shown, as in the Tenerife disaster.

On 27 March 1977, a bomb exploded in the passenger terminal at Las Palmas Airport on the island of Gran Canaria. There was a warning of a second device. Immediately the airport was closed to all air traffic and a search begun. As he slipped away, even the madman responsible could not have guessed that his outrage would form the first link in a chain of events leading to an aviation holocaust.

As the debris was being cleared, aircraft *en route* to Las Palmas were warned that they would be unable to land there. Among these were two Boeing 747 aircraft: Pan American 1736 from Los Angeles International Airport and KLM 4805 from Amsterdam, the latter carrying holidaymakers on behalf of the Holland International Travel Group.

The captain of KLM 4805 chose to divert to the neighbouring island of Tenerife, some fifty miles from their original destination. The captain of Pan American Clipper 1736, after first requesting and being denied permission to hold until Las Palmas was accepting aircraft, decided to do the same, as did most of the other aircraft *en route* to Las Palmas.

When KLM 4805 touched down at 13.38 that afternoon on Tenerife's Runway 30, the airport was beginning to fill with diverted flights, and the weather was fine. Thirty-seven minutes later, when the Pan Am Clipper landed, the apron was already crowded and some aircraft were parked on the taxiways. KLM 4805 was parked nearest to the threshold of Runway 12, followed in sequence by a Boeing 737, a Boeing 727, and a DC-8. The Pan Am Clipper was parked behind them.

Thus the factor of time and the factor of uncertainty were already being added to frustration and fatigue to combine eventually with other human factors to bring about the world's worst air disaster. A paragraph in the Spanish Inquiry which followed it says, '. . . uncertainty of the crew, who were not able to determine their limit exactly, must have contributed an important and psychological factor'. The Inquiry went on to point to 'a certain subconscious, though exteriorly repressed, irritation caused by the fact that the service was turning out so badly'.

That it was turning out so badly must have been especially frustrating for the KLM captain. He was KLM's chief flying instructor, a man of great prestige in the company. He himself had certified his co-pilot as fit to fly the Boeing 747. Correctly, therefore, he was a man to be respected and trusted. But as the chief instructor flying the route, herein lay a dangerous paradox.

One disadvantage of a senior airline post is that the holder gets fewer opportunities to fly the routes. The captain had averaged less than 260 hours a year actual flying time during the previous six years, perhaps less than one half of normal. In the past, it was often a cause of incredulity to British line pilots that when a member of royalty or a VIP was carried on a flight the service was put under the command of a management pilot. While being regarded as a natural perk for someone in authority, it resulted in the important personages often being flown by the least practised captain on the fleet.

Because of the time pressure and the hope of an early departure, the KLM captain had at first kept his passengers on board. But twenty minutes later, mindful of their comfort, he had changed his mind and arranged for them to be bussed to the terminal. The Pan Am captain kept his passengers on board. Once released into a packed terminal building, passengers are notoriously difficult to find when the time for departure comes. Perhaps, sensibly, the captain wished to be ready for a quick getaway.

It was not to be. When Las Palmas opened up again and Air

Traffic Control released the Pan Am aircraft to continue its journey, the crew found their route to the runway blocked by the KLM Jumbo. Not wishing to lose more time, the first officer and flight engineer climbed off the aeroplane to measure the distance between them and the other aircraft, reluctantly deciding that they could not get through without risk. The other aircraft parked behind KLM 4805 had, being smaller, managed to get past. There was nothing else for it. The Pan Am Boeing must wait until KLM 4805 moved off.

It was a long and frustrating wait. The KLM passengers were bussed back from the terminal and that took time. An hour later, KLM called the control tower and requested an estimated departure time. Then the captain decided to take on extra fuel. Presumably he wished to avoid refuelling at Las Palmas and thus to save time before the last leg of his journey back to Amsterdam.

At last he requested and was given permission to start up and then taxi to Runway 30. Now that their way was clear, the Pan Am aircraft followed suit.

By now, weather conditions were deteriorating. In common with many oceanic islands, Tenerife is subject to frequent low cloud which drifts in erratically off the sea. One moment the weather will be merely misty, then suddenly visibility will drop to near zero. One side of the airfield will be almost clear and the other fogbound. It was just such an evening, and conditions were expected to become worse.

At the time, the control tower had three radio frequencies available – 121.7MHz, 118.7MHz and 119.7MHz. But only two controllers were on duty, and 118.7 was used for taxi instructions and 119.7, the approach frequency, for both take-off and approach communications.

KLM 4805 requested permission to backtrack on Runway 12. Clearance was given to taxi back down the runway and exit at the third turn-off. The first officer misheard and read back 'first exit', but then the controller amended the instructions. KLM was to backtrack down the runway all the way, then complete a 180-degree turn to face the take-off direction. The first officer acknowledged the instruction, but the captain, now concentrating on the taxying, was beginning to overlook radio calls.

Meanwhile, Pan Am 1736 had been cleared to backtrack down the *same* runway, and leave at the third taxiway.

Like the KLM crew, however, they were experiencing communication difficulties. Both crews had the problem of taxying in poor and variable visibility. Both had to cope with the controller's accent. For the KLM crew, who spoke to each other in Dutch, there was the further strain of switching from the language they spoke in to a foreign language, English, in order to receive instructions from a controller who spoke that mutually foreign language with a further foreign accent.

A terrible game of blind man's buff started. The crew of Pan Am 1736 succeeded in identifying exits one and two by use of the airport chart. Then, through fatigue, or because they missed the turn-off in the fog, or considered the fourth exit might be easier, they overshot their designated exit, exit three.

Meanwhile, ahead of them, the highly experienced captain of KLM 4805 was also taxying down the runway in use. Beside him sat a first officer eight years younger than he was. Flying as co-pilot to a management captain is never relaxing. A critical report from a normal line captain can be disputed; disagreement with the assessment of the chief flying instructor is fruitless and might even make an enemy of him. This co-pilot would also have been conscious of his own inexperience on the 747. With only ninety-five hours on the type, he would not be thoroughly at home on the Jumbo. A delightful aircraft to fly, it nevertheless has features of size and mass which mark it out as different from other civil aircraft. Weighing between 350 and 400 tonnes, it has a wingspan of over 195 feet (59.6 metres) is 63 feet (19.3 metres) high, and at 232 feet (70.7 metres) is longer than the Wright brothers' first flight.

Its size creates problems for the pilot when taxying. The wing tips can barely be seen from the flight deck, and the pilots sit so high that it is difficult to be sure just where the sixteen main wheels are in relation to the taxiway edges and their projecting lights. Nor is it easy to judge how fast the aircraft is moving. Normal practice is to use the inertial navigation system as a speedometer. Recognising the problems of ground manoeuvring at the design stage, Boeing incorporated a system which allows the main wheels to turn in the opposite direction to the steered nose-wheel in order to negotiate bends. So the 180-degree turn into wind at the end of the runway needed the captain's full concentration.

When he had completed it, the co-pilot was trying to get ATC Airways clearance. But nevertheless, the captain began to open the throttles. The captain was anxious to take off, since he was scheduled to fly back to Amsterdam from Las Palmas, and there was a possibility that Dutch flight-time limitations would prohibit it unless he hurried.

The co-pilot exclaimed, 'Wait a minute, we don't have our ATC clearance!'

The captain's reply began with an implicit rebuke.

'No. I know that. Go ahead, ask.'

The comment was pointless, even defensive, and merely wasted time. He must have been aware that the co-pilot's concern was less with the clearance and more with his apparent intention to take off without one.

'Go ahead,' the captain said.

At this point, the visibility improved, but a bank of fog could be seen moving down the runway. The Pan Am Clipper moving down the runway was still hidden, but the brief break in the weather emphasised the need for a quick take-off.

The co-pilot called the tower. 'Ah – the KLM 4805 is now ready for take-off, and we're waiting for our ATC clearance.'

The controller read out the ATC clearance.

Just before the message ended, the captain said, 'Yes', and moved towards opening the throttle. The co-pilot began to read back the clearance. About six seconds before he had finished, the captain released the brakes, saying, 'Let's go . . . check thrust!' speaking over the top of the co-pilot as he read back the clearance.

They still had no take-off clearance. The unexpected start of the take-off in the middle of his read-back confused and disorientated the first officer, who became (according to the Inquiry Report) noticeably 'more hurried, less clear'.

As a result, his last sentence was quite unclear. 'We are now at take-off,' or, 'We are now . . . uh . . . taking off.'

By the time he had finished the call, the aircraft was rolling down the runway. A second and a half later, the engines were at take-off power.

The controller replied, 'OK . . . [and after a second's pause went on] stand by for take-off. I will call you.'

But in that second's gap Pan Am was calling to make their position clear. 'No, uh . . . and we are still taxying down the runway, the Clipper 1736'. Controller and Pan Am pilot spoke on top of each other, causing a squeal on the radio. Such a squeal and its cause are well known to airline pilots and the KLM captain should have been alerted to the fact that the controller might have been trying to talk to him, but had been blocked by another aircraft's transmission.

KLM had one more chance to be warned. The controller spoke to the Pan Am Clipper. 'Roger, Papa Alpha 1736, report the runway clear.'

Ten seconds later, the Pan Am 1736 replied, 'OK, we'll report when we're clear.'

This interchange clearly alerted the KLM engineer, who asked, 'Is he not clear, then?'

The engineer's question was a pivotal point as the operation teetered between complete safety and total disaster. Flight engineers occupy a unique position in the flight-deck hierarchy. Under the direct command of the captain, they must also answer to the first officer. They require no flying qualifications, although they often have training to ensure that they are *au fait* with the pilots' job. Being technically gifted, many soon become expert in piloting procedures and, indeed, many of them hold a private pilot's licence. All of them are involved closely in the operation and are normally expected to monitor the actions of both pilots at critical stages of the flight.

Outside the confines of the flight deck, they are responsible to a chief flight engineer. The checks which they undergo are naturally conducted by flight engineers. A serious disagreement with the captain will be investigated by his own chief, who might well support him. They are therefore *with*, but not *of*, the pilots.

This independence allows them a degree of latitude often not available to the co-pilot. A suggestion from the flight engineer to the captain does not carry the implied criticism that one from another pilot might. If any slight loss of face is involved, the flight engineer's suggestion can be interpreted almost as a layman's opinion if it involves piloting, and can be considered on its merits. It is one thing if the bank manager tells the doctor that his diagnosis is wrong, but quite another if a fellow doctor tells him.

The flight engineer of KLM 4805 had twenty-seven years' experience, and not far off twice as many flying hours as the two pilots put together. He was patently unhappy with the captain's unilateral decision to take off, as he had not himself heard the aircraft being given take-off clearance. He also had a high work load at this stage and knew he might just have missed it.

An aircraft the size and weight of a Boeing 747 is slow to accelerate. There was still time to close the throttles and brake to a halt. If the flight engineer was convinced that they had no clearance, there were only two options open to him. He could question the captain, or he could slam the throttles shut himself, thereby making discussion superfluous. Had any sign of support come from the co-pilot, there is little doubt that he would have done the latter. Disastrously, he chose the former.

To the engineer's query as to whether the Pan American 747 was clear, above the noise of the engines the captain said, 'What do you say?'

'Is he not clear, that Pan American?'

The captain replied, 'Oh, yes!'

On the flight deck of the Pan Am Clipper, the crew were

alarmed at the ambiguity of the situation, though they did not know that the KLM had begun its take-off run.

The captain said, 'Let's get the hell out of here!' Then, 'Yeah, he's anxious, isn't he?'

'Yeah,' replied his first officer, 'After he held us up for an hour and a half.'

'Now he's in a rush,' said the captain.

Suddenly the Pan Am captain saw the KLM's landing lights appear through the mist.

He shouted, 'There he is . . . look at him . . . that sonofabitch is coming!'

'Get off! Get off!' yelled the first officer. 'Get off! Get off!'

The Pan Am captain swung the aircraft to the left and opened the throttles to get clear.

At the same time, the KLM first officer called 'Vee One!'

Now KLM 4805 was committed to take-off.

Four seconds later they saw the Pan Am 747 dead ahead.

The KLM captain uttered a horrified exclamation. At more than 150 mph there was no time to take effective evasive action. He hauled back frantically on the control column, hoping to climb over the top of the other aircraft.

It was too late.

KLM 4805 skidded over the top of the Pan Am's rear fuselage, destroying it and shearing off the tail. It continued in flight for a short distance, hitting the runway some 150 metres beyond, slid for 300 metres and exploded. There were no survivors from the 248 passengers and crew. In what was left of the Pan Am Jumbo, 326 people died and 9 more later succumbed to their injuries.

Whilst it was clear that the co-pilot knew they had no take-off clearance, he acceded to the captain's authority and impatience to be airborne. The flight engineer had serious doubts, but he too was silenced by the authority figure's ego.

The investigation by the Spanish Civil Aviation Authority found no evidence of mechanical or electrical failure. The aircraft radios were working normally, and there was no sign of crew incapacitation. With every other avenue closed, the cause of the accident clearly pointed to those factors most difficult to quantify – the human factors. The Inquiry identified some of them: fatigue, overload, fixation, frustration, time pressure, authority in the cockpit, the desire to please the passengers.

Added to that, the captain's long stint in simulator instruction would have a bearing in that during those spells he would be taking the role of controller and issuing clearances. In many cases, no radio would be used and simulator take-offs would be carried out *without any clearance at all*. But perhaps the most important factors were his egotism and his prestige.

The search for a pilot's lost prestige was at the root of an accident to a Twin Otter near the Great Bear Lake in 1984. The maintaining of prestige and fear of failure is ingrained in the average pilot – with good reason. No profession is tested so often and so regularly as that of airline flying. Medicals and flying checks punctuate the pilot's year, and at any of them he might lose his flying licence and his job. He constantly has to prove himself to other people – and to himself. Further stress is induced by all this testing, which can produce fear of failure in other aspects of life. Most men do not take kindly to remarks about their car driving or their sex life. Pilots are particularly touchy on the subject of the latter, perhaps because flying stresses may well affect it. One of the first questions a pilot is likely to ask a doctor after an injury is, 'Am I all right down there?' The ace Adrian Warburton, double DSO, triple DFC, wounded in numerous dogfights over the Malta area during the Second World War was afraid of that – but of nothing else.

Added to the pilot's personality and the attendant stresses that may induce him to take risks is the fact that in some areas of the world, the community literally *depends* on him to take risks. Such an area is the North-West Territory of Canada, particularly in the snowy wastes of the Franklin Mountains to the west of Great Bear Lake.

At noon on 9 October an Arctic front extended eastwards towards the Great Bear Lake and the sky was blanketed by low stratus cloud. At Fort Norman, the pilot of the Twin Otter service bound for Fort Franklin with a stopover at Norman Wells was anxious about the weather. Originally he cancelled the first leg of the flight. Then he delayed it. However, by following the Mackenzie river just above the water, he managed to reach Norman Wells, where he unloaded one of his seven passengers and a load of freight.

Then he was buttonholed by another pilot who had just returned to Norman Wells after an unsuccessful attempt to reach Fort Franklin. This man reported near nil visibility and cloud down to the treetops. The pilot of the Twin Otter again cancelled his flight, but a few minutes later changed his mind and took off at 16.08. No pressure had been put on him by the company. The decision was his alone. The flight was supposed to be flown in visual, but was clearly well below Visual Flight Rules.

At 17.15, the Twin Otter was over Fort Franklin. Fog filled both the Mackenzie river and the Great Bear Lake. The inhabitants were horrified to hear the roar of an engine immediately above them, but invisible. A local resident who had a portable VHF transceiver immediately contacted the pilot to tell him conditions were impossible.

The pilot told him he would not land, but so concerned was the resident that he got into his car and drove to the airstrip. Almost immediately, he heard the aircraft returning. He called the pilot again, telling him that visibility was only around seventy yards.

Shortly afterwards, he heard a shattering crash. The aircraft had struck a 200-foot communication tower to the east of the hamlet. The pilot was familiar with the airfield and very well aware of the tower. The Twin Otter burned, sliding forward until it came to rest upside down between a row of houses. No one on board survived.

Besides the usual pressures of his particular job in transporting food, medicine, mail and other necessities of life to isolated villages, the Accident Report stated that the pilot had 'a greater than usual personal need to complete the flight'.

All pilots at some time feel the pressure of the Zeigarnik effect – the stress induced by an uncompleted task, especially acute when landing is frustrated. But what was this quiet, kindly, conservative pilot's 'greater than usual personal need'? Although he had only been with his present company, Nahanni, for a few months, he had flown with his previous company for over twelve years. With them he had earned the reputation of being an excellent pilot, and prior to March 1984, he had not experienced any known accident.

But on 6 March, seven months before the fatal crash, everything changed. While he was landing a Twin Otter on rough ice at Ward Hunt Island, the nose ski struck the ice heavily, damaging the bulkhead. This incident was followed by another only five weeks later, in which similar damage was done while he was taking off from an unprepared Arctic ice strip near the geographic North Pole. In July, a third incident occurred while he was trying to land on an unprepared surface on Somerset Island, which he overshot by 1,000 feet, landing on rough terrain and damaging the main landing gear, aircraft tail and the nose-gear assembly.

By this time, more than the aircraft concerned were damaged. The pilot's high reputation was gone. Company management began to question his ability to make operational decisions. His own confidence at a low ebb, he asked to be reassigned to another base of operations, and was sent to Inuvik, where the company believed the flying was less demanding.

But his ill-luck went with him.

On 18 August, the pilot was the captain of a Twin Otter which ditched in the Beaufort Sea when both engines failed as a result of water contamination of the fuel. He and his co-pilot had refuelled the aircraft from barrels, using an extension to the stand-pipe refuelling pump which allowed the barrel to be completely drained, thereby pumping any water which had settled in the bottom of the barrels straight into the aircraft fuel tanks. Furthermore, on completion of refuelling, they had not sampled the aircraft tanks for water contamination.

The pilot was blamed, his resignation called for and he left the company at the end of August.

However, the chief pilot of Nahanni did not share that company's condemnation. He believed that the pilot had shown a high degree of airmanship during the ditching accident, and having flown as his supervisor many years before with another company, he had considerable faith in him – a faith which, naturally, the pilot of the Twin Otter would want to justify. Besides, he had done far more difficult and dangerous flights than the one to Fort Franklin. These trips were a bit of a come-down for him. He didn't want to cry off and go back, even though someone else had already done so. The macho image and the need to prove himself were strong.

Other factors also tightened the screw – so much stress in so short a time – four accidents, a termination of employment, a new job. And though it has been pointed out that emotional stress does not by itself cause an accident, 'high *potential* for an accident is transformed into the *reality* of an accident through some act of commission or omission'. The commission was in attempting such a landing. The omission was forgetting the position of the 200-foot tower.

Most accidents leave a feeling of 'if only' – this one especially so. The resident of Fort Franklin tried very valiantly to warn the pilot and avert tragedy. If only the pilot could have allowed himself to have given up and returned to Norman Wells.

The consistent 'if only' that runs through all accidents is 'if only human factors had been more carefully studied or indeed studied at all'.

'Human factors', said the Accident Inquiry Report, 'is a subject which does not enjoy wide acceptance in the aviation industry in Canada'.

The Inquiry also cited an American study on pilots operating in similar conditions in Alaska which identified 'the bush pilot syndrome' – as a factor which contributed to the high accident rate in Alaska. This syndrome was described as an attitude on the part of Alaskan operators, pilots and passengers that ranged 'from a casual acceptance of risks to a willingness to take unwarranted risks'.

During my stays in South America, I found the custom appeared to be that for a man to admit he was wrong was to insult his own manhood – a quality hardly to be looked for in the selection of an airline pilot. This appeared to be reflected in the statistics for aircraft accidents during the period from 1973 to 1984, when Colombia topped the world airlines with 27.464 fatal events per one million flights, though of course other considerations were involved. Turkey was second with 17.369, Egypt third with 13.423 – both countries pretty male-orientated. The UK and USA were well below the average of 1.846, while Australia was at the very bottom with 0.328 fatal incidents per million flights. Yet Australians have a reputation for being macho, especially with women. But in flying this does not appear to intrude, and it is balanced by their lack of hesitation in challenging those above them, and their ability to get along with one another. Machoism is what human factor education would try to reduce in civil airline pilots.

In military flying the disciplined macho man is the chap they want. Military pilots have to risk their aircraft and their lives by putting them into potentially dangerous situations, and be quick-witted enough to get themselves out of those situations. It is also necessary to preserve in them the continual desire and ability to do so. As Jones (1986) suggested, the most notable characteristic of successful flyers is their absolute faith in themselves. Anything that shakes or destroys this belief or casts doubt on their self-control leads to a disproportionate anxiety about flying. As in the ability to swim, the ability to fly is founded on self-confidence. And the military pilot's macho ego has to be preserved by various devices. The motto of an American F-111 squadron based in Britain is: 'We are the Greatest'. The RAF 'piece-of-cake' attitude during the Second World War was the same sort of Freudian defence mechanism the other way round. The USAF elevate the man, the RAF denigrate the dangerous operation. To protect themselves from the normal reaction to large combat losses – i.e. fear – individual pilots of both Air Forces convinced themselves that 'It can't happen to me'.

Inevitably, to prove that point to themselves, military pilots do on occasion behave recklessly. Bader lost both legs 'beating up' the officers' mess, yet with great courage he became a fine leader of men and a fearless pilot.

During the Second World War, the macho image was encouraged, off duty and on. Senior officers applauded as young pilots 'walked' on the ceiling leaving sooty footprints, played High Cockalorum, drove along the Mess corridors on motor bikes and shot the glasses off the bar shelves with their revolvers.

In peacetime, such behaviour is frowned upon – but the desire for the macho image persists.

In 1983, the pilot of an RAF Gazelle helicopter practising mountain flying in Snowdonia flew at a height of ten feet over a mountain railway passenger train 'to the grave consternation of the driver'. The aircraft then circled the Snowdon summit before descending again to hover over a party of schoolchildren and their teachers, and turned south. When it was about a quarter of a mile away, it went into a near vertical climb and executed a wing-over to starboard. It then descended in a reciprocal direction, overflew the school party at high speed at a reported height of between five and ten feet, then impacted the ground seventy feet beyond the party. Both the qualified instructor and the student pilot were killed.

The verdict of the Inquiry was understandably that of culpable negligence, but there are other less obvious cases when a verdict of pilot error is arrived at by an RAF inquiry. When a Jaguar and a Tornado collided doing 'simulated attitude pro-files' in 1984, the verdict was 'pilot error' – the flight safety comment being that: 'In free airspace, pilots must accept full responsibility for their aircraft's deconfliction with others'.

Two Hercules collided in 1982 during air combat training. Both pilots were found 'culpably negligent', the surviving pilot being reproved by the Air Officer Commanding.

In Chapter 5 it was shown how difficult it can be to avoid

other aircraft in the sky. All the four pilots mentioned above were placed in a difficult and dangerous situation as a duty. But it is necessary for their training, the RAF would say, avoiding the term 'human error' and preferring the hoary old concept of 'pilot error'.

Unlike the USAF, who are very open about accidents and their causes, the RAF keep their accident reports under wraps. This is, they say, because they are classified 'restricted'; traditionally only the person who classified them can unclassify them, and he is often difficult to locate. Whittle's thesis on the jet engine is reportedly still classified.

The dilemma of the RAF can clearly be seen: risk-taking has to be encouraged and discouraged. It is not the same in civil flying, however.

Can risks be assessed? Can pilots learn that *this* is an acceptable risk, but *that* is not?

How does the pilot decide?

Nine

Decision-Making

Most of us have difficulty in taking decisions. It is one of those things we like to put off until tomorrow. It is stressful and tiring. Once a decision has been taken there is a strong feeling of relief, but the decision may be a wrong one, and then there is a tendency to stick to it through thick and thin, because unpicking a decision is even more difficult and stressful and is in some instances damaging to the person's ego. Politicians, dictators and generals are very susceptible to this disastrous habit.

Not only has an airline captain often to take a decision quickly, but it has to be the right decision for a particular circumstance – and he must try to keep his mind flexible so that he can change that decision. An analysis of FAA reports was undertaken in 1977. This showed that during a four-year period errors in pilot judgement accounted for over 50 per cent of pilot fatalities. Yet into this aspect there is very little research.

Psychologists have begun to be interested in 'decision theory'. After all, effective decision-making is a biological, sociological and economic need for our survival. Our distant ancestors coped with their environment by instinct and reflexes. We still use those on certain levels. When we burn our fingers we automatically withdraw our hand by conditioned reflex – we don't waste time deciding to withdraw it.

There are skills which a pilot learns that can become almost a conditioned reflex. By overlearning and practice, the pilot achieves a skill sequence and skill rhythm that is so well organised that it is highly resistant to wrong moves, though this skill sequence (with multiple variations built into it to cope with emergencies) may be disorganised by stress or fatigue.

There are, however, many decisions that an airline captain has to make which are *not* automatic. No flight is exactly like another flight and much conscious thought has to be given as to how to deal with different and unexpected circumstances. With a fire on board at take-off, should he try to return to the airfield or crash-land immediately? With unforeseen heavy headwinds, should he go on, go back or divert?

And what are the processes by which he arrives at the decision? First, the pilot must weigh the input from a number of information sources to help him understand the situation. Additional information will be available to him from his memory store, but, as already mentioned, there are many limitations on what we see and what we hear. As Captain Monan notes in his 1986 study, 'Pilots heard what they expected to hear and frequently did not hear what they did not anticipate hearing'.

From all this input the pilot has to make an assessment of the alternatives open to him. He then has to choose an appropriate action, balancing the pros and cons of the probable outcome. As in everyday life, the decision-maker never has complete information. We can only estimate outcomes. But perhaps the most important factor in decision-making is our degree of arousal when we take it.

Unlike aircraft instruments, the human brain is never switched off but always in a state of being 'on'. In a reaction to menace or surprise, adrenalin pours into the blood to give it the strength and energy to fight, accelerating the heart-beat, raising the blood pressure. Psychological research has shown that, under high arousal, thinking becomes more rigid, and there is a tendency to stereotype in decision-making. More than the rest of us, it is very likely that the pilot will have to take his decision in a state of high arousal, in a stress situation and when the defence mechanisms with which Man is equipped to counter the effects of a stressful environment will narrow his mental and physical vision.

For every task, there is an optimum level of arousal. Extremes of arousal, whether very high or very low, reduce any possibility of rational decision-making. Unfortunately the most difficult problems, as those sometimes encountered in the air, are often the most emotionally arousing. The result is that the more vital the decision, the poorer the pilots's state of mind when taking it. Worse still, the longer the arousal goes on, the more irrational the decisions.

This must surely have been the problem for the captain of Saudi Arabia Flight 163, a Lockheed Tristar which departed Riyadh on the evening of 19 August 1980 with 301 people on board – 287 passengers (including 15 infants) and 14 crew members.

Flight 163 was cleared via green airway number 53 to cruise at an assigned altitude of 35,000 feet. The initial climb was uneventful, but seven minutes after take-off the flight crew were alerted that there was smoke in the aft cargo hold. Cargo compartments are normally inaccessible in flight, and are monitored by an automatic system which gives an audible and visual signal on the flight deck.

The crew knew that the correct procedure to follow for a smoke warning was itemised in the checklist. Their arousal high, they couldn't at first find it. Frantically they searched through the 'Abnormal Procedures' section. All three crew members unfortunately suffered from learning difficulties. The captain was said to have difficulty in adapting to changing circumstances – a grave handicap in decision-making – the first officer had failed his training programme, though he was later reinstated, and another hidden danger on the flight deck was that the flight engineer suffered from dyslexia, which is closely related to laterality problems and the confusion of left and right. (Chapter 14) All those handicaps could hardly have speeded the search for the correct procedure.

At last they found the correct drill under 'Emergency Procedures', but it took four and a half valuable minutes to carry out the checks, and the delay put the aircraft more than twenty-five miles further from Riyadh. This was the first of the delaying of decisions which were to have such catastrophic results.

Up to that moment they had received no report from the cabin staff that anything was amiss in the passenger cabin. Nevertheless, the captain sent his engineer aft to check that all was well. In no time at all he was back to report: 'We've got a fire back there!'

There is no effective way of fighting an aircraft fuselage fire in the air once it takes hold. Flammable materials and a plentiful supply of air ensure that. Fire extinguishers are good for a small conflagration only if it is caught early. Their only hope was to get back on the ground as quickly as humanly possible. They had one great advantage. They were still only seventy-eight miles from Riyadh and the weather was clear. If the fire could be contained, they would be back on Riyadh's runway within twenty minutes.

As the captain altered course, the first officer called Riyadh on the radio.

'163, we are coming back to Riyadh.'

Riyadh asked the reason.

'We got fire in the cabin, please alert the firetrucks.'

Then began the agonising race against time. The captain increased speed and began the long descent from 22,000 feet. After the captain's decision to return, the crew's actions deteriorated further.

The flight engineer made a second visit to the passenger cabin. This time his report was more reassuring. 'It's just smoke in the aft,' then added, 'Everybody's panicking in the back, though.'

As they dived through 12,000 feet, the captain asked for the 'landing preliminary' checklist. Before it could be completed, a second smoke-detector warning sounded.

'What can I say?' asked the flight engineer.

'OK,' replied the captain.

'I think it's all right now,' added the flight engineer.

As if in reply to his optimism, a third warning sounded.

At that moment, the throttle for number two engine jammed. No amount of effort would move it. Although they couldn't know it, the fire in the aft cargo bay had burnt through the operating cable. As the captain announced his intention of shutting the engine down, a stewardess arrived to say that there was now an actual fire in the passenger cabin. Then a second rushed in to say that there was no way she could get to the back of the aircraft as 'people are fighting in the aisles'.

One of the cabin staff shouted over the cabin address system: 'Please everybody sit down! Move out of the way! Everybody sit down! Move out of the aisle! There is no danger from the airplane, everybody should stay in their seats!'

It is doubtful that she had any effect on the terrified passengers. Religious chanting could be heard amid the shouting and the cabin staff could still not persuade passengers back into their seats.

Meanwhile, the crew had been emphasising to Riyadh the importance of getting firetrucks to the back of the aircraft after landing. Riyadh tower contacted Firetruck Three, waiting by the runway: 'OK, sir, the fire on the cockpit, when the aircraft land, I want you to follow them the tail, from his tail. Drive behind it from the tail. OK, OK, Hamad.'

Seven minutes before landing, a stewardess reported that, 'There is too much smoke in the back.'

Since the captain was busy locating the runway for landing, the flight engineer acknowledged the message as he checked the smoke detector yet again. 'OK, there's both A and B loops working again and no indication of smoke.'

The sheer futility of the remark made the captain query it. The flight engineer stuck stolidly to his guns, repeating that there was no indication of smoke. Yet the passenger cabin was full of smoke.

Then the smoke detector sounded again.

Five minutes before touchdown, a cabin attendant asked the captain if they should carry out an emergency evacuation after landing.

She received no coherent reply, even though the question was repeated. Perhaps it was not surprising. The captain was busy flying the Tristar and appeared to be getting no assistance from his first officer, who so far had done little except transmit radio messages when prompted. Behind him, the dyslexic flight engineer was engrossed in repeatedly pointless checks of the smoke-detector system interspersed with optimistic comments about the lack of positive indications. The reality of an aircraft filled with smoke appeared to be irrelevant to him.

Denial is a well-known defence mechanism. When the level of stress is unbearable, we deny the existence of the stressful situation. Not only the first officer but also the flight engineer had at one point in their careers been dropped from the training programme. The Inquiry pointed out that reinstatement of terminated crew men is not desirable. As for the captain, so narrowed had his concentration become on the act of getting the aircraft down that he was unable to take any other decisions.

A minute later, a cabin attendant once again asked the captain whether they should carry out an emergency evacuation on landing. His only response was to order her back to her seat. He could not communicate with anyone trying to press him for the decision it was so impossible for him to make.

Just over a minute before landing, the flight engineer informed the captain that the cabin staff still wished to know whether to carry out an emergency evacuation of the aircraft after landing. The captain, still concentrating on his flying, replied with a request for '33 flap'.

By now, the cabin staff were desperate to know just what to do after the aircraft touched down. They knew they could be forced to cope with an aircraft full of hysterical passengers.

Half a minute before landing, the captain at last decided.

'Tell them . . . tell them to *not* evacuate!'

In the cold light of day, the decision appears incomprehensible. They had turned and fled back to the sanctuary of Riyadh Airport with a burning cargo deck, and they were not to escape to safety as soon as the opportunity arose?

Why?

There was no time for argument, though. The aircraft was

about to land. Witnesses saw smoke coming from the rear of the aircraft while it was on its short final approach.

Down on the airport the firetrucks waited in position. They expected the Tristar to brake hard on the runway. Instead, it rolled to the end, turned off up the taxiway and came gently to rest with the engines running. It was now two minutes and forty seconds after touch-down. The vehicles gave chase. Now surely the doors would be flung open, deploying the chutes and allowing 301 people (all of them uninjured) to tumble to safety.

Nothing happened. The crew seemed still gripped in a lacuna of indecision. The captain had asked the tower if any fire could be seen in the tail and was perhaps reassured that none could. After three minutes, the tower asked Flight 163 if they wished to continue to the ramp or shut down the engines.

The reply, again indecisive, was, 'Stand-by.' Then, 'OK, we are shutting down the engines now and evacuating.'

A minute and a half later, the watchers saw fire at the back of the aircraft. Immediately the control tower passed on the news. (Surprisingly, a direct line between the aircraft and the fire fighters had not been made available.)

'Affirmative,' replied the Tristar. 'We are trying to evacuate now.'

That was their last transmission.

But no attempt was made to open the emergency doors from the inside, perhaps because the toxic fumes were beginning to suffocate crew and passengers. The surrounding firemen, who were by now covering the back of the aircraft with foam and water, saw a sudden puff of white and black smoke from the belly of the aircraft. Insignificant as it looked from the outside, it was the product of a flash fire which ripped through the interior.

Attempts to gain entrance to the aircraft were at first unsuccessful. No one had anticipated the need to open the doors from outside. The height of the doors from the ground, and the difficulty caused by foam obscuring the exits delayed access. When questioned at the subsequent Inquiry, it was found that the fire-fighters' knowledge of aircraft doors ranged 'from limited to non-existent'. They were also said to be inefficient and disorganised. It was an unbelievable twenty-three minutes after engine shutdown before Door Two on the right side was opened.

By then, it was too late to save any of the occupants. All 301 people on board had died of smoke inhalation or burns. All had been alive and unhurt when the aircraft landed.

Excluding the captain's orders not to evacuate the aircraft as soon as possible, the accident investigators found many things to puzzle them. Most of the fire extinguishers on board had been used, but none of the oxygen masks. Even the flight-deck crew, whose survival was essential for the safe return of the aircraft, had not troubled to wear them.

The cabin staff were still at their allotted stations. In spite of the captain's decision against an emergency evacuation, company rules empowered cabin staff to carry one out *in extremis*. They were strictly forbidden from going ahead while the engines were running, so perhaps those lost minutes after the aircraft stopped were the reason.

The flight engineer appeared to have continued his state of denial and to have carried out his shutdown checks as though conditions were normal, switching off the air-conditioning packs and eliminating any ventilation air to the cabin interior. The crash investigators surmised that *this* could have triggered the flash fire which removed all oxygen from the air – another action resulting from the need to deny the reality of the situation.

Although there were many human factors contributing to the awful ultimate scenario, one stands out above the rest. The captain's inability to make the right decisions, culminating in the wrong decision to turn the aircraft on to the taxiway instead of applying full brake after landing and ordering an immediate emergency evacuation.

From the moment the warning of the fire in the cargo hold sounded, decisions were taken wrongly or too late. It was as if the fire warning itself triggered off the crew's psychological defence mechanisms, particularly Freud's concept of denial. They therefore found it difficult to make the right decisions because subconsciously they were denying that any stress situation was there.

Similarly incorrect decisions were evident in the Boeing 737 crash on 14th Street Bridge near Washington National Airport on 13 January 1982.

The crew had brought the aircraft in from the warmth of Miami in freezing conditions less than ten minutes before a snowstorm closed the airport, delaying their return scheduled flight to Fort Lauderdale, Florida. To add to the crew's frustration, de-icing was interrupted by delays. There was a change of mechanic halfway through the application of the methylene glycol and water solution to the aircraft, and unknown to the crew there were certain deficiencies in the de-icing. The Boeing Manual cautions that de-icing solutions can be diluted by melting snow, resulting in the mixture re-freezing as ice.

From then on, a number of mistaken decisions established the scenario for the disaster that followed. First, in spite of the bad weather, the not very experienced captain allowed the even less experienced first officer to do the take-off. Then inexperience of the winter weather conditions caused the crew to make further wrong decisions. As their name, Air Florida, might suggest, almost all their experience was in warmer climates. Therefore, to add to their visual clues, they did not have the hypotheses available from their memory store to help them interpret those clues.

So when the airport opened again, neither captain nor first officer inspected the aircraft to see if it was free of ice and snow. And when the aircraft doors were closed, the jetway retracted and the tug attempting to push her back couldn't move her, the crew decided to start the engines and apply reverse thrust. Snow and slush were thus blown everywhere including the engine intakes, where it could form as deadly ice.

The reverse-thrust ploy didn't work, and they needed a replacement tug which this time successfully pushed them back.

The co-pilot read out the start checklist. When he called out 'anti-ice' (the system which protects the engines from the effects of ice and slush) the captain incredibly answered, 'Off.' And incredibly, perhaps because stress and time pressure had narrowed their perceptions, there was no query from the first officer. With 'anti-ice' switched on, one of the probes responsible for measuring engine power has heated air fed to it. Should it freeze up because anti-ice is switched off, the cockpit instrument will grossly overread. The power set by the pilot for take-off will as a result be far too low.

The captain then took another extraordinary decision. They were taxying out behind a New York Air DC-9 joining the queue for take-off, when he decided that they would tuck themselves in so close to the DC-9 that the heat from the DC's engines would thaw out the accretions of snow and ice on their aircraft.

The following is taken from the cockpit voice-recorder.

The captain: 'Tell you what, my windshield will be de-iced, don't know about my wings.'

The first officer: 'Well, all we need is the inside of the wings. The wings are gonna speed up on eighty anyway, they'll shuck all that other stuff.'

Yet Boeing's flight manual states: 'Maintain a greater distance than normal between airplanes when taxying on ice or snow-covered areas. Engine exhausts may form ice on the ramp and take-off areas of the runway and blow snow and slush which freezes on surfaces it contacts.' The heat from Air New York's engines was effectively melting the snow and enabling it to refreeze as infinitely more threatening ice.

As the Air New York aircraft moved to the head of the runway for departure, Air Florida 90 taxied to the holding point. Here the special briefing should have included discussion of actions in case of rejected take-off.

The first officer asked, 'Slushy runway. Do you want me to do anything special for this or just go for it?'

'Unless you got anything special you'd like to do,' the captain replied.

At the end of their take-off clearance, the tower controller added, 'No delay on departure if you will, traffic's two and a half out for the runway.'

Obviously the controller wanted to get the runway cleared and the queue of aircraft moving. Thus a time pressure was added to whatever decision the captain might have to make. For early on in the ill-fated take-off roll, it seems clear that he should have decided to abandon take-off. Again perhaps as a result of lack of memory hypotheses, the crew did not seem to realise that their engine-power readings were improper because of accretions of ice and snow.

During engine spool-up, the captain commented, 'Real cold here, real cold.' And it has been suggested that he might well have thought that the engines were more efficient in the cold.

As the B-737 sped towards the boundary through the snow, the first officer commented three times, 'That's not right . . .' but Vee One (the speed at which they could still stop on the runway) was passed.

What the co-pilot felt 'wasn't right' would have been the readings on the rest of the engine instruments, RPMs and temperatures. Only the co-pilot was concerned, but still he took no positive action. Neither was the ice on the wings helping. As they rolled down the runway, a captain of one of the waiting aircraft commented to his crew, 'Look at the junk on that airplane!'

The profile of a modern aircraft wing is a very sophisticated affair, developed over decades of design and refinement. Any alteration to its shape can have devastating effects upon its ability to produce lift. Add low power to a wing distorted by ice and the mixture is lethal.

As the wheels of Flight 90 left the ground, the stickshaker operated, signifying that the aircraft was close to the stall.

'Forward, forward!' called the captain, urging the first officer to ease the control column forward and maintain flying speed.

Only at the very last moment did the pilots decide to shove the throttles fully open and gain the maximum power they still had

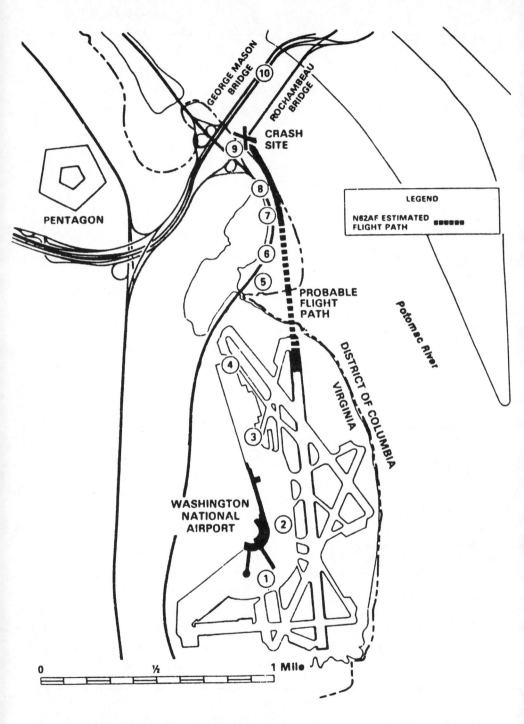

Washington Bridge Crash: Flightpath and witness location

available. Subsequent calculations showed that if they had done so when things began to go wrong, the aircraft and all on board might still have been saved.

So might many people in the line of cars along the crowded Washington Bridge. As it was, the 737 staggered off the ground, hit the bridge, tore up massive lumps of concrete and lengths of railing, then fell into the icy waters of the Sound. Only five of the seventy-nine people on board survived, and many people on the bridge were killed inside their vehicles. That anyone survived at all was due to the heroism of bystanders and surviving crew. Repeatedly they dived under the ice to drag out survivors.

One after another, wrong decisions had been taken, exacerbated by the fact that the crew were more familiar with the warmer conditions in Miami. Indeed, the ex-fighter-pilot first officer had only operated in icing conditions twice before. But the final wrong decision was *not to open the engines up to full power* until it was too late.

Yet the accident was foreshadowed. There had been a similar incident to a B-737 at Gander a month before (see Chapter 17).

After Washington Bridge, the NTSB issued a long list of recommendations for operation in snow and ice. Boeing telexed warnings to airlines and the NTSB Accident Report drew attention to the 'known inherent pitch-up characteristics of the B-737 aircraft when the leading-edge is contaminated with even small amounts of snow and ice'.

But at 16.05 on 13 January 1982, when Air Florida Flight 95 began its take-off from Washington National Airport, those lessons had not yet been fully learned.

Ten

Learning and Regression

Flying an aeroplane is a learned skill.

Learning is so involved in perception, thinking and memory that it is impossible to put it into a tight compartment. One psychologist has described learning as 'the process of being modified, more or less permanently, by what happens in the world around us, by what we do, and by what we observe'.

It can be grouped into three categories. First, conditioned-response learning, which ensures that after sufficient repetitive pairings of two stimuli the organism acquires a response to a hitherto neutral stimulus. Secondly, rote learning, where a series of words or movements is committed to memory. Thirdly, trial-and-error learning, whereby the organism learns to carry out the *correct* response from a number of responses and memorises it.

All three categories come into flying an aeroplane. The speed with which the mind of a student learns will depend partly on the communication ability of his instructor, and partly on the tools on which he is taught. The two attributes that distinguish a skill from learning a single response are its integration into a pattern and its flexible serial ordering. Practised sufficiently, it can become almost automatic. Once learned, it is rarely forgotten.

For the average healthy man or woman with few traits predisposing him or her in the wrong direction, learning to fly is not difficult. Essentially the pupil identifies with the role model, and after an average of half-a-dozen hours copying his instructor, he/she should be able to go solo in a light aeroplane.

Selecting people who are likely to be able to learn to fly quickly is therefore a fairly easy exercise. A good impression can be obtained by an interview, together with a short flight to check their motor skills and whether they can judge height above the ground.

Selecting people who are likely to become good military pilots and airline captains is another thing altogether. Because failures are so expensive, over the years a fair amount of the small sum available for research into aviation psychology has been spent in this area, with often contradictory and disappointing results.

This is not surprising. In fact differences in civil-airline-pilot ability will only manifest themselves under stress. These differences can be massive, and it is these that the selectors are somehow supposed to discover. Roscoe and North (1981) list the predicted variables as 'attention left over to take care of an emergency while not losing control of the routine; being able to estimate quickly probable outcomes of different courses of action; having a sense of relative values that allows rapid re-ordering of priorities as situations deteriorate or improve; decisiveness of action in the face of indecision in others'.

Bearing in mind each pilot's different personality, background and education, together with the numerous influences and stresses on him that differ at different times and in different situations, it is small wonder that finding tests to select the right candidate has proved nearly impossible.

In the meantime, airlines and air forces try out their own ideas on selection. Some prefer batteries of tests on cognitive load, risk perception, listening, defence mechanism tests, together with interviews and appearance before a three-day selection board. Others such as Dan Air (who only recruit licensed pilots) have a simple interview, a test on the simulator and a psychological profile designed by the Institute of Aviation Medicine.

The RAF and British Airways have the former, while British Midland and other airlines have the latter. According to Captain Jack Nicholl, ex-Manager of the Oxford Flying School to which most of the successful candidates go and ex-Chief Training Captain of BOAC, candidates from both systems show little difference in ability. And the actual *flying* skill of airline pilots throughout the world is first class. As a result of enormous sums spent on highly realistic simulators and *flying* training, together with more highly trained air traffic controllers, increasingly sophisticated traffic control equipment and operations, accidents caused by pilots' *flying skill* are now very rare.

But the world's stock of very experienced pilots is running low and Professor Earl Wiener of Miami University sounds a note of warning: 'Soon the airlines in the US and elsewhere will face the greatest peacetime training challenge in history ... very inexperienced pilots will be placed into the right (hand) seats of very sophisticated aircraft.'

Massive steps forward in engine and fuselage reliability, in radio and radar have been made, all making reductions in their share of the causes of aircraft accidents, while human factors remain almost constant, causing over 70 per cent of all aircraft accidents. Yet compared with actual *flying* training, a minuscule amount of money and time has been allotted to human factor training. It has taken disastrous accidents to trigger off long-overdue attention to human factors. The Portland running-out-of-fuel and the Jumbos colliding at Tenerife were the catalysts for human factor courses in United and KLM airlines.

At least a start has been made. But psychology is a comparatively new discipline and, because mankind is its study, it is far from being a black-and-white science. It deals in paradox and anomaly – and for nearly every plus of human behaviour and inheritance there is a minus. For instance, Man is quick to learn but, to reverse the old saw, a lot of learning can be a dangerous thing. Contrary to expectations, the pilot who is experienced and knows the aircraft well is, through over-learning and complacency, more likely to make an error on landing than one who is less experienced.

The captain of the Avianca B-747 which crashed at Madrid in 1982 (Chapter 14) knew the airport well. So did the captain of the Dan Air B-727 that crashed into a mountain on descent in Tenerife. If a pilot knows an airport well, he may stay on 'automatic thought' rather than change to problem-solving thought. This is particularly true if an unexpected event (in the Tenerife accident, an unpublished holding pattern) interrupts a well practised descent and landing.

In an emergency people regress to their mother tongue. We tend to assume that both our attention and memory are better and longer lasting than they are. We cannot keep up continuous attention. Our short-term memory is indeed *very* short-term, and though we begin to learn quickly, this flattens and drops into a downward learning curve. In a simulator, the motor acts of flying are long remembered, but the procedural skills taught by it are soon forgotten. In addition, there are 'side effects' of the concepts to beware of – 'transfer of training' and 'regression to earlier learning'. A contributory factor to the Tenerife Jumbo collision described in Chapter 8 may have been that the KLM captain regressed to his considerable simulator experience, where a clearance for take-off is not required.

The importance of regression in learning cannot be over-emphasised.

In 1983, a Malaysian Airline System crew were operating an Airbus leased from Scandinavian Airlines. At dusk, they were coming into Kuala Lumpur on the last leg of the passenger schedule Kuala Lumpur–Singapore–Kuching–Singapore–Kuala Lumpur. This round trip was reckoned by crews to be particularly hectic and demoralising. The sectors were short and demanded a high degree of concentration, and there were four take-offs and landings.

Fatigue was therefore a well-recognised human factor for the crew concerned, but it is unlikely that any of them had heard of the psychological concept of regression. They were, however, extremely well versed in the *Malaysian* version of the Airbus A-300.

The young first officer was flying the aircraft on an ILS approach to Kuala Lumpur, and he was having a hard time in turbulence and pouring rain.

'Fly the aircraft!' the captain demanded, as the A-300 rocked from side to side. 'Fly the aircraft!'

The twenty-three-year-old was doing his best to get on to the localiser and glide path, but he was being hampered not just by the weather, but by a far worse difficulty.

The ILS wasn't tuned in on the aircraft receiver.

To add to the first officer's troubles, an F-27 and a DC-10 were intent on landing. The pilot of the F-27 made a successful landing, but warned that the field was closing in rapidly, a fact confirmed by the DC-10 suddenly overshooting and going round again. Time pressure was now added to the crew's difficulties.

But the most important factor was that the Airbus, which the first officer was struggling to fly, was not the usual Malaysian Airways Airbus. The lease arrangement with SAS was for it to be flown by MAS crews only after completing a special 'differences course', for the SAS cockpit was slightly different. In particular, the ILS switches were not *exactly* alike. In the MAS Airbus, it had two positions – INS/NAV and ILS localiser. In the SAS aircraft this same switch had *three* positions – up, centre and down. The *centre* position gave the ILS function.

Miles out of position now, at last the captain suddenly noticed that they were not receiving any ILS signals. He checked with the controller that the ILS was on and serviceable.

When the crew had finally worked out what the problem was and had selected the correct position, the first officer continued at the controls, trying to find the localiser and glide-slope indications. Eventually the glide slope came up on the instruments, well to the right of the localiser.

The captain took over, but by this time the Airbus was well below the glide slope, and thirty seconds later descended into the ground and cut a swathe through the rubber trees two kilometres from the runway threshold. It eventually came to rest with both engines and the main gears ripped off and fire already sprouting from the damaged wing tanks.

What had happened was that under the stress of a long flight and bad weather, the crew had regressed to their earlier learning. They had simply carried out the response they would have done in a Malaysian Airbus. The confusion arose because the switches were *nearly* alike. The greater the similarity of the stimuli, the greater the chance of confusion, as numerous psychological experiments on Transfer of Training have shown. The ILS switches in the two aircraft were confusingly alike, so the MAS response was made by the crew – on the SAS aircraft.

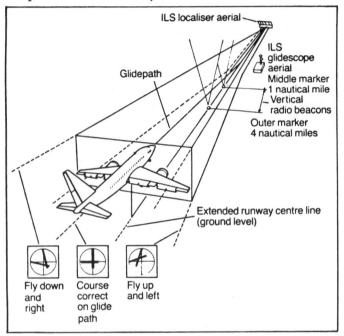

Regression is a psychological defence mechanism against a difficult or frustrating experience. Instead of facing up to a situation, we may simply unconsciously retreat away from it to an earlier form of behaviour. There have been a large number of psychological experiments showing that animals regress in various ways. Rats trained to run a maze by two different routes regressed under electric shock to the first-learned path to the goal. In 1959, two American psychologists, Barthol and Hu, performed an experiment in which nine subjects were taught how to tie a bowline knot by one method first, and another totally different method second. A further group were taught the second method first, and the first method second. A difficult stress situation was then organised for all subjects, after which they were called out of the room in random order, handed a cord and told to 'tie a knot'. As a check on the importance of the stress situation, subjects had been previously asked to tie a knot under normal conditions. Nine had tied the bowline by the method learned first, nine by the method learned second. After the artificially induced stress, however, sixteen out of the eighteen subjects tied a bowline by the method learned first.

Ex-Comet pilots being converted to Boeings showed the marked interference of their Comet experience in the new technique of flying B-707s. Just as, when people get a new car, they reach for a while for the brake or the light switches as they were in the old car, so did the ex-Comet pilots reach for switches and levers as though they were still in a Comet.

In a Comet, as soon as all three wheels are on the ground in a landing, the pilot reaches for the nose-wheel steering wheel to keep straight on the runway. In a 707, he must wait until the aircraft has slowed down considerably, keeping both hands on the stick, or damage may result. Again and again in early stages of training, the ex-Comet pilots were reaching immediately for the nose-wheel steering. Gradually this old habit was overlaid by the new learning – but it is doubtful if any ingrained habit can ever be eradicated completely. When these pilots actually started to fly the B-707 aeroplane – particularly in the stress of night-flying training – up came the old habit of immediately reaching for the nose-wheel steering.

Such interference of earlier learning and regression may have been the principal factor in an accident in Australia, when an instructor was converting another captain from piston-engined DC-4s to Viscounts in perfect weather conditions.

The conversion course had reached the three-engined stage. On the last circuit, the instructor had deliberately failed the starboard outer engine on take-off, just before reaching flying speed. The student had successfully coped wih a three-engined circuit and landing. Now he was to do a three-engined take-off with the same engine inoperative.

The Viscount was lined up on the runway. The before take-off check was completed. The inner engines were opened up to full power. The brakes were released. As the aircraft gathered speed, the pilot under training in the captain's seat gradually advanced the port outer throttle. The expected swing to starboard was corrected on the nose-wheel steering. Further along the runway, however, *another* swing to starboard developed. This one tightened into a turn. Two thousand feet from the beginning of take-off, the Viscount left the runway.

This time, nose-wheel steering was not used. The aircraft became airborne, still turning. The starboard wing went steeply down. At about 100 feet, the Viscount began to lose height and crashed into the ground, breaking up on impact and catching fire. The two pilots and one supernumerary pilot were killed. Three others were seriously injured and two were unhurt.

The Accident Inquiry Report stated that:

> The captain may have been influenced in this decision [to take off] by his considerable experience on other aircraft recently flown by him, the minimum control speed of which are lower than that of the Viscount. It is felt that in an emergency such as faced the captain, he would be inclined to react automatically under the influence of his predominant experience in the DC-4, overlooking the particular characteristics of the Viscount of which he was comparatively inexperienced.

In another accident, an Auster took off, began to porpoise, then dived into the ground. The pilot had been flying Tripacers for a long time. Both Auster and Tripacer have similar trim wheels, but while the Tripacer requires several turns of the wheel to effect a small change, the Auster requires only a single turn for the whole range. The pilot had clearly thought he was in a Tripacer and trimmed accordingly.

A Constellation 1049 was badly damaged during an emergency landing in which the captain had apparently applied neither brakes nor nose-wheel steering. The accident, however, might easily have been avoided had the emergency braking mechanism been used. The report says: 'The captain attempted to brake as he should have done, and as would have been proper and successful, with predecessor type Lockheeds (Models 049 and 749A) on which he was highly experienced.' The stress of the emergency may have made him regress to his earlier aircraft.

Incorrect identification of switches owing to regression may have contributed to other accidents besides that of the MAS Airbus. Thus a C-54G which crashed at Jacksonville had three tank-selector positions: auxiliary tanks forward, main tanks centre, 'off' positions rearward. Other marks of C-54 had two selectors: main tank forward and the 'off' positions rearward. The co-pilot had flown 209 hours in C-54B, but because he was in a C-54G, his action had opened only the auxiliaries. The twenty-five to fifty gallons in each axiliary tank were sufficient for the aircraft to take off and begin the climb. Then both engines failed through fuel starvation, and the aircraft was ditched in a small lake.

A Boeing 377 ditched after severe buffeting, apparently caused by having its cowl flaps fully opened. The cowl flap switches on the B-377 and the Constellation 1049 move in the opposite way. During the preceding year, most of the engineer's flight time had been on 1049s.

A Dakota took off from Azaiba, then immediately lost height and crashed into the ground. Both engines broke away, the starboard engine caught fire and the port wing was practically severed at the root. The aircraft had lost power because the carburettor air intake shutters had been selected to Hot Air instead of Ram Air. On this aircraft, the air intake control levers had to be positioned *aft* for Ram Air, whereas on another Dakota owned by the company which the pilot had recently been flying Ram Air was obtained by a forward movement of the lever.

The number of types of aircraft a pilot has recently flown is relevant here. During the three months before one accident, a first officer had been flying as captain or first officer *five* different types. Training captains often have a large number of different types on their ticket. A captain coming into New York, who had six different types current on his licence, elected to do a steep power-off approach which might have been adequate on Constellations (one of his types) but was hazardous on the Martin in which he happened to be flying – and he crashed.

There have been several other instances of this apparent 'interference' of previous learning in aircraft accidents. In 1964, the pilot of a DC-3 near Bogota saw another aircraft and went into a sharp right turn that became uncontrollable, and he crashed. The report stated that: 'The pilot of the aircraft had been flying DC-4s and C-46s as well as DC-3s. The psychological reaction of the pilot at this critical moment was certainly affected by habits acquired on DC-4 and C-46 aircraft.'

An accident to an RAF Vulcan clearly shows regression to earlier learning. Fire developed in the flare chute, the pilots ejected and the crew at the back struggled to open their escape door. They had frequently practised this escape exercise on the simulator as part of their safety drill. Unfortunately, they had been trained on a defective door. The catch on the simulator had been slightly twisted. Expecting this twist on a perfectly seviceable door, they were quite unable to open it.

Regression to earlier learning persists. In July 1983 an Air Canada Boeing 767, one of the most sophisticated airliners in the world, unbelievably ran out of fuel. It should have been impossible in such a modern airliner in perfect conditions so to do.

Flight 143 had originated in Montreal and was bound for Edmonton. Fuel, supposedly for the entire flight, was taken on board at Montreal. The refuelling panel in a B-767 is in a compartment beneath the left wing. The refueller simply dials in the required number of kilograms, pushes a button and the aircraft automatically accepts the correct amount of kerosene. But that day the refuelling panel was unserviceable and so were the cockpit fuel gauges. Therefore, someone had to tell the refueller how much fuel to put on board – 22,300 kilograms. Since the aircraft gauges were all blank, he had to use the gauges on his truck, but these measured *litres*, not kilograms. He had to pump in a specified volume to reach a required weight, allowing for the kerosene already in the tank. Fuel weight varies with temperature, so the refueller had to know the current ratio.

When decimal coinage came in, and when car petrol pumps showed litres instead of gallons, everyone had difficulty. The interference from the greatly overlearned knowledge is very considerable. The difficulty of the refuellers under time pressure on a forty-three-minute Montreal turnround at an airfield can be sympathetically imagined.

A mechanic eventually told the refueller how many litres to load. But he used the wrong multiplier – the old multiplier he had originally been taught, the familiar 1.77 that converts litres to lbs. But a kilo is 2.2 lbs and so the fuel on board was less than half that required.

Time was when the captain alone would say whether he was prepared to take the aircraft in the state that it was. But when Air Canada decided to operate the B-767 with only two pilots, it assured the pilots' union that it wasn't going to take the work of three and put it on to two. That meant a rewriting of the operating manuals, giving some of the duties to ground personnel. One was to give the responsibility for overseeing the refuelling previously handled by the flight engineer to maintenance personnel.

On this occasion, although the fuel gauges were blank, the captain was told that the aircraft had been cleared to go by Maintenance Control. Nevertheless, it was said afterwards that the captain should not have taken the aircraft in that state. There is subconscious pressure to conform to what management requires.

The captain, disturbed by the fact that the aircraft had been cleared to fly with blank gauges in apparent contradiction of the Minimum Equipment List (MEL), and irritated by the delay caused by the length of time the refuellers had taken over their sums, demanded their figures. These he double-checked with a pocket calculator. But although his figures agreed with those of the mechanics, he, too, assumed that the total was in kilograms when it was actually in pounds.

After an intermediate stop at Ottawa, Flight 143 took off for Edmonton. At 41,000 feet, 140 miles along the route, a warning buzzer suddenly sounded four times, followed by an amber light. There was low pressure in the fuel supply to the port engine.

Puzzled, the captain contacted Winnipeg.

More warning lights. A bang. Then the port engine stopped.

The captain put the nose down. Descending through 28,000 feet, all the instruments on the panel in front of him vanished.

The starboard engine had failed.

'Mayday' – help me – was radioed out as in eerie silence the powerless 767 began losing height at 2,500 feet a minute. Now the captain was making for Winnipeg, but calculations showed that he would never make it.

Back in the cabin, white-faced passengers were being briefed for a crash landing.

A tiny mainly disused airfield called Gimli was their only hope. But with no slats, no flaps, no instruments, no nose-wheel steering, no reverse thrust and a landing speed that would have to be 50 knots above normal, there was little chance of survivable landing.

There were two great things in their favour and both of these were the pilots themselves. Captain Robert Pearson was a real flying enthusiast and had spent his spare time not only as a glider pilot but as an instructor – and they certainly needed to glide. The co-pilot, Maurice Quintal, had served in the Royal Canadian Air Force and knew of Gimli.

Out of the countryside ahead the crew suddenly spotted the airfield – but they were too high. With no chance of a go-around, desperately the captain side-slipped the aircraft like a fighter and slammed it down on a sports-car track at 170 knots.

Brakes screaming, lurching, skidding and bumping, the 767 careered over the uneven surface. The tyres burst. The aircraft began slowing. Crouched in a crash position, the passengers lifted their heads.

They were down! Seconds later, the 767 shuddered to a stop.

Although a chain of seemingly small human errors had precipitated a potential disaster, the human being, by his learned skills, had managed to bring the highly automated but entirely powerless machine to a safe landing. The political and managerial machinations which followed are another story, which is told in Chapter 18.

What is a very present story is that the machine is getting ever more sophisticated. Mankind's propensity to make human errors remains constant.

Can the pilot cope?

Eleven

The Clockwork Captain, or Deus in Machina

Visit the flight deck of a modern airliner and you may be surprised to see the pilot, head down, pressing buttons and twirling knobs to command the autopilot to do the very things which he himself would do instinctively were he at the controls. Having done the programming, he must thereafter watch the aircraft's performance like a hawk to make sure it carries out his selections. He is only too well aware that if things go wrong it will be he, not the autopilot, explaining matters to the Inquiry. In February 1984, the captain of SAS Flight 901 – a DC-10 equipped with an autothrottle – found this to his cost.

In addition to the autopilot, most civil transport aircraft are now fitted with an autothrottle which can be used on its own or in conjunction with the autopilot. As its name implies, it controls the aircraft speed by operating the throttles to maintain the speed selected by the pilot. It sounds wonderful, not unlike cruise control fitted to some cars. When first introduced, however, it caused a few problems.

Most pilots were trained to control aircraft speed with the control column. During initial training, any attempt to control it with the throttles was certain to earn a black mark from the flying instructor. The autothrottle turned this basic tenet on its head. When it was first introduced, some airlines approved its use for manual approaches – that is, with the pilot handling and the speed controlled by the autothrottle. After some of the approach paths threatened to rival the rollercoaster at Disneyland, its use was sensibly confined to the period when the autopilot was also engaged. At least *that* didn't have any flying training to unlearn and, together, autothrottle and autopilot were capable of performing fully automatic approaches and landings. As with almost all modern aircraft systems, it became extremely reliable.

But not totally. The spring can break even on a clockwork mouse.

SAS Flight 901 began its approach to Runway 04 Right at John F. Kennedy Airport at 16.00 local time. The first officer, known to be a very capable pilot, had flown the DC-10 from Stockholm on a scheduled service. After this landing the crew would be finished for the day, and the flight had been well-nigh perfect. Until, that is, they were three miles from the threshold of the runway and passing 800 feet altitude.

Then the autothrottle decided to take a hand.

The aircraft was under the control of the autopilot and autothrottle, a standard routine with visibility at only three-quarters of a mile. As the aircraft descended through 800 feet, the autothrottle gently applied increasing power to the engines, making no attempt to maintain the speed selected by the crew.

The acceleration went unnoticed.

Target speed for this phase of the approach was 168 knots, the aim being to cross the threshold of the runway 10 knots slower. As the actual speed increased through 193 knots, the wing flaps began a controlled retraction from their landing setting, a built-in programme designed to prevent damage to them by too high an airspeed. With the engines set at 84 per cent of full power and the autothrottle making no adjustment, speed increased to 209 knots.

The crew continued the approach, still apparently unaware of their grossly excessive speed.

As the aircraft crossed the threshold of the runway, the autothrottle failed to close the throttles as normal. Much worse, the aircraft was now travelling 60 knots too fast. The captain slammed shut the throttles, exclaiming, 'It didn't take power off!'

'Fifty feet,' shouted the third pilot behind them, giving the standard height call required on each landing.

The height was good, but the speed was still 60 knots fast.

The third pilot continued his litany of aircraft height as they flew further and further down the misty runway.

'Forty.'

'Thirty.'

'Twenty.'

By now they should be on the ground and braking.

'Twenty.'

'Twenty.'

'Twenty.'

'Ten.'

'Take it down,' called the captain.

'Ten,' called the third pilot.

'Get it down!' repeated the captain.

By this time the aircraft had covered 3,500 feet of the 9,000-foot runway and was still airborne. The mist, however, prevented the crew from seeing the runway end. By the time the co-pilot finally forced the reluctant aircraft down on to the runway, they had travelled over half its length.

He started to brake.

The captain shouted for him to use all three thrust reversers instead of the usual two. It was difficult to judge just how much runway they had left. Preoccupied with stopping the aircraft, they failed to notice the colour-coded centreline and edge lighting which marked the last section of the runway. Had they done so, it would have been of little help.

When the end of the runway surged out of the mist, it was immediately obvious that they could never stop in time. The captain took the tiller and swung the aircraft over to the right to avoid hitting the approach light structure at the far end of the overrun area.

Braking hard and with thrust reversers roaring, the aircraft crossed the levelled area beyond the runway and slid into Thurston Basin, a tidal waterway about 600 feet beyond the end of the runway.

It came to rest with its front half in the water. Happily, everyone on board climbed out without serious injury.

The Inquiry not unnaturally wished to discover why a known competent crew ignored the excessive speed and doggedly continued with the landing. The captain had, in fact, called, 'Speed high' at 300 feet but taken no action to retrieve the situation. The co-pilot, even though concentrating on the imminent landing still had a responsibility to ensure that the speed was correct. The third pilot, less involved in the action and therefore free to assess the information displayed by the instruments, spoke nothing but his standard calls. At this stage of the flight his task was to monitor the actions of the other two and monitor the safe progress of the operation. A speed error of 60 knots was difficult to miss.

Or was it?

It is an anomaly that the very reliability of modern aircraft systems can bring problems in its wake. In early days pilots had an almost pathological suspicion of anything new. When an airline in Scotland introduced a new aircraft with a retractable undercarriage, one captain refused to select the wheels up, remarking that he had never retracted an undercarriage in his career and certainly wasn't going to start now. Earlier still, a pilot hacked off the canopy that had been built over the open cockpit of his aircraft.

Things have changed. Now pilots have rightly come to expect comfort in the cockpit and the aircraft systems to work consistently. When they do, it is natural for guards to be dropped a little. After all, unless there is a violent storm, we don't go outside before lighting the fire to check that the chimneypot is still in place. To suspect everything marks one out as paranoid, yet this is how an airline pilot is expected to behave.

The airline pilot also gets less and less opportunity to practise his craft. Autopilots do the job well. Indeed, they are now certificated to make approaches and landings in conditions far worse than those permitted for the human version. Increasingly, the pilot is relegated to the role of monitor, and experience has shown that human beings make very poor monitors. How often have you left the car headlights on after the fog has cleared? How many motorists do you know who have run out of fuel in spite of having a gauge and a flashing light on the dashboard? But as they drove surrounded by the strains of Beethoven on the car stereo, the little fuel-pump icon winking erratically to the Fifth Symphony, there was something which they emphatically did *not* do. They did not abruptly steer off the road into a tree.

It is not difficult to understand why. They were involved in the act of driving. They did not need to check their steering ability at intervals so that action could be taken if the car happened to be crossing the central reservation. They were an essential part of a loop which included them and the car. They would know that to break the loop would result in catastrophe. No way would they forget to drive the car, although they might forget to monitor the fuel gauge and be forced to spend the night in the middle of Dartmoor.

Pilots, being human beings, are no different. But in a machine-controlled aircraft, they are being pushed out of the loop. Training can go far to encourage strict monitoring, but until the genetic engineers wheel out an aircrew version of Mr Spock, the industry will have to make do with the 46-chromosome model. The safety record to date shows this to have been a success, but the profusion of bells and whistles to draw the attention of pilots to things amiss amply illustrate the necessity for some prompting.

There is, of course, a limit. Some aircraft types are fitted with so many aural warning devices that efficient operation almost demands a degree in music, but most warnings have been acted upon at some time. The warning lights, many in number and varied in possible interpretation are now more rationalised than the random scattering of polychromatic Christmas tree lights typical of earlier aircraft. They have all, however, become essential reminders to the pilots of the existing aircraft configuration and state of flight.

When he fails to take heed, with disastrous consequences, we all feel justified in blaming the individual. The National Transportation Safety Board decided fairly predictably that the cause of Flight 901's accident was the flight crew's disregard for prescribed procedures for monitoring and controlling airspeed during the final stages of the approach, and over-reliance on the autothrottle speed control system, which had a history of malfunction.

The crew had given too much credence to the machine – an example of deification of the machine, an unwillingness to contradict it, a phenomenon which is being increasingly noticed among aircrew. As a result of the machine taking over so much of the flying while the pilot does the monitoring, he tends to lose confidence in his own ability. Man is not by nature adaptive to hours of watching without action. If primitive man had so done, he would have starved or become a meal himself. And with automation, the pilot's precious skill is further eroded. The use of a good autothrottle tends to degrade speed consciousness, as altitude pre-select tends to degrade height consciousness.

This respect, this deference for the machine also tends to make pilots accept inferior or even incorrect performance by the system and to hang back (perhaps until too late) before taking appropriate action.

Autopilots, autothrottles, flight directors, automatic tuning radios, computer flight plans, automatic height acquire and inertial navigation systems are some of the examples in use today. The autopilot control system is the most complicated and troublesome from a pilot's standpoint. The Automatic Flight Control System (AFSC) can automatically control airspeed, altitude, descent and climb and track following through the autopilot, autothrottle, vertical navigation system (VNAV) and lateral navigation system. The problem that pilots have with this system is that there are too many options or modes of operation, e.g. climbing to a higher altitude can be made automatically in three different ways – through the vertical navigation system, vertical speed or flight level change. Each mode has different characteristics and different possible sources of error.

Pilots have told investigators that they no longer feel themselves 'in the loop'. That nothing could be more dangerous is exemplified by two RAF Tornado aircraft which crashed in 1988 on low-flying night exercises over Cumbria. Based at different airfields, they were using the same low-flying programme in their computers which fly the aircraft automatically, changing course automatically and lifting the aircraft over pylons and hills. Since they were programmed exactly the same, the computers brought them together at exactly the same height at exactly the same spot at exactly the same time. So they collided. The four crewmen were killed.

Years ago, when automation began to take over the cockpit, some senior aviation pundits declared that it would reduce the pilot's workload and free him for 'the job to which he was better suited – supervising'.

They could not have been more wrong – on *both* counts. It has changed the workload, but in many ways to a more demanding one, and the limitations on his supervisory skills are becoming all too apparent. He has now to acquire a new facility – when to come out of his supervisory role and override the machine. Pilots are becoming standby controllers who may be called upon suddenly to perform a task at which they have very little practice.

Flight computers follow the rules of logic and sequential processing. But the human mind can weigh other variables besides, such as each other's experience, air and ground traffic, weather change, the passengers' problems or sudden interference with the flight such as bird strikes – (in one year alone worldwide there were 3,887 bird strikes). When the unpredictable occurs, the pilot must be able to think quickly and creatively. He must dredge up from his long-term memory and experience exactly how to deal effectively with the situation. Therefore, besides the ability to act as supervisor, the ability to emerge decisively out of the supervisory role is of paramount importance. The question is being asked: 'Is there a warm-up period of delay in this change-over?'

A further point, with regard to the SAS 901 crash – the captain was in the right-hand seat. Research has shown that captains display *lower* efficiency than first officers in the monitoring role. Perhaps because, as a senior pilot, he will have had more time actually flying the aircraft manually than supervising the system.

Another problem of crew experience of automation is that on some airlines a number of co-pilots on the wide-bodied jets clock up enough seniority to become captains on narrow-bodied jets which do not have the sophisticated autopilot/autothrottle systems.

After the SAS 901 crash, Captain Thernhem wrote a valuable article on 'The Automatic Complacency', emphasising that the machine cannot think and is a tool which should never be allowed to work on its own without its weak spots and the limits of its capabilities being known. He cites cases of the autothrottle becoming inactive, altitude pre-set malfunctioning and other incidents, in all of which the crew failed to notice and act immediately.

A further example of the dangers of automation is that, in the Swift Aire Lines Nord 62 crash at Los Angeles, it was the automatic feathering system which actually *initiated the accident*. This device was designed to stop pilots, under stress when an engine failed, from feathering the wrong engine (see Chapter 14 on laterality). Shortly after take-off, the sensing system became unserviceable. Mistakenly, the machine feathered the perfectly serviceable starboard engine. The crew added human error to mechanical error by shutting down the perfectly serviceable *port* engine. Powerless, the aircraft ditched with loss of life and damage.

There are other incidents of automatic error precipitating an accident. On the flight deck of a DC-9 taking off from Denver, with normal airspeed and pitch attitude indications, the stall-warning system was activated. The crew took the decision to abort take-off, with resulting heavy damage to the aircraft and injury to the passengers.

Then the machine can 'go sick' suddenly. It doesn't have the stomach of the human to fight back and win in unprogrammed emergencies. A captain's report in a CHIRP describes graphically the desertion in the face of duty of the electronic crew-member.

Flying a glass-cockpit highly computerised twin to London in February 1990, he and his co-pilot found themselves in a storm with 188-knot winds. As he put it, 'the aircraft automatics started running for cover'. Both FMSs were failing and recovering and at various times both autopilots and the flight director ceased to work. The ride down the ILS was 'very wild'. In violent turbulence, the captain commanded a go-around. As he said,

> *En route* to the diversion, a combination of failed automatics, unfamiliar ATC clearances and monitoring the weather (to say nothing of liaison with the cabin crew, the very frightened passengers, and the company) precluded us from getting the weather for any ultimate/tanks dry possibilities. With just over three tonnes remaining (about thirty minutes' flying) we *had* to make it in, and with the weather deteriorating literally by the minute, it had to be the first time!

Yet there are perhaps more accidents where pilots have ignored automatic warnings than there are those where they have acted on erroneous ones.

The 1972 accident to Trident Papa India at Heathrow Airport, London, though there were other human factors involved, was probably finally precipitated by the fact that the crew did not believe the stall-warning system because the stickshaker had given spurious warnings on previous occasions. Once a device gets a bad name it is easy to ignore it. How many people take any notice of their neighbour's dodgy burglar alarm or the bell that always seems to be ringing outside a High Street bank?

In the Dan Air Tenerife crash, though the GPWS had sounded, the crew were reassured when it ceased, only because they were in fact, for a few seconds, over a ravine. People learn to ignore an alarm if experience has shown it may be false; they have a drive towards the most optimistic explanation.

The pilot of an Avianca B-727 descending over Mount Oiz for a landing heard the Ground Proximity Warning telling him to 'pull up!' Instead, he told it to 'shut up' and engaged in a shouting match. The B-727 crashed, killing all 148 people on board. *Secrets of a Superbrat* by J. MacLean has been quoted by others. The reformed thief is speaking: 'If I had a hundred dollars for every time I heard a dog owner tell their dog to "shut up . . . go lie down", while I was right outside their window, I'd be a millionaire.' As with dog-owners and dogs, so sometimes with pilots and automatic warnings.

The worst type of automatic device is not the one that is known to be bad, nor of course the one that has an excellent record, but the one in the middle which produces cognitive dissonance in the pilot as to whether he should believe it or not. In many ways we can deal more easily with a known liar than an intermittent one.

As automation advances, it is forecast that the pilot will interact with more computers than the aircraft itself. Problems of workload in the future may well be 'how little' rather than 'how much' it is safe for him to do in order to prevent him making mistakes.

The ultimate in aircraft computerised sophistication so far is the Airbus A320, as can be seen in photograph 8 of the 'clean' flight deck. The engineer and all his instruments have been swept away. If anything goes wrong, a warning will appear on a screen, together with what is to be done about it. The aircraft is 'flown by wire' – there is no mechanical connection between the pilot's controls and the control surfaces. Only the rudder and pitch trim can be used mechanically to fly the aircraft in an emergency. The pilot controls the aircraft with a sidestick, not with a control column, thus giving him an unrestricted view of the flight instrument panel. Controls are not moved mechanically but by the sidestick commands to digital computers. The aircraft is prevented from flying beyond its approved limitations and will not *allow* the pilot to stall or overstress it by his own inaccurate flying. Thus the pilot's workload is substantially reduced and he is relieved of many chores.

This would appear to make him less likely to make slips. But does it?

Years ago, the makers of a new cake-mix realised that they mustn't make it produce the perfect cake too automatically. They must leave the housewife something to do, or she wouldn't feel involved. So they left out an ingredient purposely! Trying to design the perfect aircraft, could Airbus Industrie have left the pilot too much out of the loop? Does the complicated computer system interfere too much? It flies the aircraft far more accurately than any pilot can, and is so automatic that the pilot has even less to do. There is hardly any need for captain and co-pilot to speak to each other, let alone have much joint interaction. Indeed, the captain and co-pilot controls are not mechanically linked. Communication skills (at last being taught on some airlines) will deteriorate, and the pilot's image of himself will suffer. The lack of real 'feel' militates against the pilot's sixth sense. And if he has long experience of conventional jets, he may regress (Chapter 10) under stress to his earlier machine.

But the main fear amongst pilots appears to be that the machine can *override them.* In June 1988, the A320 was being demonstrated at the Habsheim airshow. Coming down very low over the field, the captain initiated a climb, but the aircraft did not gain height fast enough and crashed into a wood, killing three people. The pilot said that he could not get the aircraft to climb (it was controlled by a computer which he could not override). The French Inquiry gave the aircraft a clean bill of health – pilot error was blamed. The pilots' union strongly objected, but the pilot was charged.

In February 1990, another A320 crashed in perfect weather coming in to land at Bangalore, killing ninety. Numerous doubts about the airport and training arose. Indian Airlines grounded its remaining thirteen Airbuses, and a bitter argument arose between them and the manufacturers. As in the Comet take-off accidents (Chapter 13), huge export orders hung in the balance. On top of that, their aircraft reliability had achieved an operational reliability of 97.8 per cent for the A-320.

The pilots' union is reported as saying that the machine 'is technically perfect, but the crews are not sufficiently aware of the changes brought about by technological innovation. Everything is fine in normal conditions, but if something goes wrong a pilot will always draw on his own experience.'

In other words, he may regress, which is what Airbus Industrie, in a warning to pilots, appear to have assumed had happened in the Indian Airlines crash. They issued a press release saying, 'We don't make the plane more sophisticated for fun. We make it that way because it's safer,' adding, 'Nothing has been discovered to support any suggestion that the accident was the result of a technical problem!' Which identifies the usual scapegoat. And this was again before the Inquiry had taken place.

Yet, as Professor Wiener points out, 'The modern cockpit solves a great many problems, but creates some as well. Pilots can find these new devices difficult to operate. It is easy to input erroneous data which lies dormant until some other factor activates it.' He also points out the tendency to blame accidents on the last person in the chain of events, usually the captain.

An experienced accident inspector has said that one of the problems on new and ever more sophisticated aircraft is that they are tested by *test* pilots – usually exceptional aircraft handlers – when all aspects of cockpit design and flying techniques should be tested by those who are destined to use them – airline pilots. The expert is often unaware of how much more he is involved and *au fait* with the systems than the pilot who will be required to operate the aircraft in the real world. He feels impatient with those he might regard as less skilled in the use of its resources.

One of the causes of the failure of British South American Airlines after the last war was that Air Vice-Marshal Bennett was totally dedicated and expert and expected the same dedication and expertise from his company pilots.

Average pilots on new and highly sophisticated aircraft often feel suspicious of the machine they fly – that it is altogether too clever by half. Automated aircraft are not merely traditional aircraft with extra boxes. They demand all the old skills and airmanship and many new ones too. Job satisfaction and prestige are being eroded, and the pilot is still a proud man. No pilot likes to feel that he is co-pilot to a wonder machine. None of us likes being in a position where we feel under-used or, worse still, helpless. This is the psychologically dangerous time when we feel threatened by something over which we have too little control. It is the time when we feel ineffectual, frustrated and bored.

One pilot said, 'I'm willing to fly it as long as it has the yellow button [autopilot disengage]. I can always turn it back into a DC-9.'

We can only hope that the button is pressed at the right moment, and that the pilot is not feeling that most dangerous side effect of automation – out of the loop, and therefore bored and absent-minded.

Twelve

Boredom and Absence of Mind

Consider the human faculties which automation makes almost superfluous. Cooped up in the cockpit, the pilot is deprived of his own individual movement and of a perspective of the outside world beyond his small automated cell. Modern instruments make his tactile sense redundant, and automation has encroached alarmingly on his flying skills and that very necessary vision of himself and his own worth.

Autopilots, alerting and warning systems and the Ground Proximity Warning system have undoubtedly had a beneficial effect on safety. Since the last named's mandatory introduction in the USA in 1974, there has been a dramatic reduction in terrain strike accidents – from thirty-three in 1969 to eight in 1984. On the debit side of increased automation has come a loss of proficiency. A marked skill loss has been noticed in pilots who regularly use automatic equipment and equally disturbing, a training captain reported that 'there is a tendency to breed inactivity or complacency'.

This is a natural human reaction to insufficient stimuli – in other words, not enough being demanded of a pilot. He gets bored.

Boredom is the result of the battle between two strong drives necessary for survival: the first, actively to explore the environment; the second, to be passive and conserve energy.

Nature seems to favour those who like novelty and gain knowledge. Many people have a hunger for stimulation. Sitting doing nothing may sound attractive to those who are continuously occupied, but insufficient stimulation and insufficient information flow impairs the functioning of the brain. Restlessness follows boredom and, in some extreme cases where there is lack of tactile stimulation, the victim can hallucinate.

Boredom on the flight deck, where highly trained, intelligent crew may sit passively for many hours, is an increasing problem. Advanced cockpit automation will be more tolerant of error, but will increase that boredom.

In September 1988, a jet captain was making preparations for a routine one-hour Brazilian domestic flight from Maraba to Belem. Reportedly, he asked the control tower how he could tune in to the football match between Brazil and Chile in Rio de Janeiro. Boredom with this routine flight and inattention caused him to set the automatic pilot on his aircraft to a south-easterly instead of a northerly course. Absorbed in the football match, he failed to notice that they were flying over ever more impenetrable jungle. Contact with Belem was lost, and the captain had to make a crash landing in remote jungle in almost exactly the opposite direction of his intended flight. Dense soaring trees sliced off the aircraft's wings and crumpled the fuselage as it cut a huge swathe through them. By luck or good judgement, the captain brought the aircraft down to the forest floor so that forty-three people survived the nightmare. Reportedly, after having hacked his way through the jungle to find rescuers, his first words were, 'Who won?'

Man requires a certain amount of arousal to remain interested. When a pilot is inactive, complacent or bored, he will find it more difficult to intervene when the machine goes wrong. We are all prone to the syndrome of attending – but not taking in what is going on.

And while boredom may cause some pilots to do nothing, in other individuals it is a time when the curiosity with which nature has endowed Man, so that he can explore other environments, can be just as lethal. After all, we accept in everyday life that boredom causes vandalism and hooliganism and that 'the devil finds work for idle hands to do'. We have a penchant for novelty, a bit of excitement, and are made to be curious.

What better way of relieving boredom than finding something out? And on the flight deck, about the instruments in front of you? As did the crew of a DC-10 at the end of 1973. They were flying at a height of 39,000 feet with altitude, speed and course automatically controlled when the flight engineer suggested. 'If you pull the number one tach, will that autothrottle respond to anything?'

The captain said that he didn't know.

Flight engineer: 'You want to try and see?'

Captain: 'Yeah, let's see!'

Flight engineer: 'You're on speed right now, though.'

Captain: 'Well, I haven't got it. There it is! I guess it does. Right on the nose!'

The conversation was suddenly interrupted by an explosion. The captain, as a result of his exploration had so overspeeded the starboard engine that the vanes of its fan assembly struck the outer casing and the engine blew up. Although the aircraft remained airborne, a fragment of the exploding engine smashed one of the cabin windows and a passenger was sucked out.

And what of the other debits? Diminution of skill is self-evident and needs no elaboration here. But loss of a pilot's image of himself is an important human factor. The necessity for a pilot to have perceived control is frequently stressed. When the human being feels himself primarily along 'just for the ride', the possibility of error greatly increases.

Perhaps the vehemence with which pilots condemn automatic warning devices when they go wrong, and the frequency with which they ignore them or switch them off, is symptomatic of a deeper disquiet and antipathy – a subconscious war of survival. There are numerous accidents where ignoring or switching off warnings such as GPWS and stick-pushers has preceded the final calamity, as in the dumping of the stick-push device which allowed Trident Papa India to stall and crash at Staines.

Subconsciously, by disbelieving a warning, the pilot may be

struggling to safeguard his own self-image. For it is self-image that holds the human being together.

Absent-mindedness is a close cousin to boredom and it scarcely requires definition. An everyday occurrence familiar to us all, it can simply mean our mind being somewhere else while our body carries on like a headless chicken, usually with routine tasks. Mostly it does so harmlessly. The absent-minded professor is a classic example, as are looking for the spectacles that are on the end of one's nose, and trying to stir the gravy with a box of matches and light the gas with a spoon.

Absent-mindedness may remain harmless while we are not engaged in highly responsible jobs or operating complicated machinery, but a momentary lapse can be lethal when we are – as in the Northern Line tube train disaster in February 1975. The train failed to stop at Moorgate station, roared through the red light into the overrun tunnel and compacted itself on the end wall with great loss of life. According to the Professor of Psychology at Manchester University, Professor Reason, the most likely cause was absent-mindedness – that the driver was behaving in place A, the half mile between Old Street and Moorgate stations, as though he was in place B, the two-mile section from Essex Road to Old Street, where trains usually reach a speed of 35 mph – a fatal speed to enter Old Street.

Public transport, as it becomes more and more automated, is an environment particularly conducive to absent-mindedness. Long ago, industrial psychologists discovered that to give a worker a job that required less than his intelligence resulted in a poorer performance than giving him a job beyond it. As the computer becomes more sophisticated, the pilot's job becomes more supervisory, with long periods when his attention can wander. He is a man who has been trained largely by overlearning and habit; he has developed scheme-sequences of linked behaviour which become largely automatic. This training will tend to make his responses habitual while his mind is able to remove itself.

Most people, quite apart from pilots, will have experienced the lull of driving a well-functioning car along a straight road to a designated destination. Many people have the car radio on and much of their mind is engaged with what they are hearing or busy with what they will say at their business appointment. How often has one come to realise that miles have gone by that have never registered, one's hands and feet automatically carrying on where the mind left off?

So in the air. In the 1950s a very skilled pilot, at the end of a flight from London to Dorval airport, Montreal, landed at a small nearby field. No damage was done except to the passengers' convenience and the airline's image, but he was hauled up in front of the irate management and asked to explain why for no apparent reason he had done so, and why he hadn't entered the erroneous landing in the aircraft's journey log. His remark was disarming. He said, 'It was just momentary absent-mindedness. I thought the less said about it the better.'

It has been shown that the greater the responsibility and the worse the risk, the more likely is the mind to absent itself. So it is in painful or monotonous circumstances. Again, this is apparent in everyday life. How many of us, faced with a disagreeable situation like having a tooth filled, or a monotonous one like washing-up, let our minds go to more congenial situations? Our imaginings, our thoughts, our fantasies become more real than the real – like the member of the audience at a very convincing play, *The Andersonville Trial*, who, when the actor playing the judge at the court-martial bade the court rise and dismiss obediently got up and dismissed, and was half-way up the aisle before she returned to reality.

So what is absent-mindedness and how does it come about? The capacity of man's brain to respond to his environment and of his memory to store information has been referred to before. So has the disadvantage of the slowness whereby this information is dealt with through a single processing system in and out of the brain. Much of what goes on in his mind and much of his memory is banished to the lower strata of consciousness, while only the distillation of his conscious processing remains – all he needs to know in a neatly packaged piece. With these schemata of his experience and knowledge, he tackles events and problems as they occur.

In everyday life, therefore, there is a vast array of things which are so habitual, so pre-processed that they hardly enter our consciousness. For just as the operation of a huge jet airliner is so heavy and complex that we need the aid of mechanical control systems and computers, so we too, in this complex and bedazzling world, need to put many ordinary routine actions on to automatic. It has been shown that we can hold only about nine items in our memory at one time, and we couldn't possibly process, yet alone retain, all the information and experiences that bombard us throughout our waking hours.

Our conscious attention can therefore be reserved for sudden, surprising or special occurrences – things that reach us through our inherited 'startle reaction', while we get on smoothly with our habits.

James has described habit as a 'great flywheel'. Once set in motion our habits require little additional energy to keep them going and are hard to stop. And of those well-learned habits we say that they have become second nature, or we could do them in our sleep. So we probably could.

For absent-mindedness frequently occurs when we are performing some well-learned, almost automatic task, and is not unlike day-dreaming. The mind is free to escape and wander and engage in its own thoughts and fantasies. The environment of forward, slightly rocking movement, of small familiar confines and agreeable temperature, favours absent-mindedness. Perhaps it represents a return to the womb and the perambulator. The train driver, the car driver, the pilot, all experience that environment. The danger, as any car driver knows, is when the ensuing absent-mindedness is broken by a sudden and startling phenomenon – an unexpected red light, a police siren or a hole in the road – and the time it takes to get through the startle reaction and *think* and *act*.

The darker side of habit is that it tends to inhibit rational thought. Safety lies in the speed of correct reaction – in other words, how quickly we can come out of the short-term memory habitual mode and get deeper down into memory and consciousness and rational thinking and come back up with the answer.

One of the theories (out of many) that have been advanced about the shoot-down of Korean Airlines Flight 007 on 1 September 1983 has suggested absent-mindedness or inattention on the part of Captain Chun Byung In and his crew. None survived and no recorders were recovered. The truth of the tragic affair was afterwards muddied by international politics, by accusation and counter-accusation, by obfuscations and cover-ups. What is undeniable and seemingly inexplicable is that the highly experienced captain flew his Boeing 747 and 246 passengers over the notorious and forbidden Kamchatka Peninsula which bristled with Soviet defences, although he was supposed to fly along Route R20, a route specially designed to take him safely to Seoul without going anywhere near the Peninsula.

When the bitter furore over the shoot-down had died away, various theories were advanced. One was that so aggressive was the Korean Airlines policy of fuel-saving that Captain Chun had risked taking his aircraft over the dangerous peninsula to ingratiate himself with the cost-conscious company. Another was that captains had been reprimanded previously for turning back, so Captain Chun would not want to risk criticism from his superiors. Another was that the wrong data had been inserted in the INS – but there would have been numerous indications even so that the aircraft was many miles off course if the proper attention had been paid.

Another, that Captain Chun was a very macho anticommunist who had been recruited by the CIA to overfly this territory so that the Soviet radar defences would be deployed and could be mapped and recorded by a special B-707 spyplane which the Americans regularly employed to invade Soviet airspace. Some credence was lent to this theory by the fact that on its regular mission that day the 707, known as 'Cobra Ball' when acting as a spy plane, had left the Soviet radar screens at about the same time as Captain Chun's 747 appeared on it.

During 1981–2, the weekly Aeroflot service to Washington had strayed off course sixteen times. And the USA had shown its interest in the Kamchatka Peninsula by continuing electronic information-gathering patrols, using not only Cobra Balls, but also specially equipped B-747s. Another theory is that the straying of Flight 007 was observed by the American radar listening post at King Salmon, 200 miles south-west of Anchorage, and accepted as manna from heaven, an espionage bonanza. King Salmon is part of a chain of military installations watching the approaches to Alaska.

No theory can be proved. But the ICAO report seemed to favour the theory of inattention. It suggests that either the holding of a constant 246 degrees magnetic or an error of 10 degrees east in longitude made in the INS would have produced 007's track. To quote the ICAO report: 'This assumes a considerable degree of lack of attention on the part of the entire flight crew, but not to a degree that is unknown in international civil aviation.'

Those are chilling words. For the inattention would indeed have to be of a considerable and alarming degree. IFALPA regretted the ICAO reference to the crew's lack of attention, pointing out that the INS itself might have been faulty, and adding that they had continually deplored the lack of facilities along the North Pacific routes. But some experts took the theory further, suggesting that the crew were asleep.

Captain Chun, one of Korean Airlines' most experienced pilots, a former fighter pilot who had logged over 6000 hours on Boeing 747s, had come on duty fresh that morning to take the regular Anchorage to Seoul service. His passengers, on the other hand, were probably tired after their flight from JFK airport, New York. Behind their flight into Anchorage had come another KAL Boeing bringing passengers from Los Angeles, and while the

passengers from both flights took refreshments in the passenger
building, Captain Chun and his crew boarded the aircraft and
began their checks.

These would include the programming of three Inertial
Navigation Systems – a triple safety device, for if a fault develops
in one, another takes over. Accelerometers for every directional
movement are sited on a gyro-stabilised platform, and every
movement is computer-processed to calculate changes in latitude and longitude, which are then shown on a taximeter-type
display in the cockpit. So throughout the flight, the pilots can
read their exact position in degrees and minutes of latitude and
longitude. The INS can also be connected to the autopilot, thus
creating a totally automated navigation system which forms the
integral part of the Flight Management System (FMS).

Before departure, the INS would have been programmed for
the route to be followed – in this case Route R20, which would
take it first over Bethel on the Alaskan coast and then across the
Bering Sea. The pilots would insert the waypoints (not actual
places, but INS locations on Route R20) – Nabie, Nukks,
Neeva, Ninno, Nippi, Nytim, Nokka, Noho, Inkfish,
Jyobonzan, Nigata, Kanchung. The question is: 'Was it programmed correctly?' or was there a dormant error in the system
awaiting a trigger?

After the INS is switched on, the aircraft must remain
stationary for at least twenty minutes to allow the gyros to
stabilise. A theory was advanced, although largely discounted,
that the aircraft was moved too soon.

Another possible inattention error might have occurred after
take-off and the direct clearance to Bethel. Captain Chun might
have turned the aircraft by means of the autopilot-control
heading knob, omitting to switch it to INS later and allowing the
aircraft to continue on a *magnetic* heading. Certainly if this had
been the case, the wind drift of only 1 degree at the time would
have resulted in a magnetic heading which would have led the
aircraft close to Bethel, and which would, if continued, have led
the aircraft to its disastrous rendezvous with the Soviet fighters.

Equally, if the INS had been wrongly programmed, if the waypoint had been incorrectly keyed in, if numbers had been reversed, such inaccuracies could also have led them over Kamchatka.

But given that they might have made such simple mistakes, how could the crew have ignored the warnings? Three green lights would have shown that the INS and the autopilot were connected. Did none of the three-man crew notice that the lights were *not* lit? The human eye does not necessarily see what is in front of it. Sometimes the message it gives the brain is that what *should* be there *is* indeed there. Flying through the night, with behind them a load of weary passengers asleep or resting, it would be easy to be inattentive, to chat together or let their minds absent themselves, and not to register the unlit lamps, or the fact that the distance-to-go meter was not counting down to zero as they passed each waypoint, but showing many miles north.

Whatever happened, it is certain that, after take-off at 05.00 local time, the flight almost immediately went wrong. Kenai Radar station, south-west of Anchorage, observed KA 007 flying westbound already six miles north. At Bethel, the first officer reported the aircraft as overhead, but KA 007 was now still further north – a fact that should have been picked up from the ADF by the crew.

KA 007 was beyond the range of civilian radar, but a radar operator at the King Salmon listening post noted 007 flying twelve miles north of Bethel. King Salmon keeps a low profile. There was no liaison with the civil flying organisations and they had no reason to doubt that the 747 was following civil or air traffic instructions.

Flight 007 was now travelling towards Nabie, the first of the waypoints. Just before each waypoint an amber light shows up on the INS to warn the crew. The INS can then be checked and a time and position relayed on VHF.

At 14.30 GMT KA 007 reported abeam Nabie. Outside VHF range itself, the call was relayed by the crew of the second 747 bound for Seoul, which had taken off from Anchorage twenty minutes later.

Afterwards the captain of the second 747 is reported as saying: 'Chun must have realised that the computer was probably wrong by the aircraft drift, but decided to go on.'

Asked why Chun wouldn't turn back, he advanced an even stranger theory: 'Chun was a very proud man. He would have lost face.'

Now passing Neeva, 007 was 150 miles off track.

Shortly afterwards, the first officer requested and was given permission to climb to 33,000 ft. Less than 400 miles away lay the coast of Kamchatka Peninsula. Flight 007 had strayed into an area supervised by Soviet controllers, and although they had not yet violated Soviet air space, they were being tracked on Soviet radar screens.

Yet the crew of 007 seemed totally unperturbed. What lulled them into this false sense of security? Were they so used to the machine taking the load? Were their minds on other things? Why did they not check the latitude and longitude? Did a collective absent-mindedness assail them all? Or were they really asleep? Because it is impossible for the human brain to cope with the billions of stimuli and countless items of information it has acquired, we have learned to make only a small percentage available for immediate scrutiny. Boredom with a learned task leads to inattention and after a while, in the womb-like cockpit, isolated from the world, warm, fed, with everything apparently going well (but perhaps feeling the fatigue and the effect of crossing time zones), it would have to be a startling stimulus that gained the attention of captain and crew. Unhappily, they were to have exactly that.

Even as they were about to cross the Kamchatka coastline, had the captain switched his radar to map mode, he might well have seen the coastal outline. But he seems to have been convinced that he was well out over the Pacific, to have been mentally in a place different from where he actually was, to have been in a state of inattention similar to the Moorgate tube-train driver. Had he received ground echoes on his weather radar, he would probably have dismissed them as cloud returns.

At 17.09 the first officer was reporting, 'Korean Air 007 over Nippi one seven zero seven, level three three zero, estimate Nokka at one eight two six.' The crew were unaware that they had just crossed the Kamchatka Peninsula, that six MiG fighters had been scrambled in the suspicion that they were a spy plane but failed to find them, and, their final death knell, that the real B-707 spy plane, Cobra Ball, had been flying in the same area.

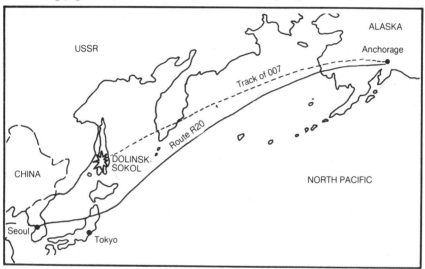

Flight Plan route and actual route of KAL 007

Now back over international waters, safe for the moment, 007 cruised towards the southern tip of Sakhalin Island, a highly sensitive Soviet area east of the famous naval base of Vladivostok, guarded by fighter, bomber and missile stations. As 007 headed over this, it had already disturbed the hornet's nest, and, because the fighters had been unsuccessful in finding them, dented the macho image of the Soviet fighter boys. The sensitive Soviet air space had been violated, the defence system found wanting and it was believed that 007 was on its way to do more damage.

The Soviet authorities might well assume that this was a deliberate act, either to test the defences, or for intelligence gathering. It was rumoured that a special Soviet weapon was to be tested that night which would have been of intense interest to the Americans.

By 18.00 hours, three more Soviet fighters were airborne, radar-vectored on to 007's tail and had the airliner in their sights. The 747 crew – over two hundred miles off track – still remained oblivious.

Shortly after 18.00, a Soviet SU-15 fighter reported, 'I see it!'

By now the fighter pilots' blood was up, their excitement plainly audible on the R/T exchanges. Flight 007 had become just a target. If the fighters identified it as a civilian airliner, which they probably didn't, that information was not passed to control. IFF (Identify Friend or Foe) was activated by the fighter, with no response. Apparently Soviet IFF are incompatible with other systems. But the Russian fighter pilot reported that the aircraft's navigation lights were on – hardly the camouflage one would expect of a spy plane.

Interspersing the excited communication of the fighters with their control, came the first officer of 007's request to ATC to climb to three five zero.

As the 007 finished the transmission, the leading fighter called, 'I'm closing on the target,' and then, 'I'm going. My ZG is lit.'

The ZG indicator showed that his radar-guided missile was locked on target. After a few seconds, he turned the lock off and radioed that he was approaching the target. And just as the 007 was about to begin the climb, the fighter pilot was reported to have fired 120 rounds from his cannon as a warning. No one knew if any of these struck the aircraft. Certainly no sign of the Soviet fighter was reported. Nor did any of 007's crew appear to see any tracers.

Why not? Were they concentrating on the climb procedure, their perceptions completely narrowed to the one job on hand? Were they still in a state of absence of mind? Was only the first officer awake?

een

ree-Headed Hydra

at another dangerous human
three-headed Hydra.
logy, conformity is difficult to
ience to a possibly mistaken
long with other people's views
is the excessive desire to please.
ne human factor of conformity.
ydra, obedience to a possibly
ipitated the Comet accident at

ain Harry Foote released the
laden G-ALYZ for take-off at
opened up the engines to full

onder plane, the first civil jet
the British were ahead of the
and already millions of pounds
de Havilland by the world's
eet was an élitist group, and
ho attended ritual monthly get-
er good relations between pilots

dest, soft-spoken man. After a
where he won the DFC and Bar,
or – a job for which he was well
rate and methodical and did

The situation is reminiscent of that described in a nineteenth-century poem, 'Death and his Brother Sleep', written after a railway collision at Eastleigh when both men on the footplate were asleep.

Who is in charge of the clattering train,
The axles creak and the couplings strain.
Ten minutes behind at the junction. Yes.
And we're twenty minutes now to bed – no less!

The poem ends: 'Death is in charge of the clattering train.'

As 007 climbed, the SU-15 overshot him. 'I am already in front of the target,' called the fighter pilot, and later, 'How can I chase it? I am already abeam of the target.'

Half a minute later, the fighter radioed, 'Now I will try rockets,' and, 'Roger. I am in lock-on. Distance to target is eight kilometres.'

Then, 'ZG.' He fired two Anab missiles which shot off the tail of the jetliner and an engine. The Boeing broke up and spiralled into the sea.

The fighter pilot called control. 'The target is destroyed. I am breaking off the attack.'

Over seven years later, the Soviet pilot, Colonel Osipovich, gave his version. He said, 'I didn't think for a moment that I was bringing down a passenger plane. Anything but that! The problem of all Soviet pilots is that we do not study the civilian craft of foreign nations. I know all the military planes, but that wasn't like any of them.' The order came from ground control: 'Destroy the target!' On his return, Colonel Osipovich was hailed as a hero. 'The young looked on me with envy. The older ones climbed on the plane and called for a bottle!'

Internationally, if ever there was an exposition of defence mechanisms and perceptual limitations, the politicians were to give it to the world. The order of the day was to ask not 'how did this happen?' but 'how can we turn this to our advantage?' When it was realised that a mistake had been made, attitudes towards Colonel Osipovich changed. Before a television interview, he was briefed on the story he must tell.

Meanwhile, the aviation world tried to find out why it had happened. For if the inattention/absent-minded theory is accepted, the implications are even more alarming in many ways than deliberate intent, because in such an environment small errors can have such disastrous consequences.

Slips, as Professor Reason has pointed out, are errors made in carrying out an intention. They occur during a largely automatic execution of some well-established routine. Particularly vulnerable to slips are routines of the act-wait-act-wait variety, and Reason cites the simple example of making tea, pointing out that the study of such banal errors may help us to limit their occurrence in more unforgiving circumstances.

Although accident-proneness in civil aviation has never been shown, there is no doubt that personality does come into the liability to make slips. If we have a tendency to be careless, not to listen, to put off decisions, to be dreamy or to be always in a hurry, the probability is that we will make more slips in certain circumstances than someone who does not show those traits. But realising their presence, since we all vary from day to day, is another matter.

Few circumstances are more unforgiving of slips and mistakes than those in aviation. Perhaps, then, the insertion of a wrong number, a programming mistake, preceded the fatal flight of 007. But if the crew *did* make those errors, theirs was not an isolated occurrence. In another incident, using NAV mode *en route*, an aircraft turned the wrong way over a checkpoint. Although the incorrect behaviour was noticed, the aircraft turned 45 degrees before the pilot took action.

In October 1985, it was a Japan Airlines 747 flying to Paris from Tokyo which strayed into danger, while trying to avoid turbulence. After making his way round it, the captain forgot to re-engage the NAV mode of the INS and found himself at almost the same spot where KAL 007 had met its fate. At first the JAL crew were unable to give warning of their position. The Russians themselves could not raise the aircraft. But *this* time, the trigger did *not* pull the finger. Restraint had been learned. Eventually

---

Conformity: the

It is in *acceding* to mistakes
factor surfaces – conformity,

Like most concepts in psyc
define. The first head is ob
authority; the second is going
rather than one's own; the thi
All these are gradations of the
It was the first head of the
mistaken authority, which pr
Rome on 26 October 1952.

At 17.56 that evening, Ca
brakes of the brand new, full
Ciampino airport, Rome, and
power.

The Comet was the new
aircraft in the world. At last
Americans in the aviation race
of orders had been placed wi
airlines. The BOAC Comet
Captain Foote was a member
togethers at the local pub to fos
and management.

Foote himself was a quiet, n
distinguished career in the RAF
Foote was to become an instruc
suited, for he was very delib

The situation is reminiscent of that described in a nineteenth-century poem, 'Death and his Brother Sleep', written after a railway collision at Eastleigh when both men on the footplate were asleep.

> Who is in charge of the clattering train,
> The axles creak and the couplings strain.
> Ten minutes behind at the junction. Yes.
> And we're twenty minutes now to bed – no less!

The poem ends: 'Death is in charge of the clattering train.'

As 007 climbed, the SU-15 overshot him. 'I am already in front of the target,' called the fighter pilot, and later, 'How can I chase it? I am already abeam of the target.'

Half a minute later, the fighter radioed, 'Now I will try rockets,' and, 'Roger. I am in lock-on. Distance to target is eight kilometres.'

Then, 'ZG.' He fired two Anab missiles which shot off the tail of the jetliner and an engine. The Boeing broke up and spiralled into the sea.

The fighter pilot called control. 'The target is destroyed. I am breaking off the attack.'

Over seven years later, the Soviet pilot, Colonel Osipovich, gave his version. He said, 'I didn't think for a moment that I was bringing down a passenger plane. Anything but that! The problem of all Soviet pilots is that we do not study the civilian craft of foreign nations. I know all the military planes, but that wasn't like any of them.' The order came from ground control: 'Destroy the target!' On his return, Colonel Osipovich was hailed as a hero. 'The young looked on me with envy. The older ones climbed on the plane and called for a bottle!'

Internationally, if ever there was an exposition of defence mechanisms and perceptual limitations, the politicians were to give it to the world. The order of the day was to ask not 'how did this happen?' but 'how can we turn this to our advantage?' When it was realised that a mistake had been made, attitudes towards Colonel Osipovich changed. Before a television interview, he was briefed on the story he must tell.

Meanwhile, the aviation world tried to find out why it had happened. For if the inattention/absent-minded theory is accepted, the implications are even more alarming in many ways than deliberate intent, because in such an environment small errors can have such disastrous consequences.

Slips, as Professor Reason has pointed out, are errors made in carrying out an intention. They occur during a largely automatic execution of some well-established routine. Particularly vulnerable to slips are routines of the act-wait-act-wait variety, and Reason cites the simple example of making tea, pointing out that the study of such banal errors may help us to limit their occurrence in more unforgiving circumstances.

Although accident-proneness in civil aviation has never been shown, there is no doubt that personality does come into the liability to make slips. If we have a tendency to be careless, not to listen, to put off decisions, to be dreamy or to be always in a hurry, the probability is that we will make more slips in certain circumstances than someone who does not show those traits. But realising their presence, since we all vary from day to day, is another matter.

Few circumstances are more unforgiving of slips and mistakes than those in aviation. Perhaps, then, the insertion of a wrong number, a programming mistake, preceded the fatal flight of 007. But if the crew *did* make those errors, theirs was not an isolated occurrence. In another incident, using NAV mode *en route*, an aircraft turned the wrong way over a checkpoint. Although the incorrect behaviour was noticed, the aircraft turned 45 degrees before the pilot took action.

In October 1985, it was a Japan Airlines 747 flying to Paris from Tokyo which strayed into danger, while trying to avoid turbulence. After making his way round it, the captain forgot to re-engage the NAV mode of the INS and found himself at almost the same spot where KAL 007 had met its fate. At first the JAL crew were unable to give warning of their position. The Russians themselves could not raise the aircraft. But *this* time, the trigger did *not* pull the finger. Restraint had been learned. Eventually contact was achieved. The aircraft was given Russian permission to proceed. Disaster as the result of a moment's slip was avoided.

In 1979 a DC-10 crew programmed the autopilot for the vertical speed mode, instead of the procedurally directed airspeed or mach command mode, and stalled the aircraft.

Another area where such simple slips of the act-wait-act-wait type might be made is in the task of fuel management. A switch is activated to open a valve and another switch is deactivated to allow fuel from the tank with the higher quantity to be used. With so many other things for the pilot to do at the same time, he might easily make a slip in the manual fuel procedure in progress.

The way to guard against such slips is to appreciate that they can happen and the environment in which they are *likely* to happen.

As our environment becomes more technically complicated, we become more distanced from the consequences of our slips or mistakes. We are more removed from the learning process of suffering by those mistakes. And in the incorrect programming of an airborne computer, those mistakes may take a long time in coming home to roost and their consequences will have increased a billionfold.

Thirteen

Conformity: the Three-Headed Hydra

It is in *acceding* to mistakes that another dangerous human factor surfaces – conformity, the three-headed Hydra.

Like most concepts in psychology, conformity is difficult to define. The first head is obedience to a possibly mistaken authority; the second is going along with other people's views rather than one's own; the third is the excessive desire to please. All these are gradations of the same human factor of conformity. It was the first head of the Hydra, obedience to a possibly mistaken authority, which precipitated the Comet accident at Rome on 26 October 1952.

At 17.56 that evening, Captain Harry Foote released the brakes of the brand new, fully laden G-ALYZ for take-off at Ciampino airport, Rome, and opened up the engines to full power.

The Comet was the new wonder plane, the first civil jet aircraft in the world. At last, the British were ahead of the Americans in the aviation race, and already millions of pounds of orders had been placed with de Havilland by the world's airlines. The BOAC Comet fleet was an élitist group, and Captain Foote was a member who attended ritual monthly get-togethers at the local pub to foster good relations between pilots and management.

Foote himself was a quiet, modest, soft-spoken man. After a distinguished career in the RAF where he won the DFC and Bar, Foote was to become an instructor – a job for which he was well suited, for he was very deliberate and methodical and did everything by the Book. On long holiday trips through France, when his wife was driving as he rested, he would tell her the exact speed she should drive at and would immediately point out to her when the speedometer needle had fallen below or above that speed.

The Comet training manual on which he had been instructed had told him that on take-off the Comet's nose-wheel should be lifted off the ground at 80 knots.

That evening it was pitch dark and raining. The wipers clanked across the windscreen to reveal muzzy blobs of runway lights, but there was no horizon. Slowly, into the damp darkness, the heavily laden Yoke Zebra moved and began gathering speed along the slippery runway, bound for Cairo.

The needle on the airspeed indicator crept round the dial: 60, 70, 75 knots, 80 knots – the speed laid down in the manual to lift the nose-wheel. Just as he had been instructed, Foote eased the control column back. The nose-wheel came off the ground. The speed built up to 112 knots, the already correctly calculated unstick speed. Again Foote moved the stick back, this time to lift the aircraft off the runway.

Yoke Zebra inched off the ground. Foote called, 'Under-carriage up.'

At that instant, the port wing dropped violently. The aircraft swung left, then began juddering. Instead of rising, Yoke Zebra bounced back onto the runway. Everything appeared normal, *but the aircraft simply would not fly.*

The Comet appeared not to be responding to the controls. Its speed was not building up. And now the aircraft was rapidly approaching the red boundary lights at the end of the runway.

Foote's only thought was to save his passengers. He slammed back the throttles and tried to stop. Seconds later, Yoke Zebra was sliding over rough ground. Both main undercarriage legs were wrenched off. The wing broke. The aircraft came to an abrupt stop.

There was sudden silence. The reek of kerosene was every-where. Although the first officer was injured, the crew shepherded all the passengers out safely and there was no fire.

The wonder plane was a write-off, yet Foote had obeyed the manual to the letter.

It is, of course, essential for our own group's survival that we *are* obedient. Chaos will result if we refuse to drive on the left-hand side of the road, and there are multifarious other benefits from group obedience. There are also, of course, as in almost all human concepts, *dangers*. Blind obedience has killed many people – on and off the battlefield. At the same time, we each believe that *we* would not carry obedience beyond our moral limits, as happened in Nazi Germany. But so ingrained is obedience in us that we very well might do so.

The experimental psychologist Milgram performed in 1974 what has since become a classic experiment. Subjects were divided into 'Teachers' and 'Learners'. The Learners were strapped into a sort of 'electric chair'. The Learner had to learn a long sequence of adjectives and nouns such as blue book, nice dog, wild duck, etc. Then he had to be tested on how well he remembered which adjective went with which noun, e.g. blue with book and nice with dog. A simple, almost party game, but the punishment for mistakes was dire. The Teacher was instructed by the Experimenter to give the Learner an electric shock every time he gave a wrong response. Worse still, with every mistake the Teacher had to move higher up the voltage scale of the shock generator until the shock level given was a massive 450 volts. The Learners shouted, groaned, screamed, cried for mercy.

So did those ordinary, kindly people stop? Not at all. They continued to obey the orders of Professor Milgram who was their authority figure, even though the Learners were apparently writhing in agony.

In fact, the Learners were in the know and had been acting. No electric shocks were delivered. But the experiment, which was repeated many times, clearly showed that subjects would obey authority to a far greater extent than had hitherto been supposed. And in a subsequent much criticised experiment, a puppy was used to which real electric shocks were given – still

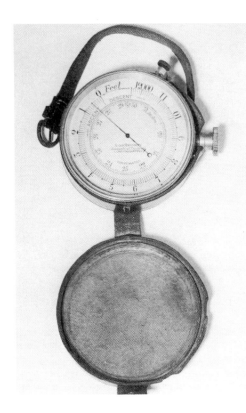

1a Balloonists' portable altimeter, c. 1912 – essentially an aneroid barometer, forerunner of all present pressure altimeters.

1b Airspeed indicator developed by Mervyn O'Gorman and used on the first BE aircraft at Farnborough in 1910. O'Gorman was the consulting engineer at the Balloon Factory and galvanised the negative government away from airships and on to heavier-than-air craft.

2a The instrument panel of the Vimy in which Alcock and Brown flew the Atlantic in 1919. The pilot sat on the right, following the precedent set by horse-carriages (the driver's right hand was the whip hand). The wheel is taken from the car. The curved spirit level seen through the spokes of the wheel was Alcock's only attitude indicator – and so inadequate that it led to a spin over the Atlantic.

2b The cockpit of the Vimy, showing the mechanisms of the controls.

3a *Left to right*: Squadron Leader E. L. Johnson (navigator), Sir Sefton Brancker (Director of Civil Aviation), Lord Thomson (Secretary of State for Air) and Lt. Colonel V. Richmond (designer of the R101) taken just before embarking on their ill-fated journey, October 1930.

3b The control cabin of the R101 – very like a ship's bridge, complete with wheel.

4a A typical blind-flying panel (this one of the mid-1950s) that originated in the 1930s remains the basis of blind-flying panels today (containing airspeed indicator, artificial horizon, directional gyro, altimeter, vertical speed indicator, and turn and bank with spirit level). The altimeter is the now notorious three-pointer. The large pointer is for hundreds of feet, the smaller one for thousands and the stub for tens of thousands.

4b Comet I instrument panel (1951). The first jet airliner instrument panel.

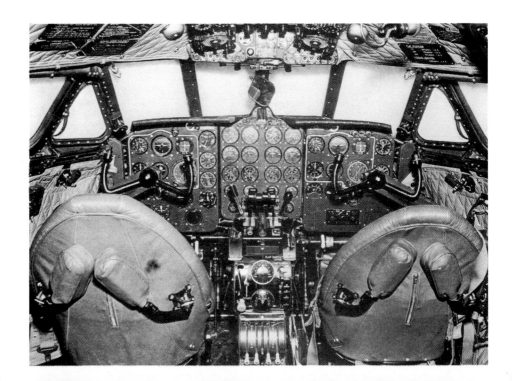

5a Comet IV panel (1959) – neater and much more modern than that of the Comet I.

5b Boeing 707 instrument panel (1960).

6a Concorde panel. The first supersonic Atlantic crossing was made on
21 January 1976. There is little difference between subsonic and supersonic
instrument panels.

6b Boeing 747-200 (late 1970s). The engineer's panel is on the right.

7a Boeing 737-300 (mid 1980s). This is the earlier version of the 737-400 which crashed at Kegworth (see Chapter 14). The engine instrument panel – but this one with pointers and easier to read – is in the centre. The modern counter-pointer altimeter with actual height in numbers in its box can clearly be seen.

7b Boeing 747-400 (1988). The long-range 747 with the two-pilot crew. The 'glass cockpit' dominates the instrument panel. On the pedestal below are the three screens of the Flight Management System which includes the three Inertial Navigation Systems.

8 The A-320 Airbus (1990) – the ultimate in flight-deck design. The neatness and clarity are obvious. Gone are the control columns, replaced by sidestick controllers outboard of each pilot. There are no mechanical connections between the pilots' controls and the control services, and the system is known as 'fly by wire'. The Electronic Centralised Aircraft Monitoring System (ECAM) quietly monitors what is going on in the system – a sort of 'subconscious aircraft mind'. If anything goes wrong, warning is given by voice, amber lights or an advisory message on the screen.

the obedient delivered real pain and suffering without dis-
obedience. In the lifetimes of many today, such blind obedience
has been cruelly demonstrated in Nazi Germany, Soviet Russia,
Rumania and many other countries of the world.

So the pressures of obedience on us are strong. Bearing in
mind his personality and military experience, they were
immensely strong on Captain Foote.

After the accident there was an immediate outcry. Nothing
could be wrong with the wonder plane. Hardly had the pieces
been picked up from the ground, let alone examined or an
inquiry held, than the Ministry of Civil Aviation produced an
interim report, and BOAC and de Havilland issued a joint
statement – all to the effect that they were satisfied that neither
engines nor aircraft were to blame for the accident. They
maintained that Foote had lifted the nose too high – there were
tail skidmarks on the runway to prove it – thus preventing the
aircraft becoming airborne.

Yet one of the things that does come naturally when flying an
aeroplane (perhaps inherited from flying animal ancestors
millions of years ago) is *not* to get the nose too high. It is possible
that a pupil might do so, but it would be impossible for an
experienced airline captain with 5,868 flying hours to do so
unless there was a very good reason.

The Ministry of Civil Aviation Inspector wrote to Foote
saying that, as a result of BOAC's Inquiry, 'blame for this
accident has been attributed to you'. The verdict was 'pilot
error'.

Foote was asked to sign a government form accepting the total
blame. Wanting it over quickly and quietly, Foote signed.

Retribution followed. Foote was formally admonished and
posted to Yorks, the oldest BOAC aeroplane, used for carrying
freight and exotic animals such as leopards and monkeys. Vast
publicity in the newspapers highlighted his punishment. The
Comet had been vindicated and could continue to be sold
worldwide untarnished.

Foote remained worried about how he could possibly have got

the nose so high, spending most of his time doing endless graphs and calculations.

Behind the scenes, BOAC and de Havilland were worried too. The manufacturers had been doing further tests and a new take-off technique was introduced. The nose-wheel had to be lifted off the ground at 80 knots, but afterwards it had to be placed on the ground again – a most extraordinary manoeuvre. When he returned from Rome, Foote found amended and undated instructions in his locker, but the training manual had mysteriously disappeared.

Comet Take-off

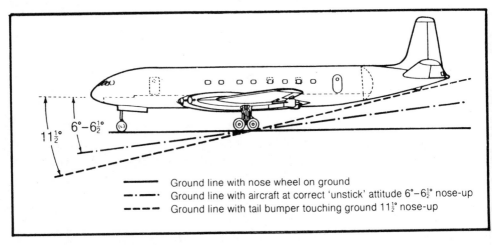

——————— Ground line with nose wheel on ground
—·—·—·· Ground line with aircraft at correct 'unstick' attitude 6°–6½° nose-up
— — — — Ground line with tail bumper touching ground 11½° nose-up

On 12 February 1953, Captain Charles Pentland, who had instructed me and my generation of pilots on flying the Atlantic, arrived in England to take delivery of a new Comet, *Empress of Hawaii*, for Canadian Pacific Airlines. Like Foote, he was a Book pilot. At de Havilland he received his training on how to fly the Comet. He was even trained on how *not* to fly it by a demonstration of 'the Foote take-off'.

On 2 March 1953, on a hot dark night at maximum all-up-weight, Pentland tried to take off from Karachi – and crashed, killing all eleven people on board. It was a repetition of the Rome accident. Pentland, too, had implicitly obeyed.

You would have thought that now there would be a vindication of Foote, but the Comet sales potential was too valuable for that. Instead, the Inquiry blamed Pentland, bringing in *another* verdict of pilot error. But now others were voicing doubts. *The Aeroplane* stated that with two such similar accidents, such a mistake as lifting the nose too high 'must be presumed to be easily possible'.

Foote was more convinced than ever that he had been unjustly blamed. He became ill with worry. Off flying, he was under his local doctor, who reported him to the BOAC doctor as suffering from 'anxiety'. This doctor had been his squadron doctor during the war, but so worried was he that he would be caught showing sympathy to BOAC's 'black sheep' that during his examination he shut Foote in a cupboard when a BOAC top official knocked at his door and wanted to see him.

Because of the anxiety diagnosis, the insurance company now refused to insure Foote's Airline Transport Pilot's Licence. Foote went to the Vice-Chairman of BOAC, Air Vice-Marshal Victor Tait, with information he had discovered that the Comet could stall at higher speed near the ground than in free air, and that the margin of safety was minute. Tait did not admit the viability of the argument. Comets continued to fly – and now, one after the other, they were (though for a different reason from his case) exploding in the air.

A *third* Comet take-off technique was now introduced. The nose-wheel had to be returned firmly to the ground until not less than 5 knots below the unstick speed.

BALPA took up the matter of what was wrong with the Comets. A meeting of the Comet sub-committee of BALPA's Air Safety and Technical Committee took place on 24 February 1954. Two representatives of the Comet fleet had been invited, but had written to say they felt unable to attend. The committee considered their absence 'a very great loss'.

Foote continued in his struggle to clear his name.

An opportunity to demonstrate his undoubted flying skill came on 1 September 1955. He was piloting a York freighter to

Bangkok when there were two sudden bangs and the aircraft swung to the right as both starboard propellers disappeared into the Bay of Bengal.

The York plunged towards the sea. All freight, mail, tools and loose gear were thrown out in a desperate attempt to remain airborne, but Harry Foote, correct and calm as always, refused to jettison his suitcase, remarking that he always liked to change after a flight, particularly in the tropics. With no starboard engines and half the starboard elevator torn off, it was Foote's skilful airmanship that brought the stricken York safely down at Rangoon. This time BOAC could do no other than give him a commendation.

Frantic modifications were now being made to the Comet. Pilots were calling for more efficient brakes, the fitting of a stall-warning device, the provision of a tail parachute, the fitting of a drooped wing and a modification to the nose-wheel oleo leg to prevent hammering at the high groundspeed required for the new take-off techniques. In Parliament, Sir Robert Perkins asked John Profumo (Parliamentary Secretary, Ministry of Civil Aviation) if he would re-open investigations into the Rome accident. This was refused, but there were loud cheers when Perkins nevertheless proceeded to say, 'In view of the fact that since this accident there have been three changes made in the take-off technique of the Comet [in fact there had only been two], will he institute a full public inquiry to enable this innocent man to clear himself?'

No such inquiry was granted.

Captain Jackson of the International Federation of Airline Pilots now took up the cudgels on Foote's behalf, threatening to call a worldwide strike of 15,000 pilot members every 3 March (the date of the Karachi accident) unless de Havilland released information on the take-off accidents.

This they initially refused to do, for why had not other pilots experienced the same difficulty? Eventually the reasons began to materialise. The conditions of high weight, high temperature, darkness and lack of horizon had been rare during the four months that Comets had operated before the accident. The only clue to correct attitude without a horizon was minute movement on the artificial horizon, not normally regarded on take-off, and the controls had only an artificial 'feel' incorporated in them.

Pilots do have an intuitive idea of how to fly an aircraft. Other Comet pilots had realised that there was a ground-stalling problem. Finding it impossible in such circumstances to judge the angle of attack for take-off, they had *not* lifted the nosewheel, keeping it on the ground until almost at unstick speed.

Richard Leakey in *The Making of Mankind* writes: 'The most notable characteristic of primates is opportunism.' Here it was used for just that, and was stronger than conformity. They had *not* obeyed authority, trusting in their instinct. Not so the very correct instructors Harry Foote and Charles Pentland.

Eventually a guarded statement was publicly issued to the effect that tests had 'revealed a hitherto unrecognised feature that the stalling speed near the ground was higher than the corresponding figure in free air, and that the disparity increased as the aircraft weight increased. The safety margin at the highest take-off weights were thus found to be smaller than that indicated by the certification flight trials.'

Pentland was not cleared of pilot error. Neither was Foote.

The strain of many years was telling on Foote. He had bouts of breathlessness and angina pain. He had to give up flying and tried various jobs on the ground, but all the time his mind remained obsessed with that totally unfair verdict of pilot error.

In the end, it killed him. At fifty-three he had a heart-attack. His memorial is now carried in jet aircraft throughout the world – the lights, horns and stick-shaker of the stall-warning devices.

The second head of the Hydra of conformity is when someone goes along with another's views although they are not in accord with his own. An experiment was carried out by Asch (1956) in which the task was to judge which of three lines – one of six and a quarter inches, one of six and three-quarter inches and one of eight inches – was equal in length to the standard line of eight inches.

There were nine subjects, eight of whom were 'in the know'. These eight gave their judgements first, and all unanimously chose the six-and-a-quarter-inch line as equal to the standard (eight inches).

Faced with a flat contradiction of his senses, the last subject hesitated, then conformed with the others who said it was the six-and-a-quarter-inch line.

This experiment was frequently repeated. And 37 per cent of the naive subjects capitulated to the unanimous majority. On almost all occasions, these perplexed subjects exhibited signs of unease, such as sweating and restlessness. Physiological tests demonstrated that the fatty acid level remained high for those who resisted and went down when they yielded. Agreement with the group also led to a lowering of arousal. The subjects wanted to conform, and obtained relief when they did. This type of conformity varies considerably with different nationalities and cultures.

Individuals also appear to vary in their conformity according to sex and occupation. Women have been shown to conform more than men. Artists, students and scientists conformed less than bankers or military officers. Crutchfield (1962) found that out of fifty American Army officers, 46 per cent expressed agreement with the higher group consensus that a star was larger than a circle – though in fact the circle was one-third larger than the star. Yet people don't like to be accused of conforming.

In post-mortems after such experiments, defence mechanisms abound. The yielding subject blames his eyesight, his angle of vision, the group, or says he misheard the question.

Krech, Crutchfield and Ballanchey in *Individuals in Society* state: 'The essence of conformity, in distinction to uniformity or conventionality, is the yielding to group pressures. For there to be conformity, there must be conflict – conflict between those forces in the individual which tend him to act, value and believe in one way and those pressures emanating from the society or group which tend to lead him another way.'

The psychologist Harvey found that the *second* highest member of a group was the most conforming. The first officer is the second-in-command of an aircraft. The status of the captain in the small group community of the cockpit may exert pressure on the rest of the crew to conform to his way of thinking. This may hinder intelligent interaction and good monitoring. Norms have refined the respective roles on the flight deck, and regulated the overall hierarchy of behaviour within the group. One of the forms of conformity is that it may inhibit action, making a person yield his right to express an opinion.

At an airport in India, A DC-3 was observed coming in unusually low at night with both landing lights on. Subsequently, the aircraft assumed a steeply banked attitude and crashed at a point 2,000 feet from the runway. Fire broke out on impact. The co-pilot, who survived, said he had seen the obstacle before the aircraft struck it. On being questioned as to whether it was not his responsibility to warn the pilot when he knew something was going wrong, he replied that he had not interfered with the captain's flying as he was only the co-pilot.

The first officer of KLM 747 in the Tenerife disaster (Chapter 8) had only ninety-five hours' flying experience in a B-747. His captain was the Chief Instructor of the KLM B-747 fleet. The higher the status of the authoritarian figure, the more chance of conformity in his second-in-command.

The problem of the subordinate conforming to the ideas and wishes of his superior, and being too scared or too wary to risk his job and promotion, is not confined to aviation. It is just more dangerous. Surgeons have been known to remove the wrong limb or eye while nurses looked on. It is not unusual, according to one authority on accidents, for 'a deck officer to remain aghast and silent while his captain grounds the ship or collides with another'.

Very few of us will, in fact, contradict authority. The usual excuses are that we can't be bothered or that it will simply cause a row. The British Cabinet itself was not noted for expressing contrary opinions to an earlier Prime Minister.

The Inquiry into the United Airlines Portland running-out-of-fuel (Chapter 6) took the bull by the horns. The report stated:

> Although the captain is in command and responsible for the
> performance of his crew, the actions, or inactions of the
> other two flight-crew members must be analysed.
> Admittedly, the status of a captain and his management
> style may exert subtle pressure on his crew to conform to his
> way of thinking. It may hinder interaction and adequate
> monitoring and force another crew member to yield his
> right to express an opinion.

The first officer's main responsibility is to monitor the captain. In particular, he provides feedback for the captain. If the captain infers from the first officer's actions or inactions that his judgement is correct, the captain could receive reinforcement for an error or poor judgement. Although in the Portland crash the first officer did, in fact, make subtle comments questioning the aircraft's fuel state, it was not until after the number four engine flamed out that in despair he expressed the direct view, 'Get this . . . on the ground!'

As regards the United engineer's contribution, the report stated that although he informed the captain that 'an additional fifteen minutes is really gonna run us low on fuel here', there was no indication that he took affirmative action to ensure that the captain was fully aware of the time of fuel exhaustion.

Amongst the safety recommendations issued to the FAA by the Safety Board was: 'Issue an operations bulletin to all air carriers' operations inspectors directing them to urge their assigned operators to ensure that their flight crews are indoctrinated in principles of flight-deck resource management, with particular emphasis on the merits of participative management for captains and assertiveness training for other cockpit crew members.'

That recommendation was immediately taken on board by United Airlines, who instituted a course on human factors which involved assertiveness training. The idea has since spread – very slowly – to other companies.

The third head of conformity – the desire to please – is more of a menace than the other two because it wears such a benign and lovable face.

Almost all of us want to please. Most of us are members of a number of different-sized groups – family, office, societies, organisations and friends. Unless there is a high degree of conformity, it is impossible to have a group. And the strength of the conformity pressure varies with the common interest of the group and the relevance of a particular issue to a group.

The group inside an aircraft – captain, crew, passengers – is a particularly cohesive one. The passengers need to believe implicitly in the crew. They want to please the father figure at the controls and the mother/mistress who comes round with food and drinks and soothing words. On their part, the crew want to please the passengers. On board, then, there is a high degree of group conformity and a strong reciprocal and interacting desire to please.

In 1966 a B-707 was almost twenty hours late for a flight from Tokyo to Hong Kong. In such circumstances, the airline try to take the edge off the natural frustration of the passengers by providing such things as extra meals and drinks. The captain had filed an IFR flight plan to the south of Fuji. But just before taxying out he changed his mind and asked control for a visual climb via Fuji.

He probably saw the snow-covered mountain against a blue sky, and thought he would give his passengers a treat. There is a Japanese saying: 'When the sky is blue, Fuji is angry.' The crew had been briefed on high winds, and prior to departure neither the captain or operations had informed the weather service of the intention to fly towards Fuji.

The dangerous turbulence from high winds over mountains is well known.

After take-off, the captain said 'Good day' to the controller – the last words heard from the aircraft.

But its course was recorded on an eight-millimetre film taken by one of the passengers. Then suddenly the film skipped two frames. Vague pictures of upside-down passenger seats and torn carpet showed next. Then abruptly the film stopped.

The B-707 had disintregrated. All on board were killed.

The Inquiry gave as the possible cause that 'the aircraft suddenly encountered gust loads exceeding the design limit and disintegrated in the air in a very short period of time'. The VFR climb may have been associated with 'the captain's desire to allow his passengers a better view of Mount Fuji, but this cannot be established with certainty'.

Similar accidents had happened before. A DC-7 and a Constellation collided over the Grand Canyon in clear weather and excellent visibility. The Board of Inquiry were unable to say why the pilots did not see each other but suggested that it had resulted from 'any one or a combination of the following factors: intervening clouds, limitations in cockpit visibility, preoccupation with normal cockpit duties, physiological limits to human vision, insufficiency of *en route* air traffic advisory information and preoccupation with matters unrelated to cockpit duties such as attempting to provide the passengers with a more scenic view of the Grand Canyon area'.

A Constellation struck the 70-degree ice slope of Mount Gilbert, Alaska. The fact that the aircraft was well off course had been established by the Alaska USAF Radar Advisory Service, set up to monitor aircraft even in the absence of a request from the pilot, and assist aircraft 'to avoid existing areas of potentially hazardous weather, terrain, restricted areas and other conditions hazardous to flight'.

The Inquiry stated that 'although a blip of the aircraft's flight had been observed for thirty minutes, those seeing it had not considered it necessary to contact the flight because it was assumed that the pilot was deviating from his course so as to show his passengers a certain glacier, as pilots allegedly often did'.

Not only are there pressures on the pilot to please the passengers, there are also pressures to please his company.

The pilot of a Lockheed on a return trip to Nice decided to

make a nightstop at Gao instead of the scheduled nightstop of Tamenrasset because he was tired. Later, he received word from the company which caused him to change his plans and leave at 03.00. The Accident Report stated that 'he seemed to dread the take-off at night very much, and went so far as to ask the controller to prohibit him from taking off. The controller would not comply with such a request, as the flight planned was normal from the regulation point of view. The pilot took off in good weather and crashed, killing seventeen.'

One would have thought that the Grand Canyon, Mount Fuji and other accidents would have taught airline managements that the aeroplane is not a sightseeing vehicle.

Unfortunately this has not been the case.

In 1977, Air New Zealand began flights from Auckland to fly over Antarctica. Ice and mountains are always a draw to sightseers, and the breathtaking views from the DC-10 attracted many customers for the eleven-hour round trip.

The flights were a great success. The company was pleased, and so were the passengers. But behind the beauty was danger. The weather was uncertain. Should any malfunction occur on the aircraft, there was nowhere to land. Around the South Pole, conventional navigation is not possible. The magnetic compass is unusable close to the magnetic pole, so inertial navigation is employed. Unbelievably, no Arctic survival kits were carried. More unbelievably, neither the captain nor the first officer had flown the route before. And most unbelievably, an illusion called whiteout, well known to polar pilots, in which sunlight refracted through ice crystals turns the sky white and results in loss of depth perception and makes it impossible to separate sky from earth, was not properly explained to the crews of the Antarctic flights. Only whiteout in snow conditions was considered, yet the illusion can occur in a crystal-clear atmosphere or under a reasonably illuminated cloud ceiling.

A further hazard lay in wait for this last trip of the 1979 season on 29 November, intended to commemorate Commander Richard Byrd's pioneering flight over the South Pole. The wrong data for the trip had been entered into the INS computer, which had the effect of moving the track closer to Mount Erebus. It was not part of the crew's responsibility to check the digits of their computer-generated flight plan. The error was hidden because the weather had been excellent for the previous trips.

It was to be otherwise for the last trip of the season. After take-off, there was to be a champagne breakfast and free booklets on Antarctic history, together with a film and explanation by a well-known Antarctic explorer and mountaineer. As the aircraft came up to McMurdo, the weather deteriorated. The cloud base went down to 3,000 feet. There were also communication difficulties in that the VHF reception was only intermittent, but the crew would feel a necessity to fulfil their obligation to the passengers and the decision was made to continue.

When the visibility improved, the captain began a VFR descent to 1,500 feet with the INS and autopilot controlling the aircraft.

At 260 knots, the DC-10 flew towards a horizon that was slowly disappearing under a whiteout.

The crew were now trying to map-read – but misinterpreting the terrain below. Further attempts to make VHF contact failed.

The flight engineer said, 'I don't like this.'

As well he might not. Their track was leading them inexorably towards Erebus, placing the mountain between the transmitters and the aircraft and blocking all signals.

The crew should never have been put into this desperate situation. Even without the previous sightseeing tragedies to warn them, the company should have had the imagination to realise the pressures that might be put on a captain trying to give passengers their money's worth in uncertain conditions – never mind the errors that had been made without his knowledge on the INS. A few weeks earlier, the 10th Antarctic Treaty Conference in Washington had noted that flights such as the Air New Zealand sightseeing trips 'operated in a particularly hazardous environment'.

A few seconds after the flight engineer's remark, the GPWS warned : 'Pull up! Whoop Whoop! Pull up!'

Immediately the captain calmly called for go-around power.

As the engines roared, the DC-10 struck Mount Erebus. All 257 people on board were killed.

The Chief Inspector of Accidents said in his report that 'the probable cause of the accident was the decision of the captain to continue flight at low level towards an area of poor surface horizon definition when the crew were not certain of their position'.

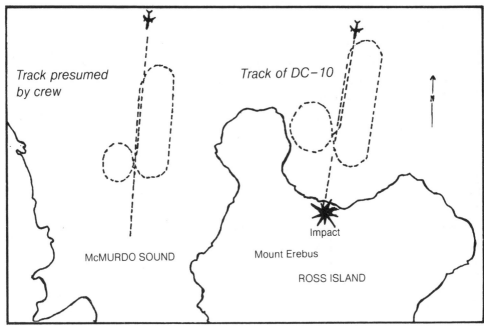

Error behind the Antarctic crash

The New Zealand Airline Pilots' Association and line pilots now fought the airline management and the executive pilots, who according to all the laws of conformity had grouped together to protect their name. In a manner reminiscent of the R101 Inquiry described in Chapter 18, the Colonel North case, the West Midlands police cover-up, and the German Inquiry into the Munich slush accident (Chapter 18), documents went missing, evidence was suppressed, pages from the captain's notebook disappeared, there was even a burglary in the dead captain's house where only a file of correspondence between his widow and her lawyers was taken.

The case went all the way up to the Privy Council. The crew was cleared. The British Law Lords summed up: 'It is an understandable weakness on the part of individual members of the airline management to shrink from acknowledging, even to themselves, that something they had done or failed to do might have been the cause of so horrendous an accident.'

Yet repeatedly pilots are not *allowed* to shrink from acknowledging that something they had done or failed to do might have been the cause of an accident.

At nine o'clock on a dark January morning in 1983, a United Airlines captain reported to O'Hare airport to take the regular scheduled cargo flight to Los Angeles via Detroit. He was an experienced and above-average pilot who loved flying and was thoroughly at home in his aircraft. He was also a kind and fatherly man who had a very happy home life.

He had spent the night before his trip at his son's home in Chicago. Mindful of his coming flight, he was in bed by ten o'clock. Next morning, he was up in time to take his son to work, and in the evening they went together to a basketball game in which his daughter was playing.

The captain also had a reputation for excellent relations with his crews. At the airport, he greeted his first officer and second officer cordially – both considerably less experienced and less able than he was.

Nevertheless, this ill-assorted crew of three had an uneventful flight to Detroit, where they landed safely. The cargo for Detroit was unloaded, the aircraft was refuelled, and the cargo for Los Angeles was put aboard.

The weather was fine – overcast at 1,900 feet with a modest south-westerly wind. Not a bad night, the kindly captain must have thought, to give his quiet, rather withdrawn second officer the experience of a night take-off.

The second officer of that United Airlines DC-8, chosen by the captain to make that night take-off from Detroit, had had a chequered career. He was described as a quiet, conservative person who was content to be a second officer. Indeed, he had to be content. For in June 1979, he had entered the DC-8 first officer upgrade training, and his instructor's comments had been: 'scan very weak ... procedural knowledge poor ... inconsistent bank in steep turns ... stall series needs more work' – until in August his training was terminated. He was precluded from bidding for any first-officer vacancies for six months.

Yet in February 1980 he was allowed to try again. He improved a little and completed the upgrade training in March, but his difficulties were not over, and despite the fact that the check-captain commented that 'his attitude could not be better and he is a hard worker', the same captain went on to say: 'His command ability is below average, and he has exhibited poor operational judgement both IFR and VFR'.

And after more training, more consultation, the Fleet Manager wrote, 'In view of the continuing problems in reaching the desired level of pilot proficiency, you have voluntarily agreed in writing to forego bidding for any pilot vacancies on United Airlines and remain in second officer status for the balance of your flying career.'

The first officer was described as of average ability, a somewhat mechanical pilot, who sometimes performed checks out of sequence, and who had once volunteered to a different captain on a previous flight, 'If you want the engineer to fly, I can work the panel.'

Once inside the aircraft, rather like a father offering his son a ball game, the captain asked genially, 'Are you guys trading?'

The second officer, quite happy at his engineer's position, was disconcerted by this offer to exchange roles.

But the first officer promptly replied, 'Do it!'

The captain repeated his probably unwelcome offer, 'Are you guys trading?'

This time the first officer said, 'Ready – you ready?' And the second officer, whose good attitude had been commended and who obviously sought to please, replied, 'Go for it!'

The first officer announced, 'Ready to trade.'

But the second officer asked, again as if both surprised and reluctant, 'Oh, we're going to trade now?'

It was not the response of an enthusiastic participator in the swap. But the change of seats was effected. The second officer became the first officer, and thus were required of him all the skills of rapid scan and division of attention in which he had been proved so significantly lacking.

Take-off at night with reduced visual cues particularly requires such skills, and the lighting of the flight deck on a DC-8 frequently required the assistance of a pen torch to read the instruments.

That the second officer was uneasy in his new seat was shown by his calling out, 'Transponder on?' (the last checklist item) as the aircraft roared down the runway, though the checklist was completed before the take-off roll began.

That both the first officer and the second officer were aware that neither of them was qualified for the duties of the position they occupied on take-off was shown in the voice-recorder. The cockpit conversation contained reassurances, cautions, reminders and uncertainties. But it does not seem that the uncertainty was unduly shared by the captain, who, being a dedicated pilot himself, believed that other crew members were too.

At home in his aircraft, he probably had no idea of how uneasy, how unambitious, a less able pilot could be. And the second officer himself, however uneasy, probably did not want to displease his captain, and chose to conform to the captain's idea of him. He would have preferred to stay put and not be winkled out of his safe engineer's seat. But in a situation such as this he did what was expected of him.

The take-off at 02.50 was normal. The aircraft rotated to take-off attitude one-half to two-thirds of the way down Runway 21 Right. Then after lift-off, the airplane's pitch attitude steepened abnormally as it climbed to a thousand feet.

There disaster struck. Some eye witnesses saw sparks coming

in short bursts, looking like 'a fireworks display which lit up the sky'. There was an explosion, followed by a fireball which spread an intense fire over what was fortunately not a built-up area, but farmland. The crash was not survivable.

At the Inquiry, a number of hypotheses that could not be proved were examined. Had the first or second officer inadvertently engaged the auto-pilot when they switched seats? Had the flight crew neglected to reset the stabiliser trim after landing at Detroit? Had the second officer frozen on the controls in those last seconds, making recovery by the captain impossible?

It was finally decided that 'the probable cause of the accident was the flight crew's failure to detect and correct a mistrimmed stabiliser before the airplane became uncontrollable'. A contributing factor was 'the captain's allowing the second-officer, who was not qualified to act as a pilot to occupy the seat of the first officer and to conduct the take-off'.

It had been a strange carousel of conformity. The first officer and the second officer wanted to please the captain. The second officer didn't want to argue with the first officer or refuse his proffered swap. Nor did he want to appear 'chicken' by not doing the take-off. The kindly captain simply wanted to please his crew, and help build up the confidence of his second officer.

It is recognised that once first officers gain experience they can often be better handlers of the aircraft than the captain. They are younger, have quicker reflexes and are probably more motivated, and it is accepted that the handling performance of a pilot on simulator checks on a modern aircraft can get worse with age.

In the old days, as Norman Tebbit, himself a BOAC co-pilot wrote in his autobiography *Upwardly Mobile*: 'I rated captains not least according to how often they were willing to play the co-pilot's role to their first officer.' But now in most airlines there is a recognised practice of alternate flying by the two pilots, called respectively Pilot Flying and Pilot Not Flying.

However, there remains one area which still needs to be addressed. Many first officers still hesitate to contradict the captain and point out flying errors. Nor are some captains grateful for such important advice. Perhaps a dim subconscious memory of civil aviation's progenitor, the merchant navy, remains with some co-pilots and captains – the notion that two hundred miles out to sea there is only 'the Captain under God alone'.

Some excerpts from recent CHIRPs, initiated at the Institute of Aviation Medicine illustrate the point.

A first officer writes of his diffidence in tackling a captain: 'Just a bad habit that I think a lot of co-pilots have of double-checking before we say anything to the captain!' Perhaps this is not unjustifiable. The co-pilot can have a hard time pointing things out to his captain.

A co-pilot told his captain that Approach Control had told them to slow down to 180 knots.

> His reply was something to the effect of, 'I'll do what I want!' I told him at least twice more and received the same answer. Approach Control asked us why we had not slowed yet. I told them we were doing the best job we could, and their reply was, 'You almost hit another aircraft.' Then they asked us to turn east. I told them we would rather not because of the weather, and we were given our present heading and told to maintain 3,000 feet. The captain descended to 3,000 feet, and kept on going to 2,500 feet even though I told him our altitude was 3,000 feet. His comment was, 'You just look out the damn window.'

Another co-pilot writes:

> At the top of descent before descending into the destination airfield – I was first officer on the outbound leg from London – I reported the latest VOLMET [Met report] to the captain, which was 8/8 cloud, 150 feet and less than 1,000 metres visibility. He announced that he would be doing all the flying on the approach, landing and possible overshoot single-handed, which was completely non-standard as the Operations Manual specified monitored approach procedures throughout.
>   I challenged him tactfully on the matter and a serious argument arose which left a dangerous, tense atmosphere among the three crew. He then carried out his approach and

landing in the conditions stated without incident. On landing there was a further argument, where I was accused of interfering with the lawful authority of the captain. I have never been involved in an argument like this in flight before or since, and the incident disturbed me. The captain did not fly the approach accurately and there could have been a more serious outcome.

'Assertiveness training' of aircrew is at last being practised by some airlines in an attempt to get people to speak out. But the reasons *why* they don't have not so far been analysed. That conformity is at the root of many aircraft accidents still waits to be acknowledged.

Fourteen

Laterality: Green for Danger

> Here lie the bones of Emily Bright
> Who put out her left hand
> And turned to the right.

If conformity, with all its dangers, is still waiting to be recognised as a cause of accidents, even more hidden lies laterality, the pattern of hand preferences, the mixing of left and right. Yet most of us have a laterality pattern and some of us have a laterality problem.

Around 88 per cent of us are overtly right-handed, 9 per cent overtly left-handed and in-between are a number whose pattern is ambiguous. On occasions, people jam on the accelerator instead of the brake, indicate left and turn right, have difficulty marching in step – the squad that doesn't know its left from right is a favourite joke. Others try to unscrew nuts clockwise, mix east and west, set the table with forks on the right-hand side, and some of us (James Bond's creator, Ian Fleming, included) have difficulty calculating times in different longitudes. Some children can't tie ties and shoelaces, reverse letters like b and d, and sometimes syllables too.

Left-handers are 'southpaws', 'cackhanders', 'culliwifters'. Professor Orton (1937) quotes thirty-five contemptuous nick-names for left-handers in England alone. Dance teachers report that children are afraid of 'confessing' to being left-handed. The Latin for left, 'sinister', and the French 'gauche' (with its English meaning of 'clumsy') say it all. The place of honour in battle and in heaven is on the right. However, there have been many famous left-handers, among them Leonardo da Vinci, Charlemagne, Julius Caesar, Holbein, Michaelangelo and Alexander the Great. Amongst well-known left-handers of today are President Bush, Paul McCartney and Gary Sobers while Prince Charles has been photographed kicking a ball with his left foot and presenting prizes with his left hand.

In the American Civil War, the majority of the North's rank and file were farm-hands who had no culture-induced knowledge of the difference between left and right. But they *did* know their agriculture and the difference between hay and straw. So in their training, hay was attached to their left foot, straw to their right. And when they drilled, instead of the sergeant calling 'Left, right, left, right . . .' he called 'Hayfoot, strawfoot, hayfoot, strawfoot . . .'

Rolf Gerhardt, a chief psychologist to the Norwegian Forces, who studied pilots in the Norwegian Air Force for many years, stressed the 'laterality personality' – pilots with varying degrees of hand preference. He found (1959) connections between laterality and maladjustment in military pilots. He quoted a number of cases – one fighter pilot feared close-formation flying because in that situation he was uncertain which way to turn. 'We found this pilot to be ambivalent as regards hand preferences. In the aeroplane he had to look for his wedding ring in order to identify left and right.'

He cites expectancies in such pilots as omitting parts of a chain of actions, wrong instrument reading, reversing numbers, uncertainty of direction in thought and space. He believes such a laterality pattern may be present in considerable numbers of people with no overt left-handedness. Overlearning has made them carry out such actions 'normally'. Only when surprised and under stress will they revert to their laterality pattern in certain behaviour situations, where for them there is a left/right confusion. He thinks the laterality pattern is basic, and if it involves a tendency to reverse, this is inevitable, saying:

A person may learn to write g and d, but when he, in fluent use of the two letters, has a marked tendency to use them in the opposite manner, he is also due to make other movements in an opposite manner. He may learn to use the right letter in the right place, if he is allowed to hesitate a little before forming the letter. But when he is in a hurry, he will inevitably make the wrong movement at one time or another.

Similar behaviour is often shown by dyslexics. The condition of 'word-blindness' was recognised in 1895 by James Kinshelwood, an eye surgeon, who published an article in *The Lancet*. As usual with any new idea, it had difficulty gaining acceptance, and it was not until the British Dyslexia Association and the Dyslexia Institute were founded in 1972 that scholastic circles began to recognise it. Even now the condition is widely ignored and there are many conflicting views on its origins and causes. Since many apparently right-handed children are dyslexic, experts hesitate to involve laterality in their arguments.

In an experiment, a thousand people were shown the two mirror-image drawings below, and 80 per cent of right-handers chose the lower one as looking happier, presumably because it is those features which arrive in the right side of the brain that determine the response.

These faces are mirror images of each other.

Stare at the nose of each – which face is happier?

Clinical data support the conclusion that in right-handed people it is the right hemisphere that decides how we feel. And it is the *left* hand (which is said to be controlled by the right hemisphere) that is called 'the thinking, feeling hand'.

In *Wind, Sand and Stars*, Saint-Exupéry wrote:

> We had been flying for three hours. A brightness that seemed to me a glare spurted on the starboard side. I stared. A streamer of light which I had hitherto not noticed was fluttering from a lamp at the tip of the wing. It was an intermittent glow, now brilliant, now dim. It told me that we had flown into cloud, and it was on the cloud that the lamp was reflected. I was nearing the landmarks upon which I had counted: a clear sky would have helped a lot. The wing shone bright under the halo. The light steadied itself, became fixed, and began to radiate in the form of a bouquet of pink blossoms.

Saint-Exupéry's description of an aircraft entering cloud in *Wind, Sand and Stars* is beautiful and vividly accurate – except for one small detail. The starboard light is not red; the bouquet of blossoms he saw would have been *green*.

There were other instances showing that Exupéry might have a latent laterality problem. After completing an air test on a civil aircraft with three 650 hp Hispano-Suiza engines, he complained to mechanics on the ground that a wing was dropping when speed was increased. As to which wing it was, he could not say. So he stood facing the sun, attempting to recreate the experience of a few minutes before by making wings of his arms and moving them up and down. He was still unsuccessful in identifying which wing it had been.

Many people have their own individual laterality pattern. I have used my left hand unconsciously for years in such tasks as opening bottles and picking or holding fruit. A number of all-round sportsmen use the right hand for some sports, the left for others.

In his excellent novel *The High and the Mighty*, Ernest Gann, a very experienced pilot, has his stewardess telling passengers, when an engine catches fire on a flight from Honolulu to San Francisco, to inflate their life-jackets and then proceed to the emergency exits. Had they done so in real life, they might well not have been able to get out through the small emergency exits.

You never inflate your life-jacket till you are *out* of the aircraft. Taxed with that, Gann is reported to have said that in a stress situation, crew make such mistakes. Quite true. But would an author put that in without explaining it to his mainly non-aviation readers? Or did he unconsciously *reverse* the actions he was describing?

Some people have a decided preference for using the right hemisphere – but cultural influences have denigrated it, linking it with the female mind, while the left hemisphere controls the 'doing' right hand so necessary for military leaders, captains of industry and politicians. It is not surprising, therefore, that laterality in all its forms is not a popular subject for research, and has hardly been studied in aviation except by Gerhardt and Gedye (1963) and discussed by Dixon (1987). Yet in aviation when pilots can suddenly be faced with a stress situation, it is one of the most important human factors.

Just after midnight on 9 August 1954, a Constellation was diverted from Santa Maria and landed at Terceira – both islands in the Azores. Lagens aerodrome in Terceira, from which I operated against U-boats in Fortresses during the war, is built in a valley on the extreme north-east end of the island, and the only long runway possible lies north-west/south-east. Facing north-west, to the right is a ridge. To the left is a high mountain which has claimed many passenger lives. As a result, normal procedure after take-off on the north-west runway is a *right* turn out over the sea.

When the captain and navigator of the Constellation called at the navigation briefing office requesting information for preparation of a flight plan to Bermuda, the briefing officer went to considerable pains to explain that on the runway in use it was necessary to make a *right* turn out and proceed to a checkpoint over the sea called Ponto Sul in order to avoid the mountain. The exact words were : 'Following take-off, turn right, climb until 2,500 on heading 160 degrees and proceed to Ponto Sul.' This procedure was included in the first stage of the flight plan.

After completing the flight plan, the two crew members went

to the meterological office before proceeding to the aircraft. The Tower cleared the Constellation to taxi to the south taxiway for engine run-up.

The clearance was acknowledged and repeated. After run-up, the captain took up position on the runway and asked for take-off clearance.

The Tower replied: 'After take-off, turn right and climb till 2,500 feet on heading 160 degrees, then proceed to Ponto Sul.'

The captain opened up the engines to full power. The Constellation took off normally to the north-west. The Tower reported time off as 02.37 and instructed the aircraft to 'turn right'.

'Shortly afterwards,' says the report, 'the aircraft not having turned to the right, the controller asked the pilot to report his position. The pilot reported that he was north-east of the aerodrome.'

The pilot could only have been north-east of the aerodrome if he had turned right. He was, in fact, north-west.

The controller looked towards the north-east and saw no aircraft. He asked the captain whether he was flying on an approach heading or was still outbound.

There was no answer. The aircraft had already collided with the mountain about five miles west-south-west of Lagens at a height of about 2,000 feet, killing all nine crew and twenty-one passengers.

No mechanical failure was found. The probable cause of the accident was given as 'the failure of the pilot to carry out the normal climb-out procedure following take-off from runway 34 on a flight to Bermuda, and his having made a turn to the left instead of the right, thus flying into the mountains instead of turning out to sea'.

Some months later, a pilot and two photographers were carrying out a filming flight of London Airport in a Dove. A successful afternoon's filming flight had been completed, and this second trip was to photograph in colour and at night the approaches, runways and take-off paths.

At 21.47 hours, when the aircraft was six miles south-south-west of London at 1,500 feet, it was diverted on to a heading of 330 degrees magnetic to bring it on to a right-hand base leg for an approach to Runway 10 Right. Established comfortably on his heading, the pilot suddenly noticed that the airspeed had decreased from 128 knots to 110 knots, although the power settings had not been altered.

The pilot checked that there was no drag from drooping undercarriage or flaps and then checked the engine instruments. He stated that he observed high oil temperature and low oil pressure on the port engine gauge. But the photographer, to whom he pointed out these indications of a failing engine, said that the gauge to which his attention was drawn was that of the *starboard* engine.

The pilot told ATC he was getting falling oil pressure on the starboard engine, and two minutes later that he was 'feathering' – that is, stopping the propeller blades turned sharp side into the slipstream to avoid drag.

He was then three miles out on final approach and was cleared to land.

The pilot then moved the *port* pitch control back through the feathering gate. When the propeller stopped rotating, he switched off the *port* engine switches. He increased the power on the starboard engine and lowered the undercarriage.

Shortly afterwards, marked vibration developed and, after warning his passengers, the pilot crash-landed the Dove just short of the first bar of the approach lights.

Telegraph poles tore off the wings, but both engines were in position – the port cowlings clean, but the starboard ones splashed with oil. The *port* throttle lever was fully closed and the pitch control was at minimum revolutions. The starboard throttle was fully open and the revolutions were at maximum. On the manufacturers' test bed, the *port* engine was found to be fully serviceable. Examination of the *starboard* engine, however, revealed that the crankshaft had fractured.

Strangely enough, the pilot had correctly identified the engine to ATC, but had then shut down the good one. The report stated: 'It is difficult to find an explanation for this mistake, particularly in view of the pilot's experience as an instructor on this type of aircraft.'

This accident is typical of many. As a result, some modern aircraft are fitted with an autofeathering device. Armed only on take-off and climb, autofeather senses a loss of power and feathers the propeller. Its purpose is to preclude the possibility of a pilot shutting down the wrong engine in the event of a power failure.

Shortly after a Swift Aire Lines Nord 62 took off from Los Angeles, its starboard propeller autofeathered (see Chapter 11). Yet the crew shut down the port (good) engine, resulting in a fatal ditching in the Pacific Ocean. Examination showed that there had been no power loss on the starboard engine, the autofeather being due to a broken hydraulic hose in the sensing mechanism. Thus the automatic device triggered off the fatal events it was supposed to prevent and left/right confusion compounded it.

Left/right confusion is not confined to operating crew. The flying accident that killed Alexander Onassis was reported as being the result of the ailerons of his father's Piaggio being reversed during maintenance. As a result, when he tried to turn left to keep straight on take-off, the reversed ailerons turned the aircraft further and further right until he lost control.

Another manifestation of laterality is reversal of numbers, called by psychologists 'transposition error.' Because numerical accuracy is so important in flying, reversals can have disastrous effects.

On a flight from London to Nairobi, the co-pilot, flying the aircraft from the right-hand seat, asked for the setting to put on his altimeter for aerodrome height at Nairobi (QFE).

Control told him 839 millibars.

The first officer set it reversed on his altimeter – that is, 938.

Nairobi is 5,500 feet above sea-level. By setting up a level almost 100 millibars higher than the true one, the pilot raised his height indications by 3,000 feet. Being 3,000 feet lower than he thought he was, he hit the ground nine miles from the threshold of the runway.

A similar reversal of numbers occurred on a South American B-747 on a flight from Paris to Madrid in 1983. The experienced captain had 23,215 hours' flying, and both he and the first-officer were very familiar with Barajas airport.

Weather at destination was 8 kilometres visibility, mist, 3/8 stratus at 1,000 feet, 5/8 stratocumulus at 1,800 feet.

At 23.56 Madrid Approach told the crew of Avianca 011 that it was still in radar contact and the B-747 was cleared to descend for an approach to Runway 33.

At 23.58, close to 9,000 feet, the first officer checked the ILS approach chart, giving the exact elevation of the airport (1,906 feet).

The captain said, 'Switch to the marker.'

The first officer then gave the final approach heading and ILS localiser frequency, which the captain repeated.

The first officer went on to indicate that the crossing altitude of the marker was 2,382 feet.

He was wrong. The correct figure was *3,282* feet. He had reversed the first two digits, putting them 900 feet below the safe height.

The captain did not check his chart. Accepting the wrong altitude of 2,382, he continued to descend.

With 5 per cent flap and wheels down, the aircraft descended through 4,000 feet.

At 00.03 Approach Control called Avianca 011 approaching the beacon saying, 'Continue Barajas 33 and Tower eighteen fifteen.'

The captain replied, 'Good night, thank you,' and called for the landing checklist.

Barajas Tower now cleared the B-747 to land on Runway 33.

Controlled by the autopilot, the B-747 continued to descend until it was about eighty feet *below* the *wrong* safe height of 2,382 feet given by the first officer.

One minute and fifty-two seconds later, the Ground Proximity

Warning system called: 'Terrain, terrain. Whoop, whoop. Pull up. Terrain!'

The captain took no notice. Ten seconds later, just before impact, he said calmly, 'OK, OK!'

Five seconds later, again he said, 'OK!', disconnected the autopilot and slightly reduced the rate of descent.

One second before impact, in what the Accident Report calls 'a mild tone', noticing that the aircraft was then about 130 feet below the *wrong* safe height, the first officer tried to get the captain to react to the GPWS and pull up by asking, 'What does the ground say, Commander?'

The ground answered his question. At 00.06:19, at 139 knots on a heading of 284 degrees, the B-747 collided with three hills successively at an altitude of 2,249 feet.

Immediately afterwards came the aural warnings, 'Spoilers out, advance thrust!'

The spoilers had automatically deployed on impact and the warning system was telling the dead pilot to apply power to overcome the extra drag.

Of the 182 persons on board 181 lost their lives. Relatives of the dead pursued huge claims against the company for 'negligence'.

The report considered that the main cause of the accident was that: 'The pilot-in-command, without having any precise knowledge of his position, set out to intercept the ILS on an incorrect track without initiating the published instrument approach manoeuvre; in so doing, he descended below all the area safety minima until he collided with the ground.' Among the contributing factors were inaccurate navigation and the fact that the approach controller, in failing to inform the aircraft that radar service had been terminated, did not maintain a proper watch on the radarscope.

The absence of any one of these factors might possibly have saved the aircraft. But surely another likely cause of the accident was the reversal of figures by the first officer when he indicated that the crossing altitude of the marker was 2,382 instead of 3,282 feet.

There is a school of psychological thought which postulates that such reversals are due to slips or mistakes in the schemata which we bring to bear on what we do. But Freud would affirm that such actions have inner, deeper origins. Certainly reversals and left/right confusions appear to follow a pattern. Though nothing yet has been proved, accidents continue to happen in which laterality might have been one of the factors involved.

Shortly before 8.00 p.m. on the night of 8 January 1989, a British Midland B-737-400 took off from Heathrow bound for Belfast. The onboard computer was programmed to take the aircraft north up Airway Bravo Three towards the Daventry Control Area.

As it was climbing through 28,300 feet, the whole airframe suddenly began to shake. Smoke and fumes filled the flight deck. Number one (left) engine instruments and vibration indicator began to fluctuate. There had been a fatigue failure of a fan blade on the port/left/number one engine.

Note the three different ways in which an aircraft engine is identified.

The first officer was operating the sector. Both pilots checked the instruments. Then the captain took over and disengaged the autopilot.

Asked by the captain which engine it was, the first officer replied, 'It's the le . . . it's the right one.' Afterwards, he was to say that he did not know how he had made that identification.

As soon as something is identified, particularly in a high-arousal stress situation, it becomes fixated in the mind.

'OK,' said the captain. 'Throttle it back!'

So the starboard/right/number two engine was throttled back.

'Seems to be running all right now,' said the captain.

But the vibration indicator on the port/left/number one engine remained at maximum.

The first officer agreed. 'Seems to have stabilised.'

Back in the cabin, horrified passengers had felt the vibration and seen sparks and smoke coming out of that same *left* engine. Three of the cabin staff – altogether there were a flight service manager, three stewardesses and two stewards – had seen them too.

The captain called the senior flight attendant. 'Did you get smoke in the cabin?'

The reply was, 'Yes, we did. The passengers are very, very panicky.'

In an attempt to calm them, the captain broadcast to the passengers that there was trouble with the *right* engine and they were diverting to East Midlands airport near Kegworth.

The flight attendants said afterwards that they had not heard the captain's reference to the *right* engine. The passengers, still seeing fire and smoke coming out of the *left* engine were troubled and confused by the discrepancy, but did not bring it to the attention of the cabin staff.

The aircraft was cleared to Runway 27 at East Midlands airport.

Engine power was reduced. The aircraft began descending.

The pilot could see the runway lights ahead and the car headlights on the M1 motorway in between. Undercarriage and flaps were selected preparatory to landing.

At 20.23:49, when the B-737 was two and a half miles from touchdown and 900 feet above the ground, suddenly there was an abrupt loss of power.

The firebell sounded.

Desperately the crew tried to restart the starboard/right/number two engine (which had been serviceable all along).

But it was too late.

And now the Ground Proximity Warning system sounded. Then the stickshaker began to operate, telling them of an imminent stall.

The captain called over the cabin address, 'Prepare for crash landing!'

The speed fell below 125 knots. Ahead lay the high motorway embankments. With luck, they might still have enough speed to stagger over them.

But the 737 was losing height rapidly and they were close to stalling. At 20.24:04, one mile short of Junction 24, the aircraft crashed into the western bank of the M1 motorway. Of those on board, thirty-nine were killed and eight died later.

The original cause of the accident was a fan-blade failure in the left engine. This had been caused by flutter. No one fully understands fan-blade flutter, which is apparently caused by a combination of speed, temperature and altitude. But the manufacturers had failed to test the engines at altitude, and subsequently two more of that type failed.

Then the display of the B-737-400 engine instruments was held to be open to confusion. The AAIB report suggested an amendment that would eliminate the possibility of special association of readings in the left column and right throttle, and vice-versa (see diagram opposite).

Also, the B-737-400 engine vibration indicators were smaller and less conspicuous than the earlier 737s. The AAIB report concluded that the light emitting diode (LED) scale markers on the 737-400's electronic secondary instrument dials are less conspicuous than the full-radius mechanical pointers on earlier 737s. (See photograph 7a of the 737-300 cockpit where the pointers in the middle bank of instruments, which includes the engine vibration indicators, can clearly be seen.) These better indicate individual pointer orientation than the 737-400's secondary dials, which have short LED cursors moving around the outside of their scale. Most pilots preferred the electro-magnetic pointers to the new EIS (Engine Instrument System) of the 737-400. A subsequent trial at the RAF Institute of Aviation Medicine found that the new variety took longer to read than the older ones.

The AAIB report stated that, although the accuracy of the 737-400's EIS is not in doubt, 'it may represent a retrogressive step in terms of presentation of information'. But why was that not discovered before? The experienced captain of the British Midland 737 had flown DC9s in which the vibration indicators were unreliable. This would influence his views on those of the 737-400, in which he had flown only twenty-three hours.

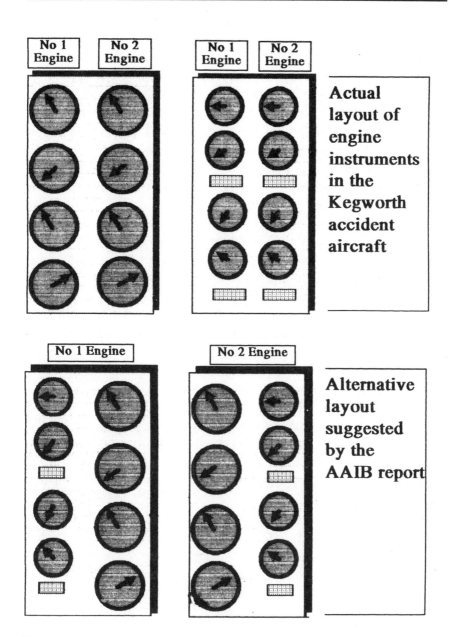

Actual layout of engine instruments in the Kegworth accident aircraft

Alternative layout suggested by the AAIB report

Throttles

184 The Naked Pilot

The captain's conversion training on the 737-400 was a very short ground-school course comprising a lecture, a slide display with voice over, together with a booklet explaining the differences from earlier 737s. The shortness of the course was a selling point to customers, but pilots have reported being uncomfortable with the training received. The very fact that the instrumentation was so similar was in fact a danger, since earlier learning will inevitably interfere. No training was given on a simulator, and the engine failure that night was the first emergency on the 737-400 that the pilots had experienced.

The cabin crew saw the smoke and sparks coming out of the left engine, as did many of the passengers. A passenger said he assumed that the captain had said it was the right engine because of his view of it from his seat. The identification of engines by left and right, bearing in mind the additional factor of laterality, as well as port-starboard and numbers 1/2, clearly makes for the possibility of confusion.

Various other points and recommendations occur in the AAIB report. The cabin crew had not come forward to report that it was the left engine which was emitting sparks and smoke and said they had not heard the captain's public-address announcement. The report recommended that operating and cabin crew should have joint training exercises. Surely the crew should be a unity whose prime responsibility is the safe operation of the aircraft.

Badly hurt after the accident, Captain Hunt was hailed as a hero by his passengers. After the Inquiry, he was retired and his co-pilot was dismissed.

Yet in that situation and against that background their contribution to the accident looks small. There is a tendency in many of us on occasion to mix left and right and reverse numbers. Although the subject of laterality confusion in aviation has hardly been studied, there far too many accidents in the air, on the roads and at sea for it to be ignored. Without actually naming it, aircraft manufacturers and instrument-makers acknowledge the existence of laterality in the automatic feathering device previously referred to, which is designed to stop pilots feathering the wrong engine after a failure.

So surely in this highly technical age, pilots should be adequately guarded against making such human error mistakes. The situation in which they will have to shut down an engine would be a stressful one. In this case, there was initial vibration – and vibration has a peculiar primeval effect on human beings. It is regarded by many pilots as more stressful than engine failure. In addition, they had the failure and the fire.

Mixing of left and right and transposing numbers usually occurs when people are tired, in a hurry, under pressure or in a state of alarm. In other words, under the influence of that little understood and highly dangerous human factor, stress and its frequent companion, fatigue.

Fifteen

Fatigue and Stress

We all know what it is to feel fatigue. But what *is* fatigue?

The condition was called Battle Fatigue in the Great War. Afterwards, it was split into the two concepts of fatigue and stress. Everyone knew what they meant – but nobody, in spite of the fact that everyone appeared to experience both, could adequately define either of them. Similarly, we all know we perform less well when fatigued or stressed.

Between the wars, psychologists studied both, but it was not until Bartlett (1939) carried out his Cambridge Cockpit experiments on workload that fatigue was considered in the aviation environment. Stress became translated into the infamous Lack of Moral Fibre system, whereby RAF aircrew who broke under danger were quarantined from their fellows lest the infection spread.

The Cambridge experiments in mock-up cockpits showed, not surprisingly, that pilots' flying deteriorated under fatigue – courses and heights were less accurately maintained, fuel checking was liable to be forgotten, there was a strong tendency to become 'set' on a particular instrument, and subjects thought they were doing well when in fact they were doing badly. These experimental laboratory findings have been corroborated in subsequent accidents to civil aircraft where fatigue may have been a contributory cause – tragedies that cost hundreds of lives and billions of pounds.

After the war, airlines were operating schedules of twenty-four hours and more. BOAC's service to New York and

Montreal was nineteen hours before the introduction of the Gander slip (when one crew takes over from another). Fatigue was never mentioned by pilots for two reasons. Firstly, because to say that you were tired somehow dented your image. Secondly, because slipping reduced your stand-off at home. There were only five Atlantic services a week, and Gander was subject to frequent sudden fog. So it was regularly overflown, leaving the slip-crew stranded for anything up to a record twenty-one days.

The management saved money by not having to position slip-crews, so there was a mutual but uneasy truce. Nevertheless, it became apparent that crews on long-distance trans-oceanic routes were on duty far too long, and that their flying, in consequence, dangerously deteriorated.

Fatigue, as has been said many times, is difficult to describe and almost impossible to quantify. Yet we know it is there.

Fired by the problem, I wrote a novel in 1953 called *The Heart of the Storm*, with the long haul over the mid-Atlantic as a background. When he was engaged in flight-time limitation discussions with the then Minister of Civil Aviation, John Profumo, the Chairman of BALPA, BOAC Captain Tony Spooner (a Second World War flying ace) gave the Minister *The Heart of the Storm* to read because, in his opinion, it presented the facts and feelings of flying fatigue.

By an unhappy coincidence, a few months later, a fellow captain and friend crashed at Singapore in a fatigue situation similar to that in my fictional accident. Thirty-three people were killed. He had been on duty for twenty-two hours.

A year later the first British flight-time limitations were brought in.

The idea of jet-lag did not surface until after the Americans had led the way in 1953 with flight-time limitations. Initially it was regarded by management as a ploy by the pilots to obtain more money, and there was considerable suspicion on both sides, until psychologists and doctors began to understand the problem of long hours on duty and the consequent effect on health and behaviour.

The problem was – and still is – what to do about it. At the heart of the matter is the enigma of what fatigue actually *is*. After a long sleep, we can still feel tired. Yet at three o'clock in the morning we can be wide-awake. A man lifting a weight by his little finger until he says he cannot lift it any more can be induced to continue by competition or encouragement. And if that fails, his finger can be made to work by electric stimulation. Fatigue thus protects us from overwork, and is a defence mechanism intended to prevent us from exerting ourselves too far and causing ourselves damage.

But a feeling of tiredness can be produced in any number of ways beside work overload – by monotony, high temperatures, alcohol and other drugs, anoxia, low arousal, habit alterations, disturbance in bodily rhythms, pressurisation changes, knowlege of bad results and a host of personal factors. It can be dispersed by alarm, excitement, interest, change of work, some drugs, high arousal and by good morale.

As aircraft flew across time zones, it began to be realised that the resultant Circadian dysrhythmia (jet-lag) contributed to fatigue. These Circadian rhythms are known to exist throughout human physiology. They have a period of about twenty-four hours and are measurable and stable fluctuations in blood pressure, body temperature, heart rate, sensory acuity, adrenal gland output and brain neurotransmitter levels.

This biological clock we inherited from our ancestors, who needed to be able to tell the natural time and recognise and allow for regular environmental events in order to survive. So does the rest of creation, as is manifest in the tidal movements of fish, the migration of birds, the hibernation habits of some mammals, and the sleep/wake rhythms and feeding habits of animals. Animals also use their biological clock to ensure that breeding occurs at the most suitable time of the year.

In the era before the widespread use of artificial light, mankind worked by day and slept by night in tune with his Circadian rhythms. So changes in the light produce changes in our internal rhythms. Research has shown how a change in the length of daylight acts on the hypothalamus part of the brain, which in turn stimulates the pituitary gland to produce an appropriate hormone for sexual development.

Because they themselves have suffered the effects of so-called jet-lag – the effect of crossing time zones – members of the public are slowly becoming aware of the danger of such decrement of performance in aircrew, often during the most critical time at the end of a flight when they most need to be alert and fresh. The pilot's sleeping and eating patterns will have been disturbed and his Circadian rhythms desynchronised.

A recent experiment has shown that sleepiness exhibits a consistent twelve-hour rhythmic pattern which remains synchronised at home, despite a two-day stay in a time zone fifteen time zones west.

Furthermore, flying skills show rhythmic variation according to time of day, with the worst decrement of performance between 3 and 6 a.m. Significantly, a number of aircraft accidents, as well as such disasters as Chernobyl, Ellesmere Port and Three Mile Island, took place in the early hours. One scientist recently called air travel 'an insult to our biology', but at least its effects upon our biological clock are being studied. The science of chronobiology, the relationship between our psychology, physiology and body rhythms, is gaining in importance: specific chemicals in the blood thought to be responsible for jet lag are being identified and, most importantly, the very real danger of fatigue recognised.

In 1962, I was the psychologist with a team of a doctor and physiologists from the Institute of Aviation Medicine in one of the first operational fatigue experiments – assessing workload on BOAC's North Atlantic Route. Captains' heart-rates were also checked, along with physiological measurements of adrenalin and noradrenalin.

I had no idea what I was letting myself in for, and no idea that so little was known about fatigue. In that highly technical environment, some sort of mechanical device to show fatigue was apparently being sought.

A start was made with BOAC captains after they had flown the Atlantic – using the Luchin's jar-filling test, which demonstrates 'set' and the Stroop test, which consists of a hundred colour names – red, blue, yellow, green, twenty-five of each – printed on a card in the four different colours. The test was to read at speed the *colour*, not the name. Continually, the printed *word* got in the way of naming the colour of the print. The more tired the pilot, the greater the confusion.

The results of the test showed the expected performance decrement, but that there was no simple relationship between frequency of errors and length of work-time. Mackworth (1948) found that after two hours of radar-screen-watching vigilance deteriorated, but other psychologists found that sleep-loss of more than seventeen hours had to be present before efficiency decrement in many tasks could be noted. Many pilots make better landings at the end of long trips, but other factors come into flying efficiency, such as longer acquaintance with their crew.

At the same time, the catalogue of accidents in which fatigue might have been involved continued.

A typical fatigue accident took place at Bahrain. At 21.15, a DC-4 called that he was on 'finals' and was cleared to land.

Nothing more was heard. The captain had flown straight into the water, 3.3 miles from the approach end of the runway.

The Inquiry stated: 'The captain, a man of fifty-two years of age, had been on uninterrupted duty since departure from Saigon, for 22 hours and a half, of which 19 hours 55 minutes were spent in flight. It therefore appears possible that he was feeling the effects of considerable fatigue just when, after a lengthy flight, he had to undergo the tension inherent in landing operations in unfavourable weather conditions.'

Two days later, the captain of another DC-4 crashed into the sea four miles from the threshold of the Bahrain runway.

In the Singapore crash already mentioned, when a Constellation undershot coming in too low for a landing, the Commissioner at the Inquiry summed up: 'Undoubtedly the captain was tired when he brought Able Mike in to land and in view of the long hours and the inexperience of his co-pilot, this was only to be expected.'

At Shannon two years later, when the captain had been on duty for twenty-three hours – the Inquiry's verdict was: 'Impairment of the pilot's proficiency due to the length of the period of duty.'

At Kerrville, Texas, a DC-3 crashed on landing. The crew had been on continuous duty for more than forty hours and had flown through snow and freezing precipitation.

At Brindisi, the captain of a Skymaster had been on duty thirty-one hours and seventeen minutes. The Accident Report said: 'He may therefore have been tired at the time of the accident.' Had he completed the trip, he would have been on duty nearly forty hours. All on board were killed.

Some time later a VC-10 crashed straight into trees coming in to land at Lagos. Again, all on board were killed. The Inquiry stated that inattention and crew preoccupation were the causes, but 'they were coming to the end of a long overnight flight involving three sectors, and short-term fatigue could well have been a contributory factor'.

General confusion persists about the whole problem of fatigue, which still lacks definition. Arguments arise regarding how to calculate hours on duty, day and night flights, sectors flown, time zones transited. Each country appears to have its own ideas on how to solve the problem.

There have been numerous committees and commissions set up throughout the world to consider fatigue. Amongst these was the 1972 BALPA Committee. Four months later, the CAA set up a Committee on Flying-Time Limitations under the chairmanship of Group Captain Douglas Bader.

Bader was a household name, but he had no experience of flying long-range civil routes. It has been typical of all governments throughout the history of British aviation, as a general rule, to appoint as Secretaries of State for Air, chairmen and other leaders of the industry, dignitaries who have little or no relevant experience of the organisations to which they are appointed. This stems from a traditional belief in the Corridors of Power that the Gentleman is better than the Player.

It was inevitable that the two Committees should have different ideas on what was or was not fatigue. The BALPA Report analysed all the accidents in which fatigue could possibly be a contributory cause. Fortunately, Bader was assisted by a very experienced airline captain, Laurie Taylor, and his report came up with the perfectly reasonable statement that 'Our attention was drawn to accidents in which it was alleged there was a possibility that fatigue may have been a contributory factor. . . . We did not accept the argument that fatigue should be assumed to be a factor, unless proved otherwise, in every case where the duty period was a long one or the flight was at night.'

As Captain Peter Bressey pointed out, 'This difficulty in drawing a line between "tiredness" and "fatigue" is typical of the subjective inaccuracies, confusion and misunderstanding, which continue to obscure the whole problem of pilot fatigue.'

Each country produced its own flight-time-limitation regulations, some of which are of breathtaking complexity. There are innumerable weighting factors and caveats, but the bare bones of present European regulations are given below.

Country	Max Hours	Min Rest	Yearly
Belgium	16	8	1000
France	14	11	900
W. Germany	14	10	1000
Greece	14	10	1000
Switzerland	14	8	1000
Spain	14	10.5	800
Italy	24	15	1000
Netherlands	16	8	1000
Portugal	12	8	850

New CAA rules came into force for British commercial pilots on 1 May 1990. They may fly a maximum of 100 hours a month (90 for helicopters) and no more than 900 a year (800 for helicopters). They must have seven days off in a four-week period. Pilots may fly no more than 55 hours a fortnight or 190 hours a month, no more than 3 consecutive night flights, and have no more than 4 early starts or late finishes. The CAA hopes that these new rules will be the basis for discussions on common European standards.

Concern over exceeding Dutch flying-time regulations certainly contributed to the Dutch captain's difficulties and impatience in the disaster of the Tenerife collision (Chapter 8). He was scheduled to return to Amsterdam that day, and had been on the phone to Holland to get their ruling on the latest possible take-off time for the homeward flight.

In 1980, a study was carried out of reports made to NASA's Aviation Safety Reporting System which showed that 21.1 per cent of 2,006 aircrew member reports were related to fatigue. But there are further complications in that experiments have shown that pilots cannot subjectively gauge their own fatigue. In fact, it is very hard for anyone to gauge their own fatigue. However, a flight-deck study by Carruthers (1976) revealed that during the early morning hours, all five crew men *on duty* displayed various brain-wave patterns characteristic of sleep or extreme drowsiness.

In 1989 Boeing revealed plans to introduce alarms to wake up sleeping pilots on long-haul flights. Yet twenty years ago, a Sunday newspaper feature was headlined 'Airline crew were asleep in mid-flight'. The text quoted a captain as saying 'On one flight I remember jerking myself awake while the aircraft was on autopilot and discovering that both the first-officer and flight-engineer were asleep. When I checked with other crews they said, "Oh, that's happened to us too."'

Recently that same captain wrote to the same paper reminding them how long ago it was since he had written. 'This alarming state of affairs . . . was then, and is now, due to aircrew having inadequate rest periods on the ground. Flight-deck alarm clocks would not be necessary if governments throughout the world would introduce, and enforce, flight-time limitations which prevent flight fatigue.'

CHIRPs confirm that little has changed in twenty years. Here is a recent contribution.

> The crew were well rested before flight, but on check-out from the hotel we were informed of a twelve-hour delay. During the subsequent flight, because of the delay, all of us were extremely tired. During the cruise across the North Atlantic, we *all* fell asleep, only to be awakened by the Mach Warning Bell! At the constant power setting, the aircraft had slowly accelerated, causing the bell to ring. I estimated that we were all asleep for about twenty minutes. Fortunately we were between reporting points.

NASA's Aviation Safety Reporting System receive many reports from pilots describing how fatigue has contributed to major operational errors, such as track deviations, landings on the wrong runway etc. A 900-foot altitude deviation was reported on a flight from Anchorage to Tokyo, due to incorrect altimeter setting before departure. The crew reported that they were unable to sleep the night before. The mistake was not discovered until Tokyo radar noticed the deviation.

In March 1987, an aircraft flying from Los Angeles to Baltimore dropped 4,000 feet below its assigned altitude, getting so close to another aircraft that alarms were set off in Flying Control. The crew were asleep.

On 12 December 1985, a DC-8 of Arrow Air, carrying homebound troops, crashed on take-off from its refuelling stop at Gander (see Chapter 17). According to the disputed majority report, the Inquiry found that the crew 'had been consistently exposed to work patterns highly conducive to the development of chronic fatigue'.

Perhaps because of fatigue and the crossing of time zones, the safety record for long-haul operators is poorer than for short-range. Approach and landing accidents account for 44 per cent of all crew-caused accidents in wide-body operations.

New laboratories and airlines of several countries, including Britain, the USA, Germany and Japan, have joined forces to obtain data from B-747 crews flying intercontinental routes.

Their research has come up with some interesting findings, including the fact that, perhaps because westward flights lengthen the day and eastward flights shorten it, sleep quality deteriorated more after eastward than westward flights. Older pilots tended to have less restful, more shallow sleep after an eastbound than younger crew, and most crew members were unable to assess their own sleepiness and alertness. It was found that pilots do nap on long night flights, though rarely (and it is to be hoped) not more than one asleep at a time on the flight deck. A nap on the flight deck, it was suggested, may act as a safety valve, and have a beneficial effect on the overall vigilance of the crew.

Another beneficial effect would be some form of exercise, for sitting for hours making minute movements does nothing for the circulation. A few trips up and down the cabin, talking to the passengers, used to be fairly standard on piston-engined aircraft. Now, on jets, with hundreds of passengers, only rarely do the pilots emerge from the flight deck.

Pertinently, in view of Chapter 12, on boredom, the researchers' subjective estimates of crew members' fatigue seem to depend on the amount of interesting stimuli present. They suggest that, as people become more fatigued, they become much more dependent on the environment to maintain their alertness.

A definition of fatigue might in fact be a dulling of the senses, thought processes and reflexes due to excess work or sleep deprivation.

Now the search is on for more innovative measures to deal with fatigue. 'Anchor' sleep, based on data relating to the timing of sleep in the home and adjusted by eastward or westward time zones, is being tried. And along with that, a 'nap anchor' based on daytime sleepiness.

Worries over fatigued pilots have been joined by those for fatigued controllers. Some of the near misses in recent years have been attributed to poor ground control. In February 1988, the pilot of a British Airways Tristar bound for Heathrow from Paris narrowly avoided a Bulgarian airliner near the Kent coast because of controller error. The number of flights handled by air traffic controllers has increased by 20 per cent in the last two years. And while business is booming, there is a worldwide shortage of controllers. A spokesman for the Guild of Air Traffic Controllers is quoted as saying, 'Although we can earn extra money through uncontrolled overtime, we do not think it safe.'

Recently, reports of fatigued maintenance staff have come in. In some companies there are so far no limitations on the amount of hours they can work over the years. The huge increase in the demand for the big jets has led to a drop in quality control. Employees blame excessive overtime, untrained workers and low morale for poor work. Workers are accused of covering up their mistakes, and inspectors of overlooking defects such as wrongly drilled holes. It began to be realised that it wasn't only excessive hours of work that caused fatigue – that there was such a thing as cumulative fatigue and that stress could be just as tiring as time on duty.

This was first pinpointed by an inquiry thirty years ago when a co-pilot made a heavy landing at Jamaica, killing thirty-seven. The report stated:

> To provide against fatigue by prescribing that the crew shall
> not remain on duty for more than twenty hours or be
> engaged in flying for more than twelve hours would seem to
> lose sight of factors that in themselves may bring on fatigue.
> The nervous strain brought on by handling an aircraft not
> functioning properly may itself be equivalent to more than
> twenty hours of ordinary duty. Also the variety of duties
> should be taken in account. The crew of HK-177 flew some
> six hours or so over the United States of America. Over such
> territory the workload is heavy. To that load was added the
> strain of a malfunctioning engine, the anxious wait for
> repairs to be done in Miami, and the renewed anxiety when
> the second engine began to give trouble, as well as the wait
> to have it repaired. The accumulation of such circumstances
> might very well have affected the pilot sufficiently to cause
> an error of judgement.

Stress still remains inadequately defined. But unlike fatigue, which might contribute to stress and which could be called a 'defence mechanism', stress could be called an 'attack mechanism'. A certain degree of stress is necessary to do anything, and in flying that degree can be high. That is its positive side. On its negative side, it produces the same decrease in quality of work performance as fatigue, and can be induced by many of the same agents, but it is particularly accentuated by emotion, frustration and distress.

Included in the stress envelope – and perhaps the most important – are the marital, home, money and job worries that the pilot always carries hidden in his 'luggage'.

The captain of a Beechcraft 99A, Flight 201, operating from Walla Walla, was described as usually capable, confident and even-tempered, a man who always operated his aircraft to established procedures and appeared to have no personal problems. He lived quietly with his family in Seattle and shared an apartment in Walla Walla only to meet his flight schedule.

But before his flight to Spokane, Washington, on 20 January 1981, he appeared to be depressed. The previous day he had flown in the morning, staying in the airport during the afternoon and talking with other company employees. That evening he had played racquetball with another pilot. He said he had had a 'bad' day, starting off with 'crummy flying' in the morning and extending to a poor performance at racquetball. He was also worried about a satisfactory performance report that he had submitted on a first officer, believing he should have given a report which could have resulted in the termination of the man's contract.

The take-off at 06.00 was normal. But after landing and taking off at Richmond and Seattle and landing at Yakima, the captain did not sign the weight and balance sheet. According to the Station Manager, 'It wasn't like him to miss that!'

Bad weather further delayed their arrival at Moses Lake, where they did not report inbound at the outer-marker, nor did the crew request or receive landing clearance at Moses Lake. The bad weather further delayed their departure when the flight

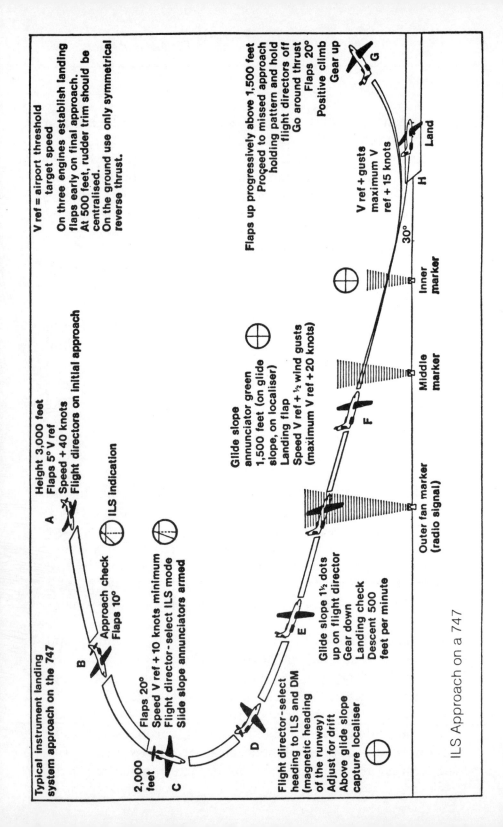

ILS Approach on a 747

Typical instrument landing system approach on the 747

A Height 3,000 feet
Flaps 5° V ref
Speed + 40 knots
Flight directors on initial approach

ILS indication

Approach check
Flaps 10°

B Flaps 20°
Speed V ref + 10 knots minimum
Flight director-select ILS mode
Slide slope annunciators armed

C 2,000 feet

D Flight director-select heading to ILS and DM (magnetic heading of the runway)
Adjust for drift
Above glide slope capture localiser

E Glide slope 1½ dots up on flight director
Gear down
Landing check
Descent 500 feet per minute

Glide slope annunciator green
1,500 feet (on glide slope, on localiser)
Landing flap
Speed V ref + ½ wind gusts (maximum V ref + 20 knots)

F

G Flaps up progressively above 1,500 feet
Proceed to missed approach holding pattern and hold flight directors off
Go around thrust
Flaps 20°
Positive climb
Gear up

V ref = airport threshold target speed
On three engines establish landing flaps early on final approach.
At 500 feet, rudder trim should be centralised.
On the ground use only symmetrical reverse thrust.

V ref + gusts maximum V ref + 15 knots

H Land

30°

Outer fan marker (radio signal)

Middle marker

Inner marker

crew misread their clearance and used the wrong flight number on several occasions during the flight.

On arrival in cloud over Spokane, the Beechcraft was expected to land on Runway 21, but because of traffic, ATC changed the runway to the reciprocal 03.

The instrument landing system on Runway 03 had no glide-path indicator. That would make a landing more difficult. They would have to use the Distance Measuring Equipment (DME) of which there were two instruments, differentiated simply by 1 and 2. The crew had to remember to which each DME had been tuned – the VORTAC/DME 4.5 miles from the airfield or the ILS DME 0.3 miles from the threshold. Thus the crew became further confused as they awaited their clearance to descend on the backbeam of Runway 21.

Noise levels in the Beechcraft 99A fell within the range where face-to-face communication was difficult, and a vocal range between shouting and maximum vocal effort was required.

At 11.24 ATC cleared the Beechcraft to make its approach, saying: 'Localiser should be up. Six miles from Olake intersection. Cleared for the approach.'

At the moment when the ILS localiser began to register on the instrument, the crew pounced on it, saying : 'There it is! We're cleared for the approach.' The first officer throttled back and forgot to put the undercarriage down. The crew completely ignored the six-mile position report and began to descend immediately.

The loud sounding of the warning horn must have further contributed to the pilots' arousal, almost always high in the landing phase, especially in bad weather. In that state of mind, the captain (it was not his normal duty anyway) must have forgotten to check the DMEs, and jumped to the wrong conclusion regarding the aircraft's position, thinking they were over the Spokane beacon instead of 4.2 miles from it.

In spite of company instructions never to descend below Minimum Descent Altitude (MDA), indeed to pull up before it in bad conditions, they continued on a rapid descent to what they thought was the airfield.

Instead, at 11.27 the aircraft crashed into a ploughed field 600 yards south-east of Spokane VORTAC.

'The flight crew,' the Accident Inquiry found, 'had not performed at the expected levels of professional proficiency on the day of the accident,' adding that any inherent human factors such as preoccupation with personal problems and other events could effect a distraction which would 'interfere with pilot performance'. In other words, stress in all its forms – of which time pressure is one.

Most of us suffer from it. There is a feeling akin almost to alarm when we are late. This may be an inheritance from our earliest ancestors, whose one and only time pressure would probably originate from a dangerous situation such as keeping ahead of a pursuing sabre-toothed tiger. For time pressure certainly seems inborn. There is something as necessary about saving time as saving money, to which it is often equated. Like many other animals, we know that the shortest distance between two points is a straight line, and we are impatient of deviation. Men hunch over the wheel of a car, cutting a corner at speed to save seconds. So it is not surprising that corner-cutting air, sea and road accidents occur all too regularly.

Airlines, after all, sell speed. Management and pilots are conscious of the need to keep to a schedules. An Inquiry into one aircraft accident said it was 'difficulty to understand why an IFR flight plan was filed direct to Buffalo under known *en route* weather conditions, while VFR was indicated on the weight and balance manifest. The only logical explanation appears to have been an effort to save time, the aircraft being already five hours and forty minutes late when it arrived at Pittsburgh.'

The Inquiry into a C-54 accident in which the captain cut a corner and crashed into the almost vertical rock face of Medicine Bow Peak at an altitude of 11,570 feet, stated: 'It is difficult to understand how a pilot of this one's experience would deliberately attempt a short cut, and even if he did, why he would have flown at such a low altitude over hazardous terrain. It is true that the flight was an hour and eleven minutes late.' All sixty-six people on board were killed.

The pressure to keep to schedule is intensified because otherwise the rhythm of the flight is disorganised. A captain, consciously and unconsciously, plans his flight. If he can keep to schedule, he may well remain most of the time in 'automatic' thinking mode, doing the correct things by routine. If he gets off schedule, he may have some real hard problem-solving to do.

Nobody likes hard work when they are tired. Indeed, one psychologist defined fatigue simply as 'a drive towards rest'. Pilots, especially of smaller airlines, may be pressurised to keep to the schedule and not tie up an aircraft. When an airport is busy and/or the weather is bad and liable to close the airport, there is sub-conscious pressure on pilots to become airborne, as in the Air Florida accident at Washington Bridge and the KLM/Pan Am disaster at Tenerife.

The pilot at the end of his flight has another stress factor to exacerbate his fatigue – the drive towards landing. This is partly the Zeigarnik effect (the psychological term for the need to complete a task once it is initiated), but it also seems to be a particularly strong sub-conscious desire, a need to get back into his own element, with his wheels and his feet on the ground. This not only increases his fatigue but is itself reinforced by that fatigue. Accidents show pilots repeatedly trying to land under adverse conditions. In June 1989, the pilot of a Surinam Airways DC-8 bound for Paramaribo from Amsterdam with 186 people on board crashed on its third attempt to land. There was thick fog at the time, manifestly unsuitable landing conditions. The airliner carried many of the country's top brass and members of the country's professional football team, so the need to land at their designated airport and not cause a diversion for his passengers must have added to the captain's stress and fatigue.

Quick fixes for stress and fatigue are drink and drugs, and though it is impossible to go into the subject in any depth here, pilots are no more immune to those problems than anyone else. In fact, they are rather less so. Fliers have a long tradition of being good drinkers. The fitting tribute to a comrade lost in the sea or shot down over Germany was a booze-up. Drinking with the boys has a manly image, and it does help you to unwind and sleep. So do certain drugs. Other drugs, as was well known during the Second World War, help you to keep awake on long operations. Many were the survival packs which pilots broke open for the Benzedrine.

Nowadays alcohol is even more readily available and cheap on trips. Alcoholism is growing. Counsellors are troubled by the number of pilot clients who confess to drink problems they are keeping secret from their employers. Many countries have advisory groups for pilots with drink or drugs problems. In 1989, IFALPA in conjunction with the RAF Institute of Aviation Medicine asked pilots to complete a confidential questionnaire on fatigue, life styles, drinking habits and drug-taking, if any. The object was to try to discover if there was a link between jet-lag, stress, alcohol and drugs and the fact that 60 per cent of pilots die before retirement age.

An extreme example was the American captain of a JAL cattle-carrying charter flight. In the dark and foggy early hours of 13 January 1977, he was picked up at his hotel in Anchorage by taxicab and was drunk. He and his crew were to take a DC-8 from Anchorage to Tokyo, and such were the symptoms of the captain's previous night's drinking that the taxi-driver became alarmed and called his dispatcher to report such observations as incoherent conversation, glazed eyes and an inability to get out of the cab without steadying himself on the car door. The dispatcher in turn called the maintenance company about the drunken captain, but was told it was logical that 'JAL would detect anything unusual and act accordingly . . . or his first officer would have stopped the flight immediately.'

Neither the Japanese first officer nor the engineer made any such attempt.

The CVR records signs of the captain's intoxication. He became disorientated while taxying and went to the wrong runway, where he reported himself ready for take-off. When he was guided to the right runway and began take-off, rotation was faster than normal, and to a higher than normal pitch attitude after take-off.

After take-off, disaster. There came a buffet which the captain failed to recognise as a stall warning. The aircraft stalled shortly after reaching V2 at a height of no more than 160 feet. The aircraft hit two crests of hills, killing the crew and the cattle-handlers.

After the tragedy, five close acquaintances declared that the captain had not had a drink in their presence and showed no signs of being drunk, while six persons not closely acquainted with him said he had been drinking in their presence and was drunk.

In March 1990, after a passenger-carrying Northwest Airlines 727 had landed at Fargo, two pilots and a flight engineer were arrested. The charge? Being under the influence of alcohol. This time someone had noticed and acted accordingly. The pilots' and engineer's licences were revoked.

A French accident investigator once stated: 'Our lack of knowledge about fatigue may well prove to be the chief explanation of those accidents which are now put down to "pilot error" or "the human factor" simply because we don't quite understand what makes well qualified, conscientious specialists like pilots commit unbelievably stupid mistakes.'

We are beginning to understand why.

Sixteen

Human Factor Education

For the last twenty-five years, about 70 per cent of aircraft accidents (76 per cent in Eastern bloc countries) have been attributed to pilot or human error. The human factors which have apparently precipitated aircraft accidents have earlier been shown to be:

1. Communication – with crews, ATC and management (chapter 4).
2. Perception – to see or not to see (chapter 5).
3. Deadly 'set' – concentration on one aspect of a situation (chapter 6).
4. On being deceived (chapter 7).
5. The male ego (chapter 8).
6. Decision-making (chapter 9).
7. Learning and regression (chapter 10).
8. Automation – the clockwork captain (chapter 11).
9. Boredom, absence of mind and slips (chapter 12).
10. Conformity (chapter 13).
11. Laterality (chapter 14).
12. Fatigue and stress (chapter 15).

In addition, there are other contributing human factors: expectancy, such as suddenly being presented with weather worse than forecast; change of plan, such as a diversion or a change of runway or let-down procedure; and interruptions in the act-wait-act task sequences.

Significant Accident Causes and Percentage Present in 93 Major Accidents

Cause of Accident	Presence %
Pilot deviated from basic operational procedures	33
Inadequate crosscheck by second crew member	26
Design faults	13
Maintenance and inspection deficiencies	12
Absence of approach guidance	10
Captain ignored crew inputs	10
Air traffic control failures or errors	9
Improper crew response during abnormal conditions	9
Insufficient or incorrect weather information	8
Runaway hazards	7
Air traffic control/crew communication deficiencies	6
Improper decision to land	6

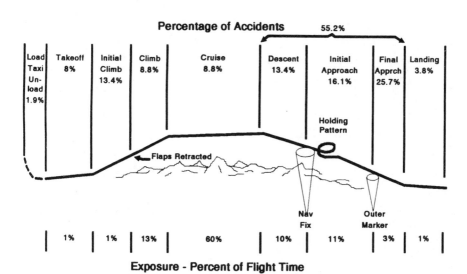

Air carrier accidents distributed by phases of flight, 1959–1983: worldwide jet fleet, all operations (excludes sabotage and military action). Exposure percentage based on an average flight duration of 1.6 hours. (Boeing, 1985)

On take-off from London Heathrow, a B-707 experienced an engine failure. The engine-failure checklist was started, and the appropriate actions had begun to be initiated when they were interrupted by the engine bursting into flames. The crew changed over from the engine-failure checklist to the engine fire checklist, but because the first few items were the same on both and the actions had been carried out, in order to save time they jumped to items that had not been done. In so doing, the closing of the valve which shut the fuel off from the engine was missed. Though the fire-extinguisher had been activated, the fire burned even more fiercely because the engine was still being fed with kerosene. Very skilfully, the captain landed the jet with the engine in flames, but five people died.

The 1975 IATA Conference called urgently for human factor education in airlines, and this call was repeated at the 1977 IFALPA Conference. Now human factor training has at last been highly recommended by ICAO and will be enforced by law by the EEC. Some airlines, such as Qantas, United, Pan Am, Swissair, Singapore, Dan Air and KLM have already instituted their own programmes. Cranfield has a basic human factors course.

ICAO hosted a valuable seminar in Moscow, in which European countries, the USA and Japan took part, and at which IATA and IFALPA were represented. It was attended by people actually working in the aviation industry and had a practical touch to it. An ICAO draft syllabus for human factor training was drawn up. The CAA now has one of its own for the compulsory examination (see Appendix). In Britain, the human factor examination for pilots was introduced in 1991, and other countries will certainly follow.

IFALPA also endorses the emphasis on all aspects of human performance relating to safe and efficient operation of the aviation system, and considers that suitable training in relevant aspects of human performance, human limitations, aviation psychology and crew co-ordination should be given to all flight crew members and trainee pilots.

All this is a beginning. The main thing is to get pilots to look at themselves and the environment in which they function. They should learn to recognise that a danger as great as clear-air turbulence, thunderstorms, icing or microbursts may be within the cockpit in the crew situation. The aviation world had to learn to cope with these meteorological hazards. Now it has to come to grips with the hazard of human factors.

Whether or not examinations on human factors are going to be effective or desirable remains to be seen. Examinations devoted to the reduction of human factor errors (especially conformity) are something of a paradox. It is a subject for 'hanging loose', for coming clean, for admitting and examining one's mistakes, for discussion and argument rather than for marks in an examination. After all, in an exam you have to conform to what the examiner reckons is the right answer.

In reality, the right aim and the right answer are self-knowledge and self-recognition. And the worst would be if human factors were made into undigested pellets to be regurgitated for the examiner.

So if it is difficult to examine on human factors, how can they be taught?

Fairly naturally, there is still some suspicion of human factor study. There are questions such as: will psychological investigation damage the pilot's ego? Will the management find out things which might lower him in their estimation, might lead to his demotion or even dismissal? Isn't this yet a further disguised medical examination? There is so much that a pilot has to absorb, isn't this added subject a bit much? Won't the study of the all too simple slips that are the main cause of aircraft accidents reduce confidence? And why, if the pilots have their errors put under the microscope, shouldn't other people, particularly management, have the same treatment?

There is also, despite the advertising industry's very profitable love affair with psychology, a natural antipathy in most industries to the subject. None of us likes the idea of the darker corners of our psyches being too brilliantly illuminated. And, for most of us, self-knowledge comes later in life: the study of ourselves is not yet taught in schools. As a result, there is for most people no groundwork on which to add the study of human factors and human errors.

Then, too, we dislike the whole concept of mistakes. We are the products of our culture and our early teaching. That teaching has made us regard mistakes with guilt and shame – school exercise books full of black crosses, like so many little deaths. Early on we learn to give the 'right' answer expected by the authority figure over us, rather than to think for ourselves, though some improvement in this area seems at last to be appearing. And it is just this expected, pleasing answer which pilots must learn now to reject.

So the teacher/learner concept has to be stood on its head. At best, pilots who do the job don't particularly like to be taught by laymen who don't. Besides, human factor study is no black and white exercise. In its own way it should be a vast research project. There should be no platform, just everyone arguing on the floor in an exercise of two-way learning. Everyone has some valuable experience and insight to offer; it is just the interpretation that can be guided. Real accidents can be re-enacted, real mistakes on video studied in real situations; those mistakes can then be interpreted and the commonalty of them recognised. Personal awareness is the theme. For pilots are as other people, but functioning in a more unforgiving environment, wherein they may be exposed to making simple human slips which on the ground might be no more than the breaking of a tumbler, but which in the air might produce a catastrophe.

It is also important that the course should not become a let-out for management in case of accident: 'You've had your course. Why did you make the mistake about which you were adequately warned?' Nor should there be quick-fix courses, which don't examine the real problems, and which look good only on paper.

After the Portland running-out-of-fuel accident (Chapter 6), United Airlines went to a management consultancy to devise their own human factor course. This lasts three days and is sold to airlines in South America, Japan, Yugoslavia and throughout the rest of the world.

It includes videos of accidents very similar to real ones, where actors play the parts of the flight-deck crews. As the drama proceeds and various errors are recognised by the viewer he will identify (or not identify) with the characters being presented. As errors start swelling up to the climax of the accident, the audience feels a growing tension that can be almost unbearable. Slips are not corrected. False assumptions are allowed to proceed unchallenged. Such situations are portrayed as a rather withdrawn co-pilot trying to bring a dangerous situation to his overbearing captain's attention – and failing. Conformity, perception, decision-making, machoism, time pressure, risk-taking, regression and the concepts of psychology can be dramatically illuminated in this way.

The Pan Am course is conducted at their Miami International Flight Academy, where the classrooms and simulators are frequently booked twenty-four hours a day, seven days a week, for programmes involving courses for other airlines, aircrew converting to new positions or new equipment, and for recurrent training.

In 1987 two new programmes were added, which became the focal point of all Pan Am pilot training. These were Line Oriented Flight Training (LOFT) and Flight Operations Resource Management (FORM), both of which, according to the Pan Am handout, focus on the human factors of the flying environment – though the details of *what* human factors are not specified. Previously there had been two trips to the Academy annually for each pilot – one for a training course, the other for a simulator proficiency course. Now there is only one trip, during which aircrew undergo both LOFT and FORM in a single integrated programme.

FORM was previously called Cockpit Resource Management (CRM), by which name it is still called by Qantas, Singapore Airlines and other airlines. Pan Am then realised that the concept applied to all aspects of flight operations, including the cabin crew, and expanded the 'crew concept' training that the airline had initiated in 1974. FORM recognises the contribution of each *crew* member to the safe operation of a flight, and is taught in a three-day seminar.

LOFT is regarded by Pan Am as a training exercise in resource management. Previously pilots did two sessions of simulator training a year. 'Every year, it was the same thing over and over again', in the words of Captain Roy Butler, the System Director, Flight Training. 'Almost like teaching old dogs old tricks.' Now it is an actual flight scenario designed to test the skill of the whole crew. The instructor does not intervene or mark the performance.

The crew prepare and fly a two-hour simulator trip, complete with flight plans, radio communications, navigation and all cockpit procedures. During the flight, the crew encounter a problem that requires a solution. A decision has to be made on whether to shut down an engine and proceed, or make an emergency landing. Or a decision has to be made on whether to land at a fog-bound airport or fly on to an alternate. There is no right or wrong solution, but areas of possible mistakes are encountered and Butler regards LOFT as an opportunity for 'mistake management'.

Afterwards there is a video critique – since the whole exercise is video-taped. The whole crew discuss among themselves what went wrong and what went right. The tape is completely confidential and after the debriefing is erased by the crew members themselves.

Proficiency training on an *en route* flight for the pilots follows; this is graded by the instructor, but mistakes are allowed, the pilot is not identified and all data is confidential. Then, in the simulator time remaining, the pilots are given the opportunity to experience unusual situations – high altitude stall, an unusual attitude recovery, take-off or landing on an ice-covered runway with maximum drift, or the use of asymmetrical thrust in a critical landing situation.

Local adaptations of LOFT and FORM are now used in the training of many of the leading airlines of the world.

Singapore Airlines follows in its own style part of the United Airlines Programme which was developed with Scientific Methods Inc. The core concept is the use of a grid scale which defines behaviour as low or high concern for performance and low or high concern for people.

Singapore Airlines developed this concept into their 'Aircrew Behavioural Compass', which is divided into quadrants, each with its own behaviour characteristics. Six types of crew member are named – the apathetic couldn't-care-less, the nice guy affiliative, the go-getter ace, the task-master, the autopilot who follows the book, and the 'acro' (the ideal pilot) concerned with both performance and people.

Singapore Airlines have engaged a psychologist who conducts a programme called Aircrew Resource Management (ARM) which will convert SAD TRIPS (Stress, Automation, Decorum, Tedium, Responsibility, Interface, Paradox, Survival) to GLAD TRIPS (Good Landings Are Developed Through Responsible Individuals Practicing the S–I–A – Skills + Interaction = Achievement) – strategy for aircrew effectiveness.

The purpose of the Singapore programme is to create a sense of awareness amongst the crew of the three C's – concern, co-operation and communication. The message is brought home through examples of 'malsituations'. It is intended to help the crew to learn more about themselves and others in order to be able to interact and communicate effectively on the flight deck – and work effectively as a team – achieving what Singapore Airlines and others like Qantas call 'synergy' – that is, the process that can make the team seem greater than the sum of individual parts.

The ARM programme covers three major topics – personal behaviour styles and their impact on crew effectiveness, the importance of communication and the need for team work. Starting at 8.30 a.m. and ending at 10.00 p.m., the three-and-a-half-day programme is crammed with films, group discussions and the 'entertainment' provided by the psychologist, Professor Korlins. The participants' wives attend the final session, after which they are invited to the dinner that concludes the course.

It is unlikely that the admirable Singapore course with its 'SIA Song' to 'Singapore's Incredible Aviators' sung to the tune of 'Swing Low, Sweet Chariot' could be used for pilots of some Western countries, and vice-versa. There are cultural limitations. American human factor programmes stress self-criticism, which goes against some Asian cultures and would be resisted by local crews, for the eastern ethic stresses obedience and hierarchy.

The aims of Qantas CRM, a course individually tailored for this particular airline, have a universality that could well be applied elsewhere. Learning about 'ourselves and how others relate to our style' is the central theme, and the course sets out to 'overcome a basic weakness that initial training has bred into pilots. Pilots have been taught to fly aircraft as sole crew members.' This is of crucial importance. 'CRM will teach us to use all the resources at our disposal to gather information, revise . . . and analyse that information, develop solutions, implement the decision and evaluate the performance as an ongoing process of education.'

Although psychology is not specifically mentioned, psychological principles underlie the course, and it is shrewdly but unobtrusively informed by them. In everyday language, it examines leadership, team work and decision-making, as well as illuminating communication skills and how other people react to us – in fact, to quote Burns again, 'how others see us'.

In terms of communication, it emphasises that fast-diminishing art of 'how to listen', especially to the underlying message rather than just the words. There are so many examples already shown of accidents where the underlying message was not understood – even the spoken words, for that matter.

This CRM also touches on the defence mechanisms we put up against seeing and hearing what we don't want to.

'Groupthink' (a form of conformity) is identified rightly as the negative aspect of team cohesiveness, something to be avoided at all costs. Examples are given of the pressures that bring about groupthink.

Peer pressure – 'We're all in this together.'
People experiencing groupthink apply direct pressure to any one individual who momentarily expresses doubts about any of the group's shared illusions or who questions the validity of the arguments supporting a strategy favoured by the majority.

Time pressure – 'Let's get on with it!'
Victims of groupthink are often more conscious of the time element than of how well the decision is processed when time pressure is critical. Time appears more important than the task.

Self-censorship – 'What would I know?'
A desire to avoid deviating from what appears to be group consensus, keep silent about their misgivings, and minimise to themselves the importance of their doubts.

Unanimity – 'We all agree . . . we're right.'
The sharing of an illusion of unanimity within the group concerning almost all judgements expressed by members who speak in favour of the majority view. This partly results from self-censorship. The effects are augmented by the false assumption that any individual who remains silent during any part of the discussion is in full accord with what the others are saying.

For the course, simulators and videos are used. As in other world airlines, Qantas CRM is practised in the simulator, then the collective performance is discussed at a de-briefing 'at which the instructor is little more than the master of ceremonies'. It is emphasised that the purpose is group learning. No assessment is given. The crew evaluate their own performance, aided by video packs. After the de-briefing the tape is erased.

CRM is done by and for Line crews. Thus, for the first time, they have a say in their own training. The ultimate aim is not to pass examinations, but the most valuable one of all – to develop the habit of constantly using CRM principles.

Qantas stresses crew co-operation, and encourages crews – particularly first officers – to express their opinions, if necessary very forcibly. The course lasts two days and there is a short annual 'refresher'. So far only pilots take it, but it is intended to extend it to cabin crews. *Retrospect*, a magazine examining past accidents and containing articles relevant to flight safety, is now issued every month. This useful publication is circulated to airlines and aviation organisations worldwide.

Qantas Safety is one complete unit in the Security Department and has considerable clout in Qantas operations. They have an excellent record and have no hesitation in fighting the 'safety' corner against the mammoth 'commercial cost effectiveness'. They have produced 'The Auditing of Accident Cost', which is reproduced opposite, a timely reminder to management, produced whenever necessary.

Captain Davenport, Director of Flight Operations, writing of CRM principles, points out an added bonus: 'You may very well find them useful in running the family business, or indeed the family.'

Therein lies the nub – despite cultural differences, human factors have by their very nature common features that can be applied not only to aviation and other forms of transport, but to almost every human activity.

Dan Air hold a two-way course on human factors that has the great virtue of simplicity and of being specifically focused on errors and how we all make them. The aim is to give pilots and flight engineers a greater awareness of flight-deck human factor problems – particularly a greater understanding of specific areas of error, a means of categorising flight-deck styles, an understanding of the influence of individual personalities on crew behaviour, standard methods to achieve effective flight-deck management, and above all, an insight into their own style of action.

Questionnaires and personality assessments are used to

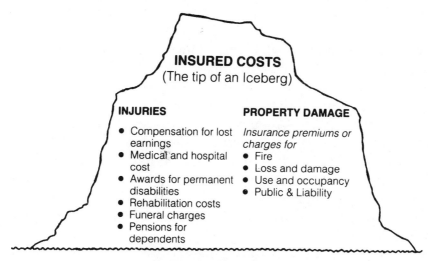

INSURED COSTS
(The tip of an Iceberg)

INJURIES

- Compensation for lost earnings
- Medical and hospital cost
- Awards for permanent disabilities
- Rehabilitation costs
- Funeral charges
- Pensions for dependents

PROPERTY DAMAGE

Insurance premiums or charges for
- Fire
- Loss and damage
- Use and occupancy
- Public & Liability

UNINSURED COSTS

INJURIES

- First aid expenses
- Transportation costs
- Cost of investigations
- Cost of processing reports

WAGE LOSSES

- Idle time of workers whise work is interrupted
- Man hours spent in cleaning up accident area
- Time spent repairing damaged equipment
- Time lost by workers receiving first aid

PRODUCTION LOSSES

- Product spoiled by accident
- Loss of skill and experience
- Lowered production of worker replacement
- Idle machine time

ASSOCIATED COSTS

- Difference between losses and amount recovered
- Rental of equipment to replace damaged equipment
- Surplus workers for replacement of injured employees
- Wages or other benefits paid to disabled worker
- Overhead costs while production is stopped
- Loss of bonus or payment of forfeiture for delays

OFF THE JOB ACCIDENTS

- Cost of medical services
- Time spent on injured workers welfare
- Loss of skill and experience
- Training replacement worker
- Decreased production of replacement
- Benefits paid to injured worker or dependents

INTANGIBLES

.051 Lowered employee morale
- Increased labour conflict
- Unfavourable public relations
- Loss of goodwill

By permission of QANTAS Airways

evaluate crew-interaction factors. Videos are shown. A fictional management human factor situation is looked at. Causes of accidents are analysed and slips discussed. In this context, quotations from CHIRPs are invaluable.

A co-pilot reports: 'At about three miles on a visual approach, I called for flaps 45 – landing flap. The captain reached across and closed the HP cock of the starboard engine. We managed to maintain a reasonable approach and carried out the landing on the remaining engine, being unsuccessful in my attempt to relight no.2. Since then, I always look at the flap lever before I select flaps.'

A co-pilot hesitated before telling the captain he had climbed through his allotted altitude, going on to say: 'I believe the main factor involved here was my reluctance to correct the captain. The captain was very "approachable" and I had no real reason to hold back. It is just a bad habit that I think a lot of co-pilots have over double-checking before we say anything to the captain.'

A captain writes: 'I called for "undercarriage up". Before I could intervene, the co-pilot selected "flaps up". He then became apparently bemused by the flap position indicator, and I shouted at him, "At least raise the undercarriage!" I now point at the selector lever whenever I am handling the aircraft on a take-off and ask the co-pilot for "undercarriage up!"'

A co-pilot took off and found the aircraft slow to climb. He reports: 'At 500 feet, I asked for the flaps to be retracted, and we then discovered what the problem was – I had forgotten to select flaps before take-off, and the captain hadn't noticed.'

There are role-playing sessions, each crew member taking the different positions of captain, co-pilot and engineer, in such situations as all engines failing, a bomb on board, co-pilot and flight engineer at loggerheads, a tired crew and take-off in a thunderstorm.

Transcripts of the cockpit voice-recorders from crashed aircraft are also analysed, showing very clearly the personalities of captains and first officers involved. In one, a Convair flying to

Pine Bluff, Arkansas, a captain says: 'First time I made a mistake in my life,' to which the co-pilot replies: 'Man, I wish I knew where we were so we'd have some idea of the general terrain round here.'

A minute later, he had obtained some idea – he is saying 'Minimum *en route* altitude here is forty-four hund –' when there is the sound of crashing, as the aircraft hits a mountain at 2,025 feet.

The course avoids bemusing its members with science and concentrates on their active participation. Criticism of themselves and each other is encouraged, and the hope is that after completing the course, each person will have a better idea of how he fulfils his own particular role on the flight deck.

The KLM course teaches human factors under various headings – the meaning of human factors; the nature of human error and meeting the challenge of human error; fatigue, body rhythms and sleep; vision and visual illusions; fitness and performance; motivation and leadership; communication, language and speech; attitudes and persuasion; training and training devices; displays and controls, space and layout; documentation; passengers, the human payload; awareness and application.

In New Zealand, there is a 'Human Factor in Airline Training' seminar. In Australia, Ansett teaches a modified KLM course in conjunction with a consultancy firm.

Swissair run a once-a-year Ground School Refresher for all their flight-deck crew. The first session of this day-long programme is given over exclusively to flight safety. The Head of Flight Safety welcomes the group, then shows a thirty-minute videotape on the most current safety issues. There follows forty-five minutes of group discussion. Working from examples, the presentation is concerned to make crews aware of 'typical' danger situations and how they might evolve.

The first presentation is called 'Better Communications for Better Safety', and focuses on four major obstacles to effective communication: 'misinterpretation, over-anticipation, rank barriers, and interpersonal friction'.

The second is 'Safety by Stress Management' and focuses on:

1. *Personality* – concentrating on an incident in Bariloche, South America, largely caused by a commercial pilot's fanatical desire to 'win' – whatever the stakes, whatever the costs.
2. *Family and partner* – i.e. 'luggage' – why should a pilot make two gear-up landings within six weeks? (The presentation looks at the death of a relative, change of partners and domestic strife.)
3. *Company and workplace* – pressure exerted by the company itself, and illustrates how fierce competition in today's air-transport world provides fertile ground for company stress.
4. *Situation* – what could prompt an experienced DC-10 captain to abort take-off with VR long exceeded and rotation already commenced? Dangerous situations all have their share of situational stress.

The programme suggests that stress management is the key to ensuring optimum performance, and that such management should begin with ourselves.

The third presentation is called 'Risk', and concentrates on:

1. The dangers of long periods without incident, illustrated by the disastrous end to a long and incident-free career of a B-747 captain.
2. The fascination of the goal – especially heading for home. The Zeigarnik effect – the tension provided by an un-completed task.
3. The follow-my-leader syndrome – leaving risk-assessment to the man in front, pointing out the numerous accidents caused by the pilot seeing an aircraft land in difficult conditions, and therefore feeling obliged to try himself – and crashing.

The fourth presentation is called 'Automation and the Monitor's Role', and shows the dangers of passive monitoring, blinkered concentration and confusion on how to respond to unexpected automation actions.

There are videotapes of all four presentations for sale at prices between $300 and $600.

The standard of airline flying – thanks to the billions of dollars spent on flying training – is excellent. A far smaller amount is at last being spent on human factor training, which airlines try to augment by selling their training products. How is it progressing?

Deregulation in America has increased the competition between airlines and enables all sorts of companies to start operating. The inflation rate is rising and there is a relation between a carrier's financial position and its safety record. Two-man crews, twin-engined ocean flying and fatigue on the long-range B-747/200 three-crew and the two-crew 747/400 are problems related to economics that are still unresolved. The two different flight decks of the 747/200 and 747/400 are illustrated in photographs 6b and 7b.

Big companies are merging and creating monopolies. At the same time, 50 per cent of the world's jet fleet is nearly twenty years old. What the engineers call BFO's – Bits Falling Off – are now more frequent than ever. There has been a pilot shortage – like bull and bear on the stock market, there is always either a glut or a famine – as many highly experienced pilots retire. But with the recession and Gulf Crisis putting enormous financial pressures on airlines, a number of which have closed down, this may no longer be the case. Pilots in the past have played 'company-hopping' for more pay, while managements hopefully dredged an already swept-clean pilot market – all in an era of aviation expanding worldwide at 10 per cent per annum. What will happen in the present financial crisis, with Gatwick Airport reporting a 20 per cent drop in business during the first three months of 1991, is anybody's guess. In the long run, however, the upward trend of civil aviation is bound to continue.

In such a climate, aircraft accidents are likely to increase (1989 was a particularly bad year) unless the nettle of the human factor problem throughout the industry is much more firmly grasped. Automation, supposedly the pilot's helpmate, has been shown to be two-faced. The spread of Artificial Intelligence (AI) is now being promulgated as an attempt to escape from the human factor problem, but it will only bring problems of its own.

You cannot get rid of the pilot – as the radio officer, navigator, and now probably the flight engineer have been eliminated. At a time when there is little crew left, managements are emphasising crew management and crew co-ordination. The label of pilot error looks like being replaced not by human error but by crew error.

In most airlines, captains are allocated crew members whom they haven't even met, let alone those whose expertise and experience they are acquainted with. It has been shown by a number of experiments that a crew who have flown together for three days or so communicate far more and are more willing to express their opinions.

Captain Roy Butler, Pan American's System Director Flight Training, says the annual flight and human factor training has significant cost benefits to Pan Am. 'We're looking in the neighbourhood of saving a million dollars in the first year alone,' he says, 'simply by reducing the number of hotel nights, the *per diem* and pay credits that put a hefty price tag on the non-training aspects of flight training.'

Pan Am expects to triple savings in the next two to three years, as 'all airmen are sequenced' into the new programme. In addition, the annualised approach to training frees up additional simulator time that Pan Am can sell to other carriers on a contract basis. Pan Am's outside training netted $3 million in 1987 and was expected to go much higher.

Human factor training in aviation is considered by some airlines to be 'a package' which they can attach to normal route and flying training, when in fact it is far more complicated and has been less studied in context than the actual art of flying.

Soon the member countries of the EEC will have to impose mandatory human factor training for aircrew. Will the airlines do this in any real depth, or will the human factor 'package' be no more than a plastic fig leaf to cover the naked pilot's human inheritance?

And just as important, will management begin to examine *their* human factor errors?

Seventeen

Human Factors in Management

Professor Reason in *Human Error* (1990) distinguishes between active error, the effects of which are felt almost immediately, and latent error, the adverse consequences of which may lie dormant within the system for a long time. This can clearly be seen in aviation, where pilots at the sharp end make an active error, while latent error lies behind the lines within the management support system. Many of these are already there awaiting a trigger, usually supplied by the pilot. 'There is a growing awareness within the human reliability community that attempts to discover and neutralise those latent failures will have a greater beneficial effect upon system safety than will localised efforts to minimise active errors.'

As long ago as 1980, Stanley Roscoe wrote that:

> The tenacious retention of 'pilot error' as an accident 'cause factor' by governmental agencies, equipment manufacturers and airline management, and even by pilot unions indirectly, is a subtle manifestation of the apparently natural human inclination to narrow the responsibility for tragic events that receive wide public attention. If the responsibility can be isolated to the momentary defection of a single individual, the captain in command, then other members of the aviation community remain untarnished. The unions briefly acknowledge the inescapable conclusion that pilots can make errors and thereby gain a few bargaining points with management for the future.
>
> Everyone else, including other crew members, remains clean. The airline accepts the inevitable financial liability for

losses but escapes blame for inadequate training programmes or procedural indoctrination. Equipment manufacturers avoid product liability for faulty design. Regulatory agencies are not criticised for approving an unsafe operation, failing to invoke obviously needed precautionary restrictions, or, worse yet, contributing directly by injudicious control or unsafe clearance authorisations. Only the pilot who made the 'error' and his family suffer, and their suffering may be assuaged by a liberal pension in exchange for his quiet early retirement – in the event that he was fortunate enough to survive the accident.

Unfair? Examples of unions fighting hard for their members are mentioned in previous pages. Managements and aircraft manufacturers have their problems and are by no means all bad, but sufficient examples of lack of foresight, cost-cutting, cover-ups, greed, buck-passing, blindness and refusal to face facts and other human factors can be shown to justify the generality of Roscoe's condemnation.

What is clear is that no aviation accident can be justifiably blamed on one individual. The mistake is a collective mistake, and the responsibility is a collective responsibility.

Yet it is only recently that very dubious management mal-practices are being identified and their contribution to accidents given sufficient weight. For though the pilot's actions are at the tip of the iceberg of responsibility, many other people have had a hand in it – faceless people in aircraft design and manufacture, in computer technology and software, in maintenance, in flying control, in accounts departments and in the corridors of power. But the pilot is available and identifiable, and, if he isn't conveniently dead, he probably feels himself responsible. Besides, he has no powerful financial lobby like the aircraft manufacturers or the big airlines.

That is not to say that there are not far too many human factor accidents on the flight deck. There are. And one of the reasons human factors took decades to be accepted is because of the pilots themselves, who understandably shied away from too much introspection. For the purposes of survival, nature appears to have endowed us with an inherited conviction that 'success' is 'good', even though success often contains its own element of failure. As a result, we draw away from those who make mistakes, lest we are associated with them. This is why mistakes are so often repeated and why it is taking us so long to understand them.

What should be stressed is that the pilot is not alone in his human condition. Nor is aviation alone in its management errors. A high proportion of recent world disasters – Three Mile Island, Bhopal, *Challenger*, Chernobyl, and the King's Cross Underground fires, the *Herald of Free Enterprise* – have occurred mainly as a result of latent management errors. In the recent Zeebrugge trial it was disclosed that no members of the marine and technical departments had a nautical or deck background and had scorned the idea of bridge indicator lights to confirm that the bow door was shut. So in aviation accidents, where the error is rather easier to cover up in the boardroom than on the flight deck.

Professor Reason points out that what is being relatively neglected are 'measures aimed at enhancing the system's tolerance to latent human failures committed by high-level decision-makers, regulators, managers, builders and maintenance personnel. In other words, we need to find ways of detecting and neutralising these fallible decisions before they come into adverse conjunction with active on-the-spot failures and local triggering factors.' How can the total organisation be managed so as to enhance its intrinsic safety?

The 'management factor' in aviation, as it is now called – *not*, it should be noted wryly, management *error* – should be measured against various parameters to get it into perspective: firstly, against the time scale of aviation endeavour; secondly against the safety measures that have already evolved.

The incredible speed of aviation evolution is self-evident. So is the ingenuity and courage of the human beings concerned in it. During the development of aviation, flight safety improved to a point where six years ago there were around 1.8 fatal crashes per million take-offs and even then a passenger would have had a 50 per cent chance of survival.

Now it has edged up to 2 per million take-offs.

Why?

The previous rapid progress in safety had been achieved because aircraft were made stronger; jet engines were far more reliable; aircraft instruments, radio and radar aids became very sophisticated; and training and operating procedures became very advanced world-wide.

The reason why the safety level resists further improvement is the human factor cause of accidents, which for decades has remained at around 70 per cent.

Various organisational and administrative measures have been taken to try to understand and alleviate the problem. The need for international standardisation, the collection and communication of information was recognised at an early date. ICAO and IATA were set up and the 1944 Chicago Convention laid down standards for overflying countries, while the countries' own administration and supervision were left to national bodies like the CAA.

The biggest difficulty that militated against improved safety was the suppression of facts about dangerous flying incidents. It is simply not possible to keep track of weaknesses in the system without having the data. For commercial, legal and personal reasons many such incidents were kept close to the chests and hearts of those involved. And that old Freudian defence mechanism, Denial, can clearly be seen at work. Don't look! It didn't really happen. Added to that there is a natural fear of reprisals – inevitably, safety suffers.

In 1976 the CAA introduced the Mandatory Reporting System, which had already been introduced in America. All concerned must report dangerous incidents, and around 4,500 are submitted annually – covering not only flying incidents and defects but any fault, problem or shortcoming of parts or people, though there is no means of enforcing this. These are processed into computers by the CAA's Safety Data and Analysis Department and published in weekly Occurrence Digests. Such reports are confidential. No names are disclosed.

The CAA makes an assurance that 'its primary concern is to secure free and uninhibited reporting and that it will not be its policy to institute proceedings in respect of unpremeditated or inadvertent breaches of the law which come to its attention only because they have been reported under the Scheme, except in cases involving dereliction of duty amounting to gross negligence'.

In addition, there is the non-mandatory Confidential Human Factors Incident Reporting Programme (CHIRP), started in 1982 and run by an under-manned but efficient staff at the RAF Institute of Aviation Medicine. The reports come to it mainly from aircrew and ATC controllers, and these are edited and reissued regularly in a valuable publication called *Feedback*. The tone struck is light.

Twenty years ago, when I published *The Human Factor in Aircraft Accidents*, pilots were denying that they ever made mistakes. Now CHIRP contains heart-searching probes by pilots into their own airmanship, and there is no shortage of people owning up to errors. Most of the reports appear to be related to fatigue or commercial pressure.

In addition, there is the Aircraft Proximity Hazard Reporting System established in 1989. When a controller considers aircraft are endangered by being too close, he must make a report.

Finally, there is the Joint Air-Miss Working Group, which examines all air-misses where a pilot considers his aircraft endangered by the proximity of another aircraft. The Group determines causes, makes recommendations to the National Air Traffic Centres and produces a report three times a year.

All these provide essential information for risk analysis and for the introduction of improved safety measures – and indeed for the further understanding of human behaviour. But all these steps forward require good practices from the next link in the chain, management.

It is a damning comment on airline management that in 1987 a Bill to increase penalties for falsifying airline maintenance records had to be passed in the US House of Representatives.

And after an investigation into airline safety by a USA Senate sub-committee, Chairman Senator Roth said: 'There is growing evidence that cost-cutting, over-scheduling and crowded conditions at airports may be eroding safety margins and posing a growing threat to the travelling public.'

If there is any doubt that mistakes and mismanagement are covered up, this same statement goes on to say that pilots and mechanics who might well be the only ones to know about potential safety hazards were 'reluctant to report those conditions because of fear of reprisals'. At another Inquiry FAA inspectors, who are supposed to uphold safety, were accused of burying an adverse report on airline maintenance.

In 1978 a Boeing 747 of JAL made a heavy landing at Osaka and dragged its tail along the runway. What followed was like the old rhyme of 'For want of a nail, the shoe was lost, for want of a shoe . . . a horse . . . a rider'. JAL asked Boeing to do the repairs but, as a result of human error, only one row of rivets was used to secure a plate that was part of the rear bulkhead web.

For seven years, because of its inaccessibility, this error on the plate was never noticed – an example of latent human error in the sytem. Then in August 1985, on a flight from Tokyo, part of the aircraft fin broke away, damaging the controls. For half an hour the crew tried to control the aircraft sufficiently to land at a military airfield, but they crashed on the southern slope of Mount Ogusa, killing all 520 people on board.

Where there is deregulation, governments have either completely removed or considerably weakened a number of the safeguards that used to protect the safety standards of civil aviation. And managements have taken advantage of that weakness.

Competition has become the name of the game, but instead of providing better service this has resulted in a greater concentration of the market in fewer hands. In America, due to unrestricted mergers and takeovers, aviation has become an unregulated oligopoly (eight airlines control 84 per cent of the traffic), within which the cost-cutting and over-scheduling which Senator Roth referred to are increasing. Problems with safety multiply as finances dominate operations. In October 1985 the annual meeting of the Flight Safety Foundation reflected a pessimistic view of the effect of deregulation on flight safety. Its President spoke of 'sharp economic competition which cannot enhance safety', and he went on to say that staffing changes resulting from economic reorganisation could 'provide opportunity for operational error'.

Cut-throat competition reducing employee costs, and aircrew free-wheeling from one company to another, are all now causing great concern to organisations like ALPA.

At the end of 1985 a DC-8 of Arrow Air, carrying 248 men of the Airborne Division, landed at Gander. They were coming home from their peace-keeping role in the Sinai Desert. After a short refuelling stop, the aircraft took off for Kentucky. Once airborne, however, the DC-8 appeared unable to climb. Skimming the ground for half a mile, it crashed into fir trees and, with full tanks, burst into flames.

No one survived.

The investigators were hampered by the fact that the cockpit voice recorder was unserviceable (allowable at the time under the Minimum Equipment List). Icing was at first suspected, but was rejected by a minority report. Witnesses testified that there had been fire before the aircraft crashed, and there was a theory that there might have been an in-flight explosion.

In the course of the investigation, various malpractices were uncovered. It came to light that the company had been previously fined for maintenance violations. Flight-time limitations had been exceeded. And a generally unsatisfactory state of regulatory control in aviation was revealed.

Such a furore was created by this accident and the revelations that followed it that a retired Supreme Court judge was brought in. He despaired of finding the real cause of the accident, but it did lead to some measures being taken and a more critical eye directed on the dangerous shortcomings of aviation.

Then, in the middle of 1990, a group of Congressmen again

rejecting the wing-icing theory, pressed for a new inquiry, pointing out the similarities of the Gander accident to the explosion of the Pan Am 747 over Lockerbie. They maintained that the original bomb theory was hushed up by the Canadian and US governments before it soured secret negotiations with Iran for the release of US hostages in Lebanon.

Certainly there was evidence of a fire on board, and the Islamic Jihad in Beirut claimed responsibility soon after the crash. In addition, an FBI report on the accident had two hundred pages blacked out, which seemed to support the cover-up theory. Now further investigations into the cause of the crash are continuing.

Cost-cutting in fuel, practices to prolong engine life, improper checking of pilots by unqualified staff, corner-cutting on maintenance, the installation of extra seats to make a more commercially profitable load, the sealing of escape hatches – the list of malpractices in some airlines is formidable and growing. Deregulation will exacerbate these problems in Europe.

It is within this error-laden environment that the pilot operates. At the apex of the flying endeavour, he has to trust rather more unseen members of the human race than he would like. He must sign a form stating that he accepts the serviceability state of the aircraft, and that the correct amount of fuel has been loaded. He signs the load sheet, although it is impossible for him to know that it is acccurate. In addition, he may have to sign for diplomatic mail, precious cargo and any live animals aboard. Although he may not altogether trust what others have done on his behalf, he has to sign, absolving them of responsibility should anything untoward happen.

On the afternoon of 25 May 1979, a DC-10, Flight 191 of American Airlines rolled down Runway 32 Right of Chicago's O'Hare Airport, bound for Los Angeles. The weather was clear, with visibility fifteen miles.

As the aircraft nose lifted, the left engine, complete with its supporting pylon, came away from the wing. The free engine barrelled forward, flew over the top of the wing and fell to the runway. The pilots, unable to see wing or engine from the cockpit, assumed that they had a simple engine failure and continued into the air using the procedures they had practised so often.

What they could not know was that the departing engine had struck the wing, severed hydraulic and electrical lines and caused the outboard leading-edge slat to begin a slow retraction. As it did, it dramatically reduced the lift from the left wing.

The appalling tragedy was the culmination of a story of mistaken assumptions, cost-cutting maintenance and ineffective regulations, and an illustration of what the Flight Safety Foundation was saying.

McDonnell-Douglas's DC-10 first flew in June 1972, eighteen months after its smaller rival, the Lockheed Tristar. Some of its early design features were the subject of controversy, not least during the Inquiry into this particular accident. That they satisfied the 1965 Federal Aviation Regulations was of little consolation to the relatives of the victims.

Those regulations allowed McDonnell-Douglas to consider the structural failure of the pylon and engine to be of the same magnitude as a structural failure of the wing. Just as there was little point in analysing the implications of a wing coming off in flight, they decided that separation of the engine could be viewed in the same light. That the pylons had failed before, fortunately without destroying the aircraft, was not taken into account. Had they examined the possibility and its potential consequences, the vulnerability of vital systems would inevitably have come to light.

The design of the DC-10 differed from most aircraft in several respects. Where most aircraft leading-edge slats were locked in their extended position by mechanical latches, McDonnell-Douglas decided to rely upon the hydraulic fluid which operated them being trapped in the lines after extension. They were aware that the fracture of a hydraulic pipe would allow fluid to escape and the slat to retract unexpectedly but, rather than fit a mechanical lock, they preferred to demonstrate to the FAA that the aircraft would still fly successfully with one slat retracted.

It would, but only at the speed normally flown with all three engines operating. At the lower speed used for take-off after engine failure, the wing would stall. It was possible to survive either an engine failure or a slat retraction at that stage of flight, but *not both*.

Nor were the possible effects of a combined failure of hydraulics and electrics examined. On the flight deck was a warning light to alert the crew that one of the slats was out of position. When the engine of Flight 191 came away, it severed the electrical supply. *It also cut the supply to the stickshaker which would have alerted them to the approaching stall.*

Unable even to see what was happening, the pilots were left in total ignorance of the true nature of the emergency.

How did the pylon come to break away? It was designed to withstand loads far in excess of those to which it would ever be subjected. Advances in design, materials and construction have ensured that the days of unexpected fractures are long gone. For the answer, it is necessary to examine the human factors involved in aircraft maintenance.

As we have seen, airlines are forced to survive in a cut-throat environment. Passengers, encouraged by newspapers and television, demand lower and lower fares. Airline employees who suggest a cheaper way of carrying out any essential task can be assured of a good reception. Indeed, many employers give awards to those who do, and the search for cost-cutting is continuous.

When McDonnell-Douglas issued Service Bulletins calling for the regular replacement of bearings in the pylon wing attachments, they suggested that the engine first be removed from the pylon before the pylon was removed from the wing. Airlines, however, remove engines at irregular intervals, often unexpectedly. It just didn't fit in with the work pattern. When someone realised that removing the engine and pylon in one piece would save 200 man hours, it was an attractive proposition. The manufacturers didn't like the idea, but United Airlines had been doing it for some time, using a crane for the task.

American Airlines decided to use a fork-lift truck to take the weight of the 13,477-lb engine together with the 1,865-lb pylon. It was not an easy job. The forks had to be placed exactly at the centre of gravity of the combined engine and pylon unit, and the forks would inevitably sag slightly as they held the weight. Nevertheless, the procedure was considerably cheaper than removing the engine first.

The accident aircraft had undergone this procedure prior to the disaster. When the mechanics had the fork-lift in position, they found it impossible to disconnect the front attachment holding the pylon to the wing.

Rather than waste time, they dispensed with the normal laid-down sequence and tackled the rear attachment with more success. Subsequent investigation showed that the engine and pylon then pivoted on its forward bearing, pushing back with enormous force on one of the rear attachment flanges and cracking it.

No one spotted this. No one heard it fracture above the noise of the fork-lift truck's engine. And there was no one responsible for inspecting it before it was replaced on the DC-10's wing. Out of view, it was just waiting for the application of take-off power to the engine before breaking.

The first officer did the take-off. The weather was clear with a blustery wind, suggesting some turbulence after lift-off. On the roll, the aircraft needed a little juggling with the rudder pedals and some aileron to keep it straight in the crosswind, but it was no more than routine.

The captain called, 'Vee One', the decision speed, then, 'Rotate.'

At that moment, someone on the flight deck said 'Damn!'

The first officer lifted the aircraft off the runway at a speed a little higher than normal. Maybe it was the recognition of something wrong which caused him to delay rotation a fraction. It was of no consequence, and some pilots prefer to have a little extra speed in hand when conditions are likely to be turbulent.

As they became airborne, however, the engine instruments

and the yaw of the aircraft left them in no doubt that the left engine had failed.

Coping with an engine failure on take-off is a routine affair. Aircraft are designed and loaded to ensure adequate power in the worst of conditions to enable them to climb away safely. It requires accurate flying and speed control, but pilots practise the procedure over and over again in the simulator until they can do it almost by second nature. It was no more than a nuisance which would probably lead to disruption of their flying schedule.

The DC-10 took off in a slight left-wing-down attitude which the first officer corrected with a little aileron and rudder. It began to climb at a very healthy 1,150 feet a minute. During the climb, the first engineer eased the throttles forward to make sure that they had all available power from the two operating engines.

The speed was 172 knots.

Procedures after an engine failure at that time called for the pilot to maintain a speed of V2 until a safe height was achieved. (This was later modified.) Realising that his speed was 10 knots higher than laid down because of the slightly late rotation, the co-pilot eased the stick back a little, allowing the airspeed to decay slowly to the correct figure.

Unfortunately, when the engine and pylon came off they severed the hydraulic lines serving the leading-edge slats. With the hydraulic lock broken, the slats on the port wing began a slow retraction. With the electrical line severed too, there was no way that the crew could know.

The dreadful irony of it was that now the first officer, doing his job professionally and accurately, was unwittingly leading them into danger by following the flight manual to the letter and reducing airspeed.

As the speed reached 159 knots, the aircraft began to roll to the left. The first officer tried to counteract this with the ailerons.

He had no success. The DC-10 began a left turn and the roll increased. By now the controls were hard over and having no effect.

On the flight deck nothing was making sense. With two good

engines delivering plenty of power, the aircraft should be climbing well and under full control.

The aircraft continued to turn and roll to the left. With wings now over to the vertical, it entered a dive, plunging into the ground and scattering wreckage across a trailer park.

Not one of the 271 people on board survived. Two people were killed on the ground and two others injured.

The NTSB Report stated that the accident was caused by 'a combination of three events. The retraction of the left wing's outboard leading-edge slats, the loss of the slat disagreement warning system, and the loss of the stall warning system – all resulting from the separation of the engine pylon assembly.'

This was not an isolated case of a company not taking action after an incident or accident. There had been a similar incident to a DC-10 in 1972 in Pakistan. Then in 1981 at Dulles there was another. Over two years after the accident, as a DC-10 took off from Miami, it happened yet again.

In 1982 McDonnell-Douglas installed a mechanical lock costing only a few thousand dollars that would prevent slat retraction in such emergencies. As Charles Perrow points out, it had taken the company three years since the Chicago accident, five years and 273 days since the Pakistan accident, for the company to make the modification.

The slats problem was by no means the only difficulty encountered on the DC-10. There had been others, including the now infamous cargo door. Here again, fierce competition with Boeing and Lockheed made for undue haste and consequent errors.

When the first DC-10 was tested in 1970, the cargo door blew open. Modifications were made to the latching mechanism. Then three other operators reported cargo doors blowing out, and a Service Bulletin (SB) was issued; this suggested further modifications including a support plate. A Service Bulletin is not mandatory.

A month later, in June 1972, an American Airlines DC-10 stopped at Detroit *en route* from Los Angeles to New York. The loader on the ramp had difficulty shutting the cargo door, and in the end shoved it shut with his knee.

Five minutes after take-off, still on the climb and over Windsor, Ontario, the pilots heard a heavy thud, dust swirled round the cockpit and the cabin filled with the white 'smoke' that follows decompression. The rear end of the cabin floor collapsed, damaging the control cables beneath. The cargo door had opened yet again.

After the incident further modifications were made; a subcontractor for work on the DC-10, Dan Applegate, prophesied that unless the fault was cured, the door would open again and, 'I would expect this usually to result in the loss of the airplane.'

The fault was not cured, his comments never reached the FAA (which had certified the plane as fit to fly), and his prophecy came true.

At 12.30 p.m. on 3 March 1974, a Turkish Airlines DC-10 took off from Orly airport, near Paris, its intermediate stop between Istanbul and London.

In an almost exact replica of the Windsor incident, while they were still climbing, unbeknown to the pilots the cargo door had burst open. Again, the cabin floor had collapsed, severing the control cables. As they struggled to avoid disaster, the pilots' last words on the CVR show that they did not know what had crippled them.

The DC-10 crashed in the forest of Ermenonville, killing all 345 people on board. When the door was recovered, it was found that the McDonnell-Douglas modification had not, presumably because of time pressure, been made.

Worse followed. The aircraft documents showed that three McDonnell-Douglas employees had certified by signature and personal stamp that the modification had been carried out before the aircraft in question left the factory. None of the three remembered either doing the work or certifying it.

Denials, arguments, accusations and cover-ups continued. There was even an attempt to blame the loader at Orly for not closing the door properly. But in 1975, McDonnell-Douglas made an out-of-court settlement and abandoned their defence.

In June 1981, the crew of a British Aerospace 748 on a mail flight from Gatwick to Castle Donington saw a red warning light signifying that the rear door was unlocked. That did not cause too much alarm, because the system was known to be fallible. However, severe vibration and decompression followed almost at once. Sending out a Mayday, the crew tried desperately to bring the aircraft down safely. But disastrously, the door had not only blown off but hit the tail plane. The aircraft became deformed and disintegrated. The investigation found that this had happened twice before to other B.Ae 748s, and B.Ae's records showed that doors of 748s had come open thirty-five times.

In April 1988, an old Aloha Airlines B-737 lost an eighteen-foot piece of the fuselage in flight and a flight attendant was sucked out. A Tristar virtually had triple engine failure returning to Miami when the O-ring seals were omitted from the oil systems during servicing, resulting in almost total loss of oil.

Because of cost-cutting, there is an irresistible trend to *extend* the operating lives of aircraft at a time when maintenance budgets are being sharply *cut*. Ageing aircraft and cut-price maintenance make a grim equation. Furthermore, in some cases pilots conform to practices they either know or suspect are dangerous.

Such were the circumstances leading to the crash in May 1979 of Downeast Airlines Flight 46 near Knox County Airport.

The captain was Downeast's chief pilot, a man who had been given so much work by the management that 'his chronic fatigue' was cited by the Inquiry as one of the causes of the accident. He was always complaining of chest pains, difficulty breathing, exhaustion and loss of appetite. It is not difficult to see why. From the list of all his duties, it would seem that he had to do pretty well everything – provide ground and flight training, schedule crews and aircraft, enforce regulations and policies, maintain a pilot personnel file and be responsible for the up-to-date status of all aircrew, interview and hire new pilots, maintain records, and take responsibility for all phases of training and testing both written and oral.

He was a deeply unhappy pilot. Witnesses testified to the Inquiry that the Downeast president was a difficult man to work for. The chief pilot was criticised frequently and feared for his job. He repeatedly told other pilots that he felt powerless.

The Inquiry further stated: 'It is believed that inordinate management pressures, the first officer's marginal instrument proficiency, the captain's inadequate supervision of the flight, inadequate crew training and procedures . . . were all factors in the accident.'

In fact, the first officer had only been hired by Downeast two months before. There was a great turnover in pilots. The sensible ones left, making more work in recruitment and training for the unfortunate chief pilot.

The first officer, prior to his joining Downeast, had only had experience in single-engine aircraft and, perhaps because of that, had the dangerous habit of moving switches without being asked, and had, to quote the accident report, 'little appreciation for the crew co-ordination concept'. He had been found by other captains he had flown with to have significant problems while making instrument approaches, though none of these were reported to either the chief pilot or the airline manager.

What *was* known was that both captain and first officer were uneasy about the fatal flight. They had flown the aircraft from Rockland to Boston and had encountered not only bad weather but vibration in one of the engines. The bad weather had caused a delay in arrival at Boston and consequently a late departure for their return flight from there.

It was 20.55 when they finally took off from Boston with sixteen passengers aboard, under Instrument Flight Rules with the first officer in the left-hand seat. To make matters worse, the cockpit lighting was totally inadequate. Burned-out bulbs were replaced with random colours – again to save money.

An hour and a half after departure, the flight received clearance to cruise at 3,000 feet for an approach to Rockland, where it was told to report when it wanted to cancel IFR. There was low visibility in fog and cloud and the weather was expected to deteriorate. Just before nine o'clock, New Brunswick radar showed the flight's position just south of Sprucehead at an altitude of 1,500 feet. Two minutes later the flight was telling New Brunswick: 'Looks like we're probably going to have to miss the approach here at Rockland. We're going down, but maybe you could pull us out a clearance for Augusta.'

They were told that clearance was 'on request'. The flight then made a radio transmission to the company facility at the airport on Unicom frequency. It was the last reported contact with the flight.

Flight 46 crashed into a heavily wooded area south-west of the approach end of Runway 3. Only one passenger survived.

In the course of the investigation and public hearing, fourteen former Downeast pilots and several other employees provided written statements and/or sworn testimonies which were critical of the Downeast president's management practices and policies as they related to safety.

According to the ICAO report, these practices included the following: ignoring take-off and landing visibility minimums; directing pilots to make repeated instrument approaches and to 'get lower' during adverse weather conditions; pressuring pilots into flying over gross weight limits and repeatedly permitting ground personnel to overload aircraft and provide pilots with knowingly inaccurate baggage weights and counts; discouraging the training officers or chief pilots from providing adequate flight training by suggesting that training was unnecessary; permitting grossly exaggerated or inaccurate flight and ground training records to be presented to FAA inspectors; pressuring pilots into flying aircraft with known mechanical defects; firing a pilot for cancelling a revenue flight which in his judgement could not be conducted safely because of weather conditions.

The president of the airline and a few other current employees denied most of the allegations or offered explanations for them.

The Safety Board's investigation determined that past and present company personnel perceived the company president as a particularly strong-willed individual who dominated the course of day-to-day operations of the company and was the final authority in all matters. The Safety Board investigators heard that employees who did not unquestioningly accept the president's decisions were often subjected to various types of coercion, ranging from ridicule and verbal abuse to fines, seasonal layoffs and, in some cases, dismissal. They stated that these factors, along with their observations of the president's explosive temperament, created an atmosphere of hostility, intimidation and fear of loss of employment.

Though the accident to Flight 46 at Rockland may seem an extreme example, it is by no means an isolated one. Worse still, there are management practices occurring now which are simply waiting for some human errors on the part of flight crews to turn into disasters. Why has it taken so long for the searchlight to focus on human error in management?

It is only when disasters grab the headlines that the long, sad story of such human error is brought to light. Then unbelievable practices are for a time examined but soon forgotten.

Firstly, management is part of the Establishment. Even small bits of the Establishment stick together, and there is a political and economic necessity not to rock the boat, nor to lower management status in their own eyes and those of other people.

Secondly, management controls the operation, hiring, firing, promotion and, above all, the money.

Thirdly, management controls most of the relevant papers (which sometimes go missing) after an accident, will rarely admit they are wrong, and duck for cover after any catastrophe.

So after an accident it is extremely difficult to trace back, possibly for years, the people within the management who might have some responsibility. At the same time, it is a human factor in society itself to demand retribution.

Then the errors of management are hard to identify. On the other hand, the errors of the pilot are self-evident and are often quick slips. The environment in which the errors are made are also different – in one case a comfortable office, and in the other a cockpit possibly surrounded by storm and darkness and with an engine on fire.

There are also violations – deliberate floutings of safety. Pilots and managements can both commit these. Pilots can take quite unacceptable risks and under time-pressure cut corners, but it is managers under political or economic pressure who are most likely to be tempted. They of course have their own *special* problems – the most important of which, following nature's earth mother of all human factors, survival – is how to stay in business and in their jobs in an increasingly competitive market.

Deregulation, according to ALPA, allows anyone to start an airline and operate anywhere in the US at whatever fare he likes. In the ten years before US airline deregulation, there were twenty-two fatal airline accidents. In the ten years after, there were nearly double that number, though the number of take-offs had not doubled. Economists, accountants and management pressure sometimes cause operators to economise, sometimes unsuccessfully.

The price of fuel is erratic. The ageing fleets need replacement. Experienced pilots are becoming difficult to obtain. The tourist market fluctuates.

Safety and economy are opposing sides of the same coin. Balancing them is very difficult, particularly as the general public don't understand that this is so. You can't yet sell airline safety – the public take it for granted. As ALPA has commented, 'The public is not saying to airlines: 'We will not fly – it is too dangerous.' It is saying to government: 'We will not fly – it is too expensive.'

So human factors not only exist in the causes of accidents, they are also present in the public attitudes to safety in which an element of machoism exists, clearly shown in the macho driving on our roads. They are also present in public demands for retribution, in the way that accidents are judged (for too long in an adversarial, holier-than-thou court-room situation) and in the punishments the 'miscreants' suffer.

It is usually the pilot who is in the dock. It is far easier to attack than to defend – hence the saying 'the best defence is attack'. So the old court-type Inquiries were doubly unjust.

After recent catastrophes, some attempts are now being made to bring the managers to book – in the cases of the *Herald of Free Enterprise*, the *Marchioness/Bowbelle* collision, and the - Clapham Junction rail disaster – but it is usually the driver, ship's captain or pilot who is the scapegoat. The train driver who passed the red light at Purley was jailed.

The co-pilot in the M1 crash was summarily dismissed. A pilot who has had a crash, particularly a fatal one, never forgets it. Nor does his family. We sympathise with the traumas of the survivors and the families of victims, but we can also sympathise with the families of pilots, sea captains, and rail drivers who have been branded (often unfairly) with blame for an accident.

Taking a hard line is, in any case, usually counter-productive.

A Chinese B-737 pilot had been hijacked and had obeyed the hijackers' instructions to fly to Taiwan, for which he was punished by the management. Incredibly, he was hijacked again. This time, he refused to obey the hijackers' orders and, in the ensuing turmoil, hit a B-757 in Canton; this resulted in a heavy loss of life.

When management error plays lesser roles than in these examples, it tends to get little attention. Low morale and inept handling of aircrew laid the foundations of the Trident Papa India crash at Staines, and though many more human factors came into play, the stress induced by bad relations enabled them to do so.

In his book *Safety is No Accident*, Bill Tench, head of Aircraft Accident Investigation from 1974 to 1981, writes that recommendations uncovered by recent inquiries have been slow to be followed up and implemented. This would appear to be particularly true with regard to the provision of fire-resistant materials for aircraft seats and furnishings, where passengers have been suffocated by smoke.

The accident to the British Airtours 737 at Manchester was one example. Initiated by faulty maintenance and communication (there had been similar failures of combustion chambers in that engine type), this accident was turned into a disaster by inadequate management practice, and poor liaison between Boeing and the operator, made more devastating by an insufficiently co-ordinated fire and rescue service.

Both pilots for that charter flight to Corfu were experienced. When, at take-off power, twelve seconds after the routine 80 knots call, a loud thump sounded, they thought a tyre had burst. Although they knew there had been an entry in the technical log about number one engine's slow acceleration, they did not associate the noise with that. They could not know that within it there had been a combustion chamber failure and that the dome had been hurled from the engine and fractured the underwing fuel access panel, nor that it had already been the subject of repair.

The captain at once ordered a stop, and was informing ATC that he was abandoning take-off when the fire bell sounded.

Six seconds later, to clear the runway, the commander turned the aircraft into link Delta, and there, disastrously, it was positioned so that a light wind fanned the flames and thrust them against the fuselage, melting and cracking the windows.

Even before the aircraft came to a halt the passengers could see the flames and feel the radiant heat. Surviving passengers testified that 'the smoke generated an immediate sense of panic'. One of them said he was aware of a mass of people tangled together and struggling in the centre section, apparently incapable of moving forward, adding that 'people were howling and screaming'.

When the purser hurried to open the right forward door to release the inflatable chute the door opened, but as it was moving out through the aperture the slide container lid jammed on the door frame, preventing further movement of the door. The purser turned to the left door, cracked it open, made sure the forward spread of the fire permitted evacuation and opened the door fully, inflating the chute.

All the cabin staff struggled heroically to evacuate the passengers. But as the Inquiry remarked,

Apart from the purser, the only cabin-crew member who was reasonably experienced, having completed a season's flying on aircraft which included the Boeing 737, was the number four stewardess, positioned in the forward cabin with the purser. Of the two stewardesses at the rear, only one had limited experience of flying as a crew member the previous year and that on a different type of aircraft.

Airlines no doubt regard it as economical to employ in this way, but is it adequate or safe for the public? Or in fact to the girls themselves? Both rear stewardesses died at their posts. Having researched many accidents in which stewardesses have behaved superbly, I can only marvel at the courage of women.

The major question which the Inquiry set itself was: 'Why did the passengers not escape sufficiently quickly?'

The answer lies in that dangerous interface between safety and profit. Too often airlines regard passengers as no more than bums on seats and inadequate seats at that. The survivors complained of inadequate exits and overcrowding. Those who have been on a package holiday must have asked themselves, 'How do we get out *if*. . . ?'

Manchester was the answer. No one had been injured until smoke filled the cabin. Then people were asphyxiated. Only six people died of burns. Yet there have been numerous warnings that this might happen after a cabin fire. In July 1973 on board a Brazilian Varig 707 approaching Paris, when a fire started in a lavatory a cigarette end in a non-standard wastebin was blamed. The 124 victims died before the emergency landing as a result of deadly fumes. Much of the smoke came from burning fabric on the seats. Air Canada began replacing their 17,500 passenger seats with fire-blocking fabric several years before Manchester. After the Manchester crash, the CAA enforced a higher standard of fire-resistant seat covers in July 1987.

The Manchester Inquiry found that: 'Access to the exits was dangerously restricted . . . existence of the twin forward bulkheads with only twenty-two and a half inches between effectively restricted passenger flow to a single file.' Extra seats had been put in to make a more profitable payload. There was only a ten-and-a-half-inch gap available between rows nine and ten to the overwing exit (which at last had been forced open by passengers).

Then, as far as the fighting of the fire was concerned, the efficacy of the immediate application of foam outside was found to be a 'fallacy'. In the course of the firemen's brave attempts at rescue, some of the hydrants ran dry and there was a delay in the arrival of the Greater Manchester City fire tender because of insufficient liaison, which left no police escort vehicle to accompany them.

Perhaps airlines should spend less on glossy advertising, and spend more money and imagination on investigating what might go wrong. Above all, they should learn from past experience. For accidents have a disastrous habit of repeating themselves, a habit made more sad because mourning relatives often comfort themselves with the belief that 'they' will immediately discover the cause and put it right so 'it can't ever happen again'.

But it does.

The Air Florida crash into Washington's 14th Street Bridge in January 1982 was an example. It happened in snowy conditions and was caused by ice-formation on engine thrust-sensing probes, resulting in false engine pressure ratio (EPR) gauge readings. Management by the airline in terms of crew assignment, dissemination of icing-effect information was called into question.

Yet only a month before, the accident had been foreshadowed by the Sterling Airways Boeing 727 incident at Gander, Newfoundland. The crew had again not used the engine anti-ice (EAI). The aircraft became airborne with the stickshaker operating, announcing an imminent stall. It struck threshold lights and nine sets of approach lights before staggering away. Once again the crew had not pushed the throttles hard forward because even in those dire straits they were not willing to exceed EPR limitations.

The EPR limitations are intended to extend the life of the

engines, and thus we come back to the potential enemy of safety, saving money. Boeing was asked if there was a thrust penalty associated with EAI. They replied that it was minimal – take-off field length would have been increased by only 80 feet and climb reduced by 35 feet a minute.

The Inquiry concluded that the accident was due, as in the Air Florida crash, to erroneous engine gauge readings caused by icing of the engine inlet pressure probes. The Inquiry also found that the EAI criteria in the Aircraft Operations Manual provided inadequate protection against P2 probe icing, that the crews had no direct way of knowing that the take-off acceleration was below normal until too late, and noted that the crew had not pushed the throttles hard forward.

A further fact was noted. As on the Air Florida flight, the crew had not pushed the throttles hard forward because even in those dire straits they were not willing to exceed EPR limitations – 'indicating,' as the Inquiry went on to say, 'a dangerous hesitancy to exceed perceived EPR limitations, *at the expense of the safety of the flight*'.

Most international airlines have safety officers who attend regular meetings, although there is evidence that safety staff are being cut down because of cost pressures. Management practices vary, some are very good, and the Manchester crash brought improvements.

But it is in Australia that managements appear to have achieved the best co-operation with their staff – a corollary of the Australian reputation for speaking their minds. A researcher called Gordon Redding has put Qantas's unrivalled safety record down to the PD factor – power distance, the extent to which the boss will allow you to dissent. He says that Australians argue with their superiors while at the same time respecting them. In other words, they have a low PD.

At the regular Qantas safety meetings, their cost-of-an-accident diagram is very much in the minds of all heads of departments. On the flight deck, strict operating discipline is maintained according to carefully laid-down rules, and they are the only airline management that I have heard affirm belief in the corporate mistake and the corporate responsibility.

Aviation earns billions of almost every currency, and to turn the old Yorkshire proverb on its head, 'where there's money, there's muck' – and a lively breeding ground for human error.

Eighteen

In the Echelons of Power

'Whoever heard of a politician
preaching the long view?'
John Galsworthy

Airlines are prestigious – the flag-fliers, the window-dressers of many countries, huge powerful companies with access to governments well versed in behind-the-scenes dealing. It follows therefore that the dread hand of politics is felt throughout aviation. And politicians, though powerful, are no less liable to human error than the rest of us – in fact, according to Norman Dixon, former Professor of Psychology at London University, rather more so. He paints a grim portrait of prototypical political leaders. Besides a strong narcissistic streak, 'they may bring to their high office a tendency towards absent-mindedness (through information overload) and risk-taking (through a predisposition towards boredom), residue of early traumatic experiences such as threat of castration and the Phaeton complex: a plethora of ego complexes such as those to please, keep up with the Joneses and boost self-esteem'.

For a leader needs a strong ego and a deep inner drive to get him or herself to the top. Having got there, he tends to surround himself with people of like mind so that the ego can be assiduously stroked. A pity, therefore, that those in charge of the safety of transport should so often be political appointments.

It is more than sixty years since the crash of the airship R101 on 5 October 1930 demonstrated the scenario of human errors and political interference, many of which still exist today. Not that these errors were permitted to be highlighted sufficiently at the time, but over the years they have emerged, and it is instructive to look at them from such a distant perspective and to see how they still survive. The findings of the Inquiry were that the forward gas bag had ruptured, causing substantial loss of gas in bumpy conditions, a loss compounded by a strong down-draught.

Despite the lavish expressions of public mourning, the special train draped in black bringing home the victims, the service in St Paul's, the lying-in-state at Westminster Hall, the Inquiry was a whitewash. And there was much to whitewash.

Sir John Simon, who appeared on behalf of the Crown, was a smooth and capable lawyer. The moving spirit behind the fatal flight to India was a member of the government, Brigadier-General the Right Honourable Lord Thomson, Secretary of State for Air and Viceroy of India designate. As Secretary of State for Air, he desperately needed to justify government expenditure on the state-owned R101, which the privately built R100 had just pipped at the post by making the first double crossing of the Atlantic. Thomson had been a soldier of great courage and a diplomat of distinction. During the Great War he had brought off the diplomatic coup of persuading the Romanian royal family to enter the war on the side of Britain, a matter of great strategic importance to the Allies.

While doing so, however, he had fallen in love with a Romanian princess. At forty-two he was unmarried, devoted to his elderly mother and had deeply romantic ideas about women. He cherished the notion that the new Viceroy would arrive in India on the maiden voyage of this aerial Leviathan, and would lay the vice-regal crown at his princess's feet. He took with him, along with his extensive luggage, crates of champagne, a large Persian carpet and his lady's silver slipper. With hindsight it is clear that he would not allow anyone to stand in the way of his dreams, and he viewed any delays over the R101 with mounting impatience.

The delays were many. For there were basic faults in R101's design which the designer and director of Airship Development refused to admit. The valves of her huge gas bags chattered, letting out the gas. There was chafing of the girders against the goldbeater skin of the bags. The year before, she had been found to be so heavy that she could only lift an inadequate thirty-five-ton payload. So she had been cut in half and an extra bag installed. And for all the holes that the chafing of the girders made, maintenance workers made 4,000 pads, and when the wind cut a tear 140 feet long in her outer skin, they did a quick-fix job with stitches and rubber solution.

This was seen by the author Nevil Shute, himself part of the rival private-enterprise R100 design team. He said the effect was to make 'the skin so flaky you could put your finger through it'. The aircraft inspector, Mr McWade, tired of having his reports ignored at Cardington, where the airship was built, wrote directly to the Air Ministry, but his letter was returned to his superiors at Cardington, and no action was taken by the Air Ministry.

The captain of R101, Flight Lieutenant 'Bird' Irwin, an ex-Olympic runner and pilot of great skill, similarly filed an adverse report after R101 had executed an unintentional deep curtsey over the royal box at Hendon Air Display. That too was ignored. The crews were aware of deficiencies, as were the maintenance staff, but it was a time of unemployment and many in Bedford depended for their livelihood on the airship project, in which they desperately wanted to believe.

On 1 October, opening the Imperial Conference, Prime Minister Ramsay MacDonald announced that the R101 was at the masthead awaiting air tests prior to her flight to India.

Bird Irwin had spent a considerable amount of time while R101 was in the hangar being refitted in working out a series of tests that he wanted before she embarked, including bad-weather trials. He was not to get them. Instead, on the same afternoon of the opening of the Imperial Conference, the giant dirigible took to the air in near perfect weather. Air Vice-

Marshal Dowding, now in charge of airships, was to give his approval. He had never been inside an airship and was unaware of the disquiet of the crew and some technicians. He spent part of the smooth, gentle journey asleep. There could be no high-speed trial because an air cooler failed and one of the Beardsmore engines had to be shut down. But on the strength of that trial, R101 was pronounced airworthy.

Captain Irwin had conveyed his deep disquiet to his wife, and had seriously considered refusing to go and resigning his short-service commission in the RAF. He knew that if he refused, his great friend, Squadron Leader Ralph Booth, who had com-manded the R100, would be asked to take it in his place. Could he rely on him to refuse also? Mrs Irwin and Mrs Booth discussed it together. But Ralph Booth, as his wife pointed out, held a permanent commission. He couldn't resign. If ordered to, he must obey or be court-martialled. Bird Irwin decided that he must go.

As for any further delay or any more tests, Lord Thomson himself immediately scotched that idea. He phoned Bird Irwin and accused him of being 'an obstructionist'.

He used the same technique on Sir Sefton Brancker, the Director of Civil Aviation who was to accompany the flight. Brancker had the effrontery to come into his office to tell him point-blank that Wing Commander Colmore, Director of Airship Development at Cardington, wanted more mooring masts *en route*, that R101 wasn't ready and that the flight should be postponed. He suggested that it was better to leave R101 at the mooring mast and let the delegates to the Commonwealth Conference come to see her, admire her and dine aboard.

Thomson's retort was, 'Of course, if you're afraid you need not come along.' Those words to a macho air pioneer were enough.

Other people besides Lord Thomson had their ambitions bound up with the flight to India. The designer, Colonel Richmond, and Wing Commander Colmore were expected to receive honours, while Major Scott, who had assisted with the

R100 flight, hoped for the long overdue K to put in front of his CBE.

Major Scott was another problem for Flight Lieutenant Irwin. Privately, Ralph Booth had confided to Irwin that Major Scott, though once an excellent airship pilot, had been a liability on the transatlantic flight, once running them headlong through a thunderstorm. Scott had resented being in an inferior position to Booth, so Irwin was determined to avoid the danger of divided command.

Officially, the captaincy was Irwin's, but Scott was his senior in rank, in experience and in the airship hierarchy. Both Scott and Irwin had separately seen the Cardington administrator on the question of command. Irwin was a first-class pilot. Scott was a very popular figure but somewhat over the hill. The administrator played it both ways. Of course Irwin was the captain. So what was Scott? Official-in-charge of the flight was too vague for him and not good enough. 'Passenger' was worse.

Scott made his complaint vociferously. The administrators and the press officer agreed a wily compromise. The first communiqué to be sent out to the world when R101 slipped the mast was drafted while Irwin and his crew were safely on board making their final checks. It read: 'Airship R101 left the mooring tower at Cardington at . . . hours GMT, 4th October on the first stage of her flight to India. The flight is being carried out under the direction of Major G. H. Scott, CBE, AFC, Assistant Director in charge of Airship Flying.'

On the day of the flight Scott, previously a passenger, appeared in uniform. Scott read the release and told the press officer that: 'It was entirely satisfactory and accurately represented his own view of his position.' But there was no time, as preparations for departure were proceeding, for the press officer to show the release to Irwin and speak to him on his position in relation to Major Scott.

On the afternoon of their departure, the Met Office issued a dismal report of an occluded front of cloud, increasing to ten-tenths and falling to 1,000 feet, with rain spreading from the west to reach Cardington that night. As the storm of rain was approaching them, Irwin must have seriously considered a delay, but Scott was rushing around like a bull in china shop shouting, 'For God's sake, let's get off! Where the hell are the passengers?'

Lord Thomson was one of the last to arrive. Although weight was severely restricted, Lord Thomson arrived with his valet and, as well as the champagne and Persian carpet, nine pieces of personal luggage, silver and napery and a specially fired Wedgwood dinner service to impress the King of Egypt. The crew, restricted to one change of uniform and underwear, a pith helmet and a tooth-brush and shaving-brush, were furious.

Fatally, because there was no room in the hold for all this baggage, the roll of carpet and the cases of champagne were stowed in the worst possible place – right in the nose.

It was only minutes before she departed that the Certificate of Airworthiness was delivered. When R101 slipped from the masthead, she almost immediately had to release ballast in order to gain height. Then, while torrential rain thundered on the envelope, she set a slow laboured course to France, where she crashed and exploded in flames on a ridge near Beauvais.

After that came the public and national expressions of grief. Perhaps we have now become used to disaster – and the R101 was one of the first of so many in the air. Perhaps, too, both government and people had an uneasy conscience that brave men were sent to their death through incompetence, tunnel vision and ambition. The relatives received little beyond the public display. Out of a fund to help dependants, one mother was given enough to buy a pair of spectacles.

Sixteen days after the lavish funeral the Inquiry opened, under the Presidency of Sir John Simon, and the spotlight immediately turned not on Scott, but on Flight Lieutenant Irwin. The influential *Flight* magazine said, 'an officer of the Royal Navy who loses his ship is, if he survives, court-martialled and we feel it right that it should be so. It may be that in the case of aircraft accidents we have been too squeamish.'

252 The Naked Pilot

Major Teed, a friend of Barnes Wallis, volunteered to appear for Mrs Irwin to protect Irwin's good name. He was needed for, mysteriously, vital documents showing Irwin's concern had vanished – including a manifold book of all his reports, including the carbon copies. There was nothing to be found about the last test flight, nor a report Irwin had written on the gas bags. Day after day Sir John complained about missing documents, and the newly appointed Solicitor General, Sir Stafford Cripps, echoed his astonishment. Although Irwin's report on the Hendon flight was allowed to come to light, and throughout the Inquiry Irwin was shown to have been correct, no mention was made in open court of Thomson's telephone call to him. And when the findings were promulgated, the cause was assessed as the bursting of the gas bag, bringing the nose too far down for the coxswain to control it. There was no criticism of Lord Thomson or the Air Ministry or the Royal Airship Works.

It is true that no criticism was levelled at Irwin either, but nor were his efforts praised, and the traditional implicit responsibility of the captain remained. To absolve him from this, the report would have had to state that the government in the person of Lord Thomson, the Secretary of State, with the acquiescence of the Air Ministry had assumed responsibility. Lord Thomson's name would have had to be impugned. Instead, a road at Shorts Town, Cardington, where many of the victims had lived, was named after him.

Sir John complimented himself and his assessors with the words, 'We have reached the truth without offending anyone', and he wrote to one of the assessors, Colonel Moore-Brabazon: 'My dear Brab, it has been great fun doing this with you. If only I could play golf as well as you, the world would be a pleasant place.'

Years later, Moore-Brabazon admitted that the assessors had never really arrived at the true cause of the R101 disaster. The Inquiry was by then regarded as a gigantic Whitehall whitewash to save the memory of Lord Thomson and protect the establishment. As Professor Dixon pointed out recently, 'maintaining the solidarity of a group may on occasion take precedence over the calls of justice and rationality'.

So how have things changed? Certainly the inquiries in most countries go deeper, have mostly sloughed off Sir John's desire to please, and have realised that the search for truth usually displeases many people. But political pressure and behind-the-scenes dealing continues.

The astonishing incident in 1983 when the Air Canada flight from Montreal to Edmonton ran out of fuel at 41,000 feet arose partly from political interference (Chapter 10).

Air Canada had been pressed to order its new Boeing 767s built to metric specifications – thus they weighed their fuel in kilograms while other aircraft in the Air Canada fleet went on weighing their fuel in pounds.

After the captain's and first officer's magnificent airmanship in bringing the powerless aircraft to a safe landing they received Certificates of Merit from the Canadian Air Line Pilots' Association, and Outstanding Airmanship Awards from the Fédération Aeronautique Internationale. From Air Canada there came an internal investigation. The company allotted the blame to the captain and first officer and to the two refuelling mechanics. They announced disciplinary procedures.

Pilots and mechanics fought through their respective unions. The Canadian press responded with tremendous support, and this was an occurrence that caught public imagination. The outcry was sufficient to force the Canadian government to hold an Independent Board of Inquiry.

When the Board issued its findings, the pilots and mechanics were more than exonerated – they were praised. The Board spoke of corporate and equipment deficiencies being overcome by the skill and professionalism of flight crew and flight attendants, which, the Board rightly reckoned, had averted a major disaster.

The Board cited the corporate deficiencies, naming the decision to introduce a new aircraft that weighed its fuel in kilograms while other aircraft still weighed their fuel in pounds:

'If Air Canada had been at all concerned about flight safety, it would have resisted pressure from any direction, including the government of Canada . . . and would have retained gauges in imperial pounds.' Failure to make clear the responsibility for fuel calculation, failure to train cockpit or ground crew to calculate fuel, and confusion in the Minimum Equipment List were cited amongst other deficiencies.

The Chairman of the Board then added: 'The evidence of a failure of communication at all levels of Air Canada is alarming. While this may in fact be a problem with all large corporations, it is of particular concern in an industry which is daily responsible for untold numbers of human lives.'

That is not the end, however. The errors continue. Without the influence of public opinion, the Board of Inquiry would perhaps not have been set up, and the two pilots and mechanics would have remained scapegoats, while dangerous practices and errors might well not have been addressed.

Public disquiet in Canada has had a further effect.

On 10 March 1989, Air Ontario Flight 363 from Thunder Bay to Winnipeg rolled down the runway at Dryden Airport, Ontario with sixty-five passengers and four crew aboard. It was cleared so to do by an air traffic controller eighty miles away in Kenora because Dryden does not possess a control tower of its own. Dryden is also subject to sudden changes of weather, especially in winter, which the controller on Kenora could not know about. A hot-line for this purpose had been discontinued the previous year.

It was snowing hard and the Fokker F-28 had acquired a heavy coating of snow on its upper surfaces.

Flight attendant Sonia Hartwick, the sole surviving crew member, said that take-off was 'very slow, very sluggish . . . without power . . . I sat there and stared at the wing. The snow was turning to ice and freezing on the wing. The fluffy layer of snow just crystallized. There was a sheen.'

Before take-off captain Morwood did not have the wings

de-iced, probably because of the logistics of so doing. After take-off, the iced F-28 skimmed a bluff west of the runway end and plunged into a dense wooded area, where it broke into three blazing pieces.

An Air Canada pilot among the passengers described how he had 'watched in horror' as the jet began its take-off roll. He said, 'I knew we were going to crash and I had my family aboard.' He went on to say that if he had known that the airliner did not have a working de-icing system he would have broken down the cockpit door.

Prior to the take-off, the aircraft had been hot-fuelled – that is, refuelled while the passengers were on board and with an engine running. The captain's logistic problem was Dryden having no ground equipment to start engines, and the auxiliary power unit on the aircraft having been unserviceable for several months. Another factor which may have influenced this decision was the familiar one of time pressure – the service was late.

Investigators arrived at Dryden on the day of the crash and began their inquiries according to procedures adopted by the Canadian Air Safety Board (CASB). On 28 March, after over a hundred people had been interviewed, the CASB investigation was suspended, because, it was said, of public controversy and anxiety about the Canadian Air Safety Board and the method of aircraft accident investigation. So, again, public opinion demanded action.

As a result a Commission of Inquiry was set up into the Dryden crash. The Commissioner reactivated the investigation, requesting that the original investigators be reassigned to it and that all their information be made available to the Commission.

Disturbing evidence emerged. Although Air Ontario had promised ground staff formal training in the de-icing of the F-28, they never received it. Sonia Hartwick gave evidence that there were other problems aboard the airliner. The handle on an emergency door had to be taped to hold it in the locked position, and the lights on two exit signs didn't work. She said that after saying that there had been ice on the F-28's wings she was

told to keep her mouth shut, 'and if anybody asks you anything
. . . just say you don't feel you are capable of talking about it at
the moment'.

It was reported that the previous year a federal review of Air
Ontario had found sloppy maintenance and poor record-
keeping, and the airline was ordered to improve. And on the very
day of the crash, Dryden Airport officials were told by the
Federal Transport Department that their disaster and emergency
procedure manual was inadequate; this is the bible for co-
ordinating fire, police and ambulance services at the scene of any
crash.

The Federal Transport Department was immediately proved
right. Although the burning wreck was only just over a hundred
yards from a road and the nearest firetruck, it was two hours
before a hose could be brought to the plane. By this time the
inferno had melted the flight-recorder tapes. There was a
communications mix-up which resulted in the fire chief at the
scene being out of radio contact with his superior. Nor did
airport fire and rescue crews have crucial 'crash rescue charts'
showing the aircraft's emergency exits, the best routes for rescue
and the location of fuel tanks and oxygen bottles which might
explode.

It was alleged that Transport Canada had been trying for
years to cut the airport's fire-rescue service by half, and that
federal money intended for training fire-fighters was not spent
on training. It was also alleged that, although emergency crews
had access to the necessary expertise and equipment for training,
they simply didn't want to train. An emergency services
specialist said, 'It was an attitude problem as opposed to a skill
or knowledge problem.'

The same old attitude of not wanting to know. And when
those ill-trained, unprepared fire-fighters reached the scene, they
were 'distracted to a man' by the horrors that confronted them.

Four months later, the Commissioner submitted interim
recommendations to the Minister of Transport. The first was
that 'hot-fuelling' should be prohibited. The second was that an

Air Navigation Order be promulgated prohibiting take-offs when any frost, snow or ice is adhering to the lifting surfaces of the aircraft. The third was that the Department of Transport should develop and implement a mandatory education programme for all aircrew on the effects of ice.

The Commissioner quoted John H. Enders, the former Manager of Flight Safety at NASA and President of the US Flight Safety Foundation, who spoke during the 1988 conference on icing. Enders had cited data showing that the fatal accident rate per million departures over the past decade is approximately the same for take-off icing accidents as it is for windshear accidents. Much had been achieved by education to overcome the windshear hazard, so icing merited an equally extensive education programme. It seems incredible that it had not received it, in that the danger of ice was recognised decades before windshear, while icing accidents continue with a relentless similarity.

The interim report contained a further, and what might be far-reaching, recommendation that in the event of a member of the cabin crew, based upon his or her observation, reporting a concern regarding wing contamination to the pilot in command, it shall be the duty of the pilot in command to check the wing condition, either personally or via another member of the cockpit crew before take-off.

The commission had heard a poignant plea from Sonia Hartwick for a mandatory joint training programme related to aircraft-wing contamination for members of both cockpit and cabin crews. She expressed concern that some airline pilots fail to recognise the fact that flight attendants are primarily on board an aircraft to ensure the safety of the passengers. Many airline managements also fail to recognise this fact. Too much time and advertising are spent in projecting the stewardess as a sex symbol. Make-up and grooming, how to walk gracefully and how to pamper the first-class passengers take too much precedence over safety.

In the Ontario Inquiry the Commissioner called on the Department of Transport to implement a mandatory self-

awareness programme for all personnel involved in flight
operations. If this is implemented, perhaps other governments
will follow suit.

The Inquiry has yet to find on the evidence about government,
management and rescue errors.

Other political hazards await the pilot. Governments are adept
at finding scapegoats to avoid blame, but pilots may find
themselves subject to laws and procedures more draconian than
their own.

In 1968, a B-727 on a scheduled flight for Civil Air Transport
of Taiwan and piloted by two Americans, Captain Hicks and
Captain Drew, crashed in bad weather while making an ILS
approach to Taipei Airport. Captain Hicks's wife was among
the fifteen people killed. Although IFALPA subsequently sub-
stantiated their claims that there had been malfunctioning of the
ILS, both pilots were charged with manslaughter and had their
licences revoked. Only IFALPA's threat to call a ban on all
international flights to Taiwan caused that government to
change its mind.

Similarly, two Swissair pilots whose DC-8 overran a slippery
runway at Athens, fell into a road trench and burst into flames,
were subsequently found guilty of manslaughter and negligence.
Despite IFALPA's strenuous efforts, despite complaints about
the danger of the trench which turned a survivable accident into
a fatal one, despite the slippery rubber on the runway and
Athens' non-standard lighting system, the pilots were
imprisoned.

As with West Germany's attitude regarding the Munich
accident, the Greek government did not wish to have its facilities
blamed. The truth, meanwhile, is disregarded as countries
engage in 'groupthink'. So with other inquiries where, though
the pilot is not criminally charged, there is international haggling
about accepting blame, and countries dissatisfied with the
results of inquiries held by other contries in the territory where
the accident occurred submit their own findings. So it was after

the Tenerife collision, the government of the Netherlands declared that the accident had been caused by the failure of the Pan Am B-747 to get off the runway, and in the case of the Dan Air crash in 1980 (Chapter 4) the British government submitted its own version of events.

Yet international protection is needed for pilots, and international regulations for safety. It is the narrow, tunnel-visioned money-orientated interference that is so disastrous.

Political interference was the underlying factor in the explosions of the second and third Comets. Government policy (widely believed to be Winston Churchill's directive) decreed that even before the cause of the first Comet explosion (Yoke Victor) on 2 May 1953 at Jangipara had been found, the Comets should continue flying. As a result, on 10 January 1954, BOAC's Yoke Peter exploded over Elba and the Navy began looking for the pieces in the sea. But so many orders were riding on the wonder-jet that the government wouldn't wait and the Comets still continued to fly. On 8 April 1954, the *third* Comet, Yoke Yoke, exploded over the Bay of Naples. Only then were the Comets removed from service until the cause was found. After an extensive and brilliant investigation, this proved to be metal fatigue producing explosive decompression.

It is only right to add that after such disasters as the take-off and metal fatigue accidents, de Havilland courageously pressed forward and produced the excellent Comet IV that began the world's first scheduled jet service across the Atlantic on 4 October 1958 and did sterling service in world airlines for many years.

The dangers of 'groupthink' have been analysed by the psychologist Janis. Among the dangers especially relevant to the politics of civil aviation are collective efforts to rationalise in order to discount warnings, a shared illusion of unanimity and a tendency to protect the group from adverse information. All these tendencies were seen at work in the political and managerial influence on the crew of the R101, and they are seen in the case of Captain Thain.

On 6 February 1958, Captain Thain attempted to take his twin-engined Elizabethan off the runway at Munich. The runway was slush-covered. Canada and KLM had already circulated airlines on the danger of slush, but BEA had taken no notice.

The aircraft failed to accelerate and the take-off was abandoned. The aircraft careered off the runway, struck a house, broke up and caught fire. Because the Manchester United football team were aboard, and several of them were among the victims, there was much publicity. The press was full of possible causes. The chief executive of BEA flew to the scene, and on his return made a statement to the effect that the house should not have been there.

The West Germans immediately countered by issuing a statement that the accident was 'possibly the result of ice on the wings, and the captain had not given a satisfactory explanation of why he did not discontinue the attempt to take off'.

Captain Thain was held to be responsible. He had already been suspended. BALPA took the matter up, and further incidents on slush-covered runways came to light.

In 1960, Captain Thain obtained a British Court of Inquiry, but it was given only limited terms of reference lest it offend the Germans. The findings were ambivalent, yet Thain's airline transport pilot's licence was taken away and he was sacked by BEA. Six months later, the Ministry of Aviation published a paper on slush.

For years IFALPA, BALPA, Captain Thain and his wife, who was a scientist, struggled to identify the culprit as slush on the runway. His wife did her own experiments. Meanwhile, slush trials were carried out in America which confirmed the inhibiting effect of slush on take-off.

In April 1968, there was another British Commission, which cleared Captain Thain of all blame. However, in spite of vital evidence being shown to have been suppressed by the German Inquiry, the Germans repeatedly refused to reopen the case. Therefore, the 'pilot error' verdict on Thain stood, and still stands today, as it does on Captain Foote.

After his ordeal, Captain Foote had written: 'A pilot, not in a position to defend himself, had been used as a public scapegoat. This has happened again at Karachi since the accident in question and will no doubt continue.'

Like Harry Foote, James Thain was worn out by his struggles against authority. Like Foote, he died of a heart attack. His age was fifty-four. There is an old saying in flying circles: 'If the accident doesn't kill the pilot, the Inquiry will.'

A British aircraft accident inquiry used to bear too close a resemblance to a court of law. A QC was Commissioner and he was assisted by two Assessors, one an expert on the engineering side, the other an experienced pilot. When Geoffrey Lane, now the Lord Chief Justice, was appointed to the 1972 Staines Trident Inquiry, here at least was a Commissioner who had been a pilot. He was in the RAF on the same twin-engined flying course as myself during the Second World War. We shared the same hut at Bibury during our night-flying training on Oxfords over the Cotswolds. I sent him a copy of *The Human Factors in Aircraft Accidents*. His Report indicated not one but twelve salient factors in the cause of the accident.

In the UK, aircraft accidents and their causes are the responsibility of the Air Accident Investigation Branch, which unlike the CAA is under the Ministry of Transport but by its terms of reference is largely independent. The NTSB is very outspoken vis-à-vis the FAA, and sometimes they are in an uneasy partnership not experienced (at least at present!) in relations between the AAIB and the CAA.

Inquiries are expensive and can show government inadequacies. The report on the August 1989 sinking of the *Marchioness* in the Thames with the loss of fifty-one lives says that the Department of Transport was aware of the risk six years before the collision. An MP cited it as witness of 'failure on the part of the government over a considerable number of years', and a survivor said, 'The reason why Parkinson, the Secretary of State for Transport, never wanted a public inquiry is that the report is so damning of the Department.'

Although the Secretary of State for Transport can call one if he thinks it necessary, the Staines Inquiry was the last public inquiry into an aircraft accident. That has not been so much a desire to avoid one as a demonstration of confidence by government and the public in the competence and integrity of the Air Accident Investigation Branch (AAIB), which has an enviable worldwide reputation.

After considerable research, the Inspector circulates a draft report to all interested parties for their comments. Anyone or any organisation can call for a review if they think they have been unfairly treated, but all potentially dangerous findings are immediately relayed world-wide. Quite apart from the field work, which can be up mountains, in jungles or trying to salvage wreckage from the bottom of the sea, draft reports have to be produced which are circulated to manufacturers and operators whose goods or services might be considered a cause of the accident. Their comments in response have to be scrutinised. Inevitably arguments arise. With millions of pounds sometimes at stake, the pressures on the investigator are considerable. Evidence is sometimes difficult to obtain and investigators have to argue with coroners for its release.

Two further areas of investigation have now come into their orbit. In 1977, a US Committee of Public Works and Transport called airline-passenger education 'the missing link in air safety'. According to them, 30 per cent more passengers could be saved from fatal crashes, so the AAIB has now turned its attention to surviveability and a Survival Studies Group meets regularly.

After the recent widely publicised sea and rail disaster reports the AAIB are investigating 'management factors'. The difficulties in tracing managerial decisions are immense. Who took what decision and when? Errors in the system are buried deep. This extra time needed to assess management factors will inevitably be added to the already much criticised length of time it takes for aircraft accident reports to appear. Already, because maximum agreement between participating bodies has to be achieved before they do so, accident reports take far too long.

The final report on the Manchester disaster took three and a half years to appear and contained thirty-one recommendations. These included the need to position an aircraft on the ground with the fire downwind of the fuselage, the provision of a device whereby the crew could obtain an external view of the aircraft, the provision of an evacuation alarm, a mandatory international code of practice for promulgating manufacturers' safety information, the removal of all 'row ten' seats to facilitate overwing exit, the distribution of the most experienced cabin crew throughout the cabin, a more management-orientated approach for fire officers with the chief wearing high-visibility clothing, the introduction of on-board fire-extinguishing systems, the provision of smoke-hoods for passengers, a recommendation that cabin furnishing materials should have limitations on smoke and other toxic emissions, and the provision of audio-attract devices to guide passengers deprived of sight and hearing to viable exits.

It is easy to be wise after the event, but why hadn't the need for some of these safety provisions been envisaged earlier? The CAA accepted almost all these recommendations and started extensive research into implementing them. The recommendation of an external device to give pilots a view of the engines was to be implemented either by a mirror or closed-circuit television. The latter was considered more effective and arrangements were made with a manufacturer. However, other manufacturers also wanted to bid for what would be a valuable contract, so the CAA had to put the project out to tender.

Had closed-circuit television been in operation or, possibly as an interim measure, had a mirror been fitted, it is unlikely that the crew would have shut down the wrong engine in the Kegworth accident.

In Australia, there is no requirement for the Bureau of Air Safety Investigation (which is independent of government) to circulate provisional findings amongst those involved. The Bureau publishes and then awaits reactions. As a result, final reports are generally in circulation three months after an accident, but arguments over the possible responsibility of interested parties then take place and may take a long time to resolve.

In his last review of RAF accident investigation, Bill Tench recommended that there should be a tri-service (RAF, Navy and Army) accident investigation branch – but this was turned down. However, his recommendation prompts the question – why are there so many little cells of accident investigation when the main cause of accidents, wherever they happen, are human factors. These are common to air, roads, railways, sea, factories, power stations – in fact everywhere that human beings operate.

Investigation of accidents at sea used to have a low profile. In the Department of Transport's hierarchy 'tree', accident investigation came right at the bottom, far away from the Secretary of State's 'control room'. Accidents were usually investigated locally by a master mariner, an engineering surveyor and a naval architect. Their report was not published, so few people could learn from it. Only rarely was there a public inquiry. Then came the *Herald of Free Enterprise* tragedy, when the cross-Channel ferry moved away from the dock at Zeebrugge with its bow doors open.

After that accident, and *only then*, the Marine Accident Investigation Branch was created. The central office is located within a hundred yards of the Titanic Memorial in Southampton which is a poignant tribute to the ship's engineers who stayed at their posts after a human factor error (time pressure to win the Atlantic Blue Riband) had caused the collision with the iceberg that sank her. Progress as usual followed disaster. A new Department of Transport 'tree' was produced. From being bottom, the Investigation Branch was now promoted in the batting order to be above Ministers and the Permanent Secretary, on a level with the Secretary of State.

The railways for some reason have a tradition whereby accidents usually appear to be investigated by retired Army officers. These are nearly all collisions caused by signal failures or by going through red lights, or derailments caused by going too fast. In this highly technical age, devices eliminating such human factor errors should surely before now have been invented and applied.

Road accidents are investigated by the Road Research Laboratory at Bracknell, which has its own psychologists. There are so many road accidents that statistics rather than reports are issued. It is generally accepted that these are chiefly caused by aggressiveness, fatigue, time pressure and drunkenness – all human factors.

Each accident investigation department should keep in touch and learn from each other. Because of his training, had he been the captain of the *Herald of Free Enterprise*, no airline pilot would have dreamt of moving away without reassurance from a status light and human reassurance from a crew member that the doors were shut and locked. Similarly, in transfer from sea to air, the knowledge that over decades 'radar-assisted collisions' (that is their technical term) are repeatedly a common cause of ship accidents might have been a warning to aircraft manufacturers and airlines of the dangers inherent in trusting, interpreting and relying on machines.

Knowledge of human factors advances far more slowly than technology itself. New evidence is always coming to light, and so often we find the wrong culprit has been identified. As with criminal convictions – the Christie murder where the wrong man, Timothy Evans, was hanged, the Birmingham Six, the Guildford Four imprisonment – gross miscarriages of aviation justice continue. A Chief Inspector of Accidents once called for the past files of aircraft accidents and began reviewing them. The first file he looked at called, in his opinion, for further investigation. So did the second. So did the third. Others called for the same further attention, so he sent them all back and called for no more. The task of taking them all up again would have been Herculean, for both him and the Investigation Branch.

There was at one time in Britain an independent Director of Flight Safety, but that was abolished by the CAA. Bill Tench says that the suspicion is that 'it was an economy measure'. 'The only way,' he adds, 'that a positive step forward in the pursuit of air safety can be made is by reinstating the office with a dynamic and imaginative Director of Flight Safety.'

Why not extend his further recommendation of a tri-service investigation branch into an independent Department of Safety for all modes of transport equipped with specialists in all aspects of accidents, since the human factor elements are similar in all types?

The CAA has the same duty of regulating civil aviation in the UK as the FAA does in the USA, and Tench believes it is vital that the accident investigation authorities like the NTSB and the AAIB are totally independent of the big organisations that regulate the industry. The CAA has been criticised as trying to avoid controversy, and the FAA has been accused of being in the pocket of the aviation industry – it has nearly two hundred outstanding claims of 'negligent certification' against it.

Japan has been criticised for having the accident investigation branch and the regulating branch practically in bed with each other, and the authorities appear much too ready to blame the pilot. Japanese culture discourages criticism of the boss and encourages humiliating acquiescence in accepting blame.

In developing countries, top aviation managers are often political appointees. Air accident investigators are sometimes part-time or even non-existent. These countries suffer from huge financial problems. There are reports of bribes and wholesale corruption and inadequate maintenance. At the same time, these airlines are trying to compete and pursue growth.

So will the Eastern bloc airlines, now that the Iron Curtain has come down. They will have acute financial problems, but will be doing everything they can to take a bigger share of international air traffic.

When 1992 brings deregulation to Europe, these problems will loom larger and nearer. And what happened in America may well happen here. In effect, deregulation has made it almost as simple for anyone in America to try to run an airline as to run the village bus. This has led to fierce commercial competition and more motives for additional economies. Furthermore, a philosophy of 'let industry do it' tends to work against formalised safety programmes. If the government's safety posture is weak, industry's will also be weak.

The Reagan administration had the declared intention of getting the government 'off the people's back'. Its budget for controlling aviation was cut. Yet there was a surplus running to billions of dollars from aviation taxes.

New airlines are setting lower standards for professionalism and experience. To economise, some of the big established airlines are making their more experienced pilots redundant. As big airlines strain to be more competitive and smaller ones struggle to survive, financial nudging may dictate a further lowering of safety standards.

In American cost-benefit analysis there is a cool algebraic sum. The cost of a human life is reckoned to be x dollars. In deciding if a new regulation shall be allowed, the Department of Transportation requires that the savings must exceed the costs expected. The expected number of lives saved multiplied by x must exceed the outlay on the safety equipment.

Another hazard of American deregulation is that airlines have been more free to set arrival and departure schedules which reflect public preference. This results in more aircraft departing and arriving at peak times, with more danger of collision and more strain on ground services.

Equally dangerously has come about the policy of 'pilot pushing', whereby managements lean on pilots to make marginal flights and compromise safety, and, with the increase in fuel prices, the policy of fuel conservation.

Economics were at the heart of the two- versus three-man crew debate, during the certification of the B-767/757 as two-pilot aircraft, which reached a climax in 1979 with the production of the McDonnell-Douglas MD-80, which McDonnell-Douglas needed to market as a two-pilot aircraft. Into the debate stepped Ronald Reagan, eager to make political headway before the Presidential election. He promised, if elected, a Presidential Task Force on Aircraft Crew Complement. This was duly empanelled in 1981. The Task Force upheld the FAA's certification of the two-pilot Super 80. But it went further. To the delight of Boeing and others, it decided that future aircraft, including wide-bodied jets, could be designed and certificated for two pilots.

The debate continues, and various pilot groups object. The results of the Presidential Task Force may be a long time in making themselves apparent.

Swifter in its result was the mishandling by Ronald Reagan and his aides of the KAL 007 shoot-down (Chapter 12). It happened in 1983, well before the thaw in the Cold War, and at a time when certain advisers were reluctant for Mr Shultz to meet with the Russians in Madrid.

At first, the President's advisers kept him in ignorance of the fate of the Boeing 747 and the Korean and American nationals aboard it. Officials at Misawa listening post had observed the demise of the 747 without being able to identify it, but had sent a Criticom (a top-priority signal) of the occurrence to Washington. Then things happened quickly. Another listening post found out that a B-747 was missing, and then a plane landed at Misawa with tapes of the Russian fighter's radio conversations on the shoot-down. It became clear that the Russians had regarded the B-747 as a suspicious intruder and the presence of the Cobraball in the area at almost the same time had been of critical significance.

Washington went to ground. The National Security Council cancelled all Criticoms and said the news was 'Not enough to wake the President.'

Nineteen

The Knock-On Effect

When the President did wake and he and his men got their heads together, all hell broke loose.

The politicians pressed for a confrontation with the Russians. There were demonstrations against the Russians in America. There was an international outcry. The Canadians were the first to cancel Aeroflot flights into their country. President Reagan closed Aeroflot offices in New York and Washington and a sixty-day ban was called for on all flights to Russia.

The American politicians could not understand how a B-747 could be mistaken for a B-707. Although the American generals declared that it was an isolated incident, President Reagan denounced the shoot-down as 'an act of barbarism by a nation that wants to dominate the world'.

The Russians, who, it later transpired, had displayed a whole catalogue of human error, indecision, incompetence, tunnel vision and conformity (flurried consultation of rule books and reference to higher authority) in their dealing with the intruder, still stuck to the theory that KAL 007 was spying.

It was left to a refuelling pilot and Major X, one of the officers at the Pentagon, to let in a breath of reason and sanity. They pointed out that at night a B-747 could easily have been mistaken for a B-707. In fact, the refuelling pilot said, he himself had on occasion come within an ace of making that same mistake. The idea that the shoot-down was deliberate was, Major X said, in Granada's *Coded Hostile* 'a fairy tale', adding: 'They want to make out man is an animal.'

So he is, but the word should not be used in a pejorative sense. And in the circumstances, he is a very naked one.

The sorry tale of denial, indignation and accusation continued. Both sides, having made considerable errors, refused to admit that the other side could make a genuine human error.

There is another human factor relevant to this disaster which affects the echelons of politics and to which the Russians are especially prone – the acute sensitivity to the guarding of territory.

Mankind is a species with a fixed home base and a highly developed territorial instinct. Now, in the age of technology, man's methods of marking and defending his territory exceed in sheer nastiness those of any of the so-called lower orders. We do not urinate on bushes, or have a specially adapted tail to scatter our faeces. We have rockets and nuclear bombs for our trigger-happy fingers. Sensitivity to our territorial instinct is heightened, not lessened, by them.

The finger of the naked pilot in the cockpit is also the finger on the nuclear button, as the 007 tragedy so starkly demonstrated. A terrible tragedy could have become a global one. It is more than likely that a simple human error will one day, unless we study the whole vast subject thoroughly, cause the end of the world.

Within a few days the heat died down. It began to be tacitly assumed that the Russians had, in fact, made a human error. But President Reagan did not rescind his 'barbarous act' speech, and Major X was reportedly found by his superior officers not to be the sort of guy they wanted around.

Eventually, however, and inevitably, human error manifested itself again, this time on the other side of the Curtain. And this time in the even more dangerous circumstances of the Iran/Iraq War and America's patrolling of the waters.

On Sunday morning, 3 July 1988, an Iran Airbus 300 took off from Bandar Abbas on the delayed shuttle service to Dubai. In command was Captain Mohsen Rezaian, an experienced Airbus pilot who had flown this particular short route dozens of times.

He was also well aware of the necessity of staying within the twenty-mile commercial airway over the Gulf, code-named Amber 29. Like any other pilot, he had no desire to go anywhere near the American warships. And before take-off, the aircraft's transponder had been activated to identify it on any radar as a passenger flight Iran Air 655.

Many of the passengers were on a shopping spree, and there was no reason to expect trouble, but down below on the waters of the Gulf, trouble was always expected. Often with good reason. American ships, bases, embassies and personnel had been the subject of attack the world over. And, this being the weekend of American Independence Day, it was especially emotive to the US Navy men serving abroad, and also a time when those who bore the USA ill-will would find it especially pertinent to attack.

Almost in the middle of the waters below airway Amber 29 lay one of the latest, most powerful warships, the *Vincennes*, and its captain, Will Rogers, had other reasons to develop a 'set', and expectation of trouble. He had been given a warning that Iran might stage an attack, and had received a report that American-made F-14 fighters were being deployed by Iran in the area.

Earlier that morning, operators in the *Vincennes*'s sophisticated control-room had been monitoring gun-boats near a convoy of merchantmen negotiating the Gulf of Hormuz. When the *Vincennes* had sent up a helicopter to take a look, the gun-boats had turned on a Norwegian tanker and then opened fire on the helicopters. The *Vincennes* and another American warship replied with fire on the gun-boats and sank two of them. So blood had already been drawn.

Captain Rogers had yet another reason to reinforce his expectation of trouble. A fellow captain, the commander of the USS *Stark*, had been court-martialled and held responsible when he had allowed an Iraqi jet, seemingly friend rather than foe, to approach and fire two Exocet missiles, resulting in the loss of thirty-seven American lives. Captain Rogers must have been very conscious that he must not be found wanting. Not just the safety of the ship, but his own self-image and esteem were at stake.

When, a few minutes after it took off, Flight 655 appeared on the *Vincennes*'s radar screens, it was immediately under suspicion. The blip seemed to be heading fast for the *Vincennes*, and for all its sophistication the *Vincennes*'s Aegis radar could not identify the type of plane, nor if it were an enemy. But one thing was clear: it was approaching fast. The *Vincennes* had only minutes to decide what action to take.

On the flight deck at that time, the captain of Flight 655 was talking to air traffic control, requesting a climb from 7,000 to 14,000 feet. Yet to the watchers on *Vincennes*, the aircraft appeared to be descending. This was later admitted to be a 'misinterpretation'. They hastily consulted an airline timetable but could not find a flight for that time. And the transponder did not help them distinguish friend from foe. The apparition on the radar screen was declared hostile. Yet the crew of the *Vincennes* apparently had the facility to listen in to civilian air traffic control. Had they done so, they would have found out that it was an Airbus. They did not do so because a 'set' had been formed: mental processes had been narrowed by stress and time pressure and the seeing, even on a radar screen, of what they expected to see.

Having declared it hostile, Captain Rogers, like his Russian counterparts, sought advice from higher authority – in this case the US Joint Task Force Commander, Rear Admiral Anthony Less, at that time on his flagship in the Gulf.

Rogers was told to decide for himself.

He decided in the same way that the Russians decided with regard to the Flight 007 intrusion. With the aircraft less than a minute's flying time from his ship, he ordered the firing of two surface-to-air Standard missiles.

Only one was needed. The aircraft exploded.

This time the President was allowed to sleep for only another two hours. Just before five, he was awakened by his National Security Adviser. The full weight of the unhappy truth was not at that time known. The President was told that an F-14 had been shot down by an American warship in the Gulf. It was another three hours before the President was told that it was a civilian airliner. This, ironically, he had to announce at lunchtime on Independence Day.

Then as with the Korean shoot-down, meetings were hastily covened. Damage limitation was the order of the day. Like the Russians, the Americans at first said, as the Russians had about KAL 007, that the Airbus was deliberately courting trouble. That it was human error was undeniable – 'set' – expectation, seeing what you expect to see, narrowing mental processes, the ego and the macho image.

The US Department admitted that crew-error on board the US *Vincennes* might have contributed, but it said the mistakes were 'not crucial'. The Department did not examine its own mistakes.

'Iran,' said the President's spokesman, Mr Carlucci, 'had to take its share of the blame.' He admitted that the tracking crew had misinterpreted climbing as descending, and that the aircraft had been on the civilian airway. Afterwards, he tied it all up neatly with the words: 'This tragic accident was ultimately the result of a conflict between Iran and Iraq.'

Quite rightly, the American study of the incident had concentrated on 'the context', the 'four-minute time span for a decision', the battle with the Iranian gunboats, and the 'earlier attack on the USS *Stark*'. But the buck-passing after an incident is counter-productive. Errors *are* made, and they should be examined and analysed.

For other errors take place further up the hierarchy: the building up of hostility; the image, as with 007, that the enemy is an animal; the creation of a situation where it is all too easy for the trigger to pull the finger – this exacerbated by the paranoid reaction of the politicians on both sides.

There is also the possible criticism that the *Vincennes*, for all her fire-power and sopistication and size (indeed, *because* of her size), was ill-equipped for the Gulf duties assigned to her; that she was designed for open-seas conflict, and therefore needed to attack first; and that her radar could not tell the difference between a civil airliner and an F-14.

Of course, the greatest error of all is insufficient study of the dangerous human factors that drive the finger on the explosive button, and the errors in the system which make that button explosive.

International acts of terrorism spawn others. Revenge is a powerful human drive. Was the bomb that exploded in the Pan Am 747 over Lockerbie a knock-on effect of the shooting-down of the Airbus by the *Vincennes*? And was the shooting-down of the Airbus the knock-on effect of the international paranoia over the shooting-down of KAL 007?

As has been shown, throughout the organisation of an airline, human error surfaces not just among its operating crew, but in operational and commercial management, in political wheeling and dealing, in aircraft design and maintenance and in the protection of passengers from terrorist attack.

Before the end of the Second World War, the acute vulnerability of aircraft was recognised, but international action against terrorism was slow to be addressed and is now bedevilled by governments who from time to time indulge in the odd spot of terrorism themselves. Thus a hideous chain reaction can begin. Even now, ten years on, it is again being asked if the DC-9 aircraft that exploded between Rome and Palermo was downed on the orders of the Italian government itself, and if so, why?

Aircraft are larger and in many ways more vulnerable to attack than they used to be. Explosives are more sophisticated and harder to detect. And where there is prey in the shape of what a terrorist would regard as a propaganda coup, there will be predators. Nevertheless, airlines and airport security staff are aware of the danger, and although I do not propose to study terrorism in this book, the questions should be asked. Are they sufficiently trained, equipped and alert? And what of all the hidden international security services? Those faceless people answerable to no democratic process – how are human failings monitored in them?

Many of these issues are now tragically being brought home. Inquiries are being demanded, suits are being filed in an attempt to unravel the ins and outs, the blunders, the international wheeling and dealing, and spying and counter-spying, the rivalries and stupidities that led to the loss of 270 innocent lives.

The date of 21 December 1988, when the Pan Am jet from Frankfurt to the USA via Heathrow was blown up over Lockerbie, is ground into most people's minds. Ever since then the argument has raged.

Almost a fortnight earlier an FAA security bulletin warned that a Pan Am jet from Frankfurt to the USA would be a terrorist target within the next two weeks. Reportedly, the warning was passed to Paul Channon, the then Minister of Transport, but he told the House of Commons early in January that he had not passed on the warning to Heathrow because the FAA had told him that it lacked 'credibility'. And although the Frankfurt jet story was later attributed to a jealous husband, there are only two services a day from Frankfurt to the USA via Heathrow, so could the baggage not have been thoroughly examined, just in case? The FAA did at one time regard it as credible enough to warn the US Embassy staff.

There had been other warnings, one of which was particularly significant. On 18 November, Pan Am in common with all other US airlines was warned by the US Federal Aviation Authority to look out for a new type of bomb which could be concealed in a certain type of radio-cassette player. The actual make was specified.

Two months before, in the famous operation 'Autumn Leaves', West German police had raided a property connected with an Arab terrorist group, and found a fully constructed bomb together with a half-made one. It consisted of Semtex plastic explosive and a barometric pressure detonating-device concealed in a Toshiba Bombeat Model 453 radio-cassette player. This device and others found in other raids was put on show to journalists. The press gave it wide publicity, emphasising the significance to air safety.

BKA (the German Federal Office for Criminal Investigation) held a conference a few days later, inviting all interested countries. British representatives attended and information and photographs of the bomb were handed out. Four days later, the Department of Transport informed British airports and airlines of the cassette-player bomb. On 19 December, just two days before the Lockerbie outrage, they distributed more details and German pictures of the bomb that showed the actual mechanism. The FAA had the same information, but Pan Am stated that they relied on receiving it from the British authorities 'as a courtesy'. It arrived at the airline's London office by post on 17 January, three weeks after the crash.

It would seem that if all the baggage were X-rayed, and an alert operator knew what he or she were looking for, the radio-cassette might well have been discovered. Instead, an hour and a half out of London, without warning and with the sending of a Mayday call, Pan Am flight 103 disappeared from the radar screens, wreckage from the aircraft devastating the village of Lockerbie below.

After the heroism of the rescuers, there have followed buck-passing, rumour and accusations, and ominous evidence of international manipulation and cover-ups. Many strange details have emerged, such as the fact that BKA arrested known terrorists as far back as October and then released them, supposedly to protect a Jordanian who was a double agent. There is a theory that Ahmed Jebril of the Popular Front for the Liberation of Palestine was behind this cell, that he was sponsored by Syria, that the German police raid upset the plans to bomb an aircraft, but that then some other terrorist group moved in on the project.

It later emerged that several CIA men were aboard the fateful flight, and there is speculation that their presence was connected with hostage-release negotiations. There was, witnesses said, suspicious activity in Frankfurt around the baggage-loading area, and it was suggested that this was overlooked or ignored because surveillance of a drug-dealing network was going on. A

Turkish bomb-maker was held at one time to be the culprit. There is also the account of a white helicopter that landed on a farmer's field close to Lockerbie, the pilot of which took away a suitcase that had survived the wreck.

Another newspaper-publicised theory involves an Arab who was supposed to have bought a random variety of clothing in a back street in Sliema, on the outskirts of Valetta in Malta. Gallant Malta, GC has always had a very significant but uneasy role between east and west, and these days its eyes have tended not to turn westward. In some quarters it has been said to be sympathetic to Libya, and anyone carrying a bomb or explosive device might have hoped for less stringent searches than at a major airport. However, it has been shown that Malta's security, passenger and luggage handling were exemplary. The Arab in question was suspected of being an associate of two secret agents who were arrested in Senegal and who were in possession of detonators identical to those believed to have been used to destroy Flight 103.

The theory was that a bomb was made in Germany and brought to Malta by a well-known terrorist, where it was packed into a suitcase among the clothing bought in Sliema. The supposed Arab checked in and boarded a flight from Malta to Frankfurt on the morning of 21 December 1988. No passenger from Malta boarded Pan American 747 Flight 103. But when, eleven hours after the flight left Malta, the 747 exploded over Lockerbie, pieces of torn and burned clothing purchased in Malta were said to have been found among the wreckage. Over two years after the disaster, new theories on who was behind the outrage are constantly being produced, and while there are numerous suspects, the assassins have still not been named.

Suspicion for master-minding the bombing switched from Ahmed Jebril's Popular Front for the Liberation of Palestine to Syria, then to America's arch enemy, Colonel Gaddafi himself, seeking revenge for the American bombing that killed his adopted daughter. A fax has reportedly come to light, originating in the Libyan interests section of the Saudi Arabian Embassy in London, which speaks of revenge achieved. But was it for the shooting-down of the Airbus or for the bombing?

All this to add to the agony of the relatives of the victims of Lockerbie. Relatives fear that politicans will find it inconvenient to probe too deeply while the Gulf crisis lasts. Our new friends may really be our old enemies. Dare we confront them and ask them about Lockerbie? Syria has not yet been exonerated, nor Iran, and who knows what the next turn of the political screw may bring, or who we will be holding hands with next on this grim magic roundabout? And which politicians will pursue such uncomfortable truths? One thing, however, is certain – politicans and management have failed to protect the public.

A report from a security firm, KPI, called in several years ago by Pan Am, was highly critical of the security arrangements at the time. KPI was particularly critical of the screening of baggage before it went into the hold, and concluded that there were no adequate safeguards at most airports under the present security system 'to prevent a passenger boarding a plane with explosives on his person or in his baggage'.

In 1989, at President Bush's Commission on Aviation Security and Terrorism, a loadmaster gave evidence that there were 'no rules'. 'Even today,' he said, 'we don't count all the bags.'

The US Ambassador to the United Nations, speaking earlier about terrorist warnings, said, 'Disclosure could wreak havoc in air travel.' Another way of saying: 'If passengers knew, they wouldn't travel.' But if they knew, as with human error, the passengers might demand that something be done about it. They might demand that not only terrorism but the last frontier of safety, human error in all its forms, be effectively tackled.

Now that the Iron Curtain is down, terrorists and pocket dictators with or without nuclear weapons are the greatest threat to world peace. The Western strategy on how to deal with terrorism is confused. All that seems clear is that governments expect it to increase. And with situations like the Gulf War, airlines will suffer knock-on effects – fuel prices become de-stabilised and passengers are reluctant to travel. In January

1991, Eastern Airlines went out of business, and Pan Am and Continental have financial problems. Britain's second-biggest travel company, International Leisure Group, which includes Air Europe, went into receivership in March 1991.

Juan Trippe, the founder of Pan Am, always maintained that the world's future was a race between the passenger aircraft and the atom bomb.

A little while ago, politicians were claiming that they and nuclear weapons had kept the fragile peace and brought the Iron Curtain down. Alas, they were too quick with their claims. What credit there is for what international understanding there is should go to civil aviation, for in the furtherance of Trippe's hope, it has spread a communications network around the world.

But what is the way forward from here?

Twenty

Forward to the Last Great Frontier

In 1991 human factor study became part of the CAA pilot qualification syllabus. This is in line with EEC regulations. So at long last human factors are identified as the potential killers they have always been. Pilots are now accepting that they do on occasion, like the rest of us, make mistakes. Management and politicians have yet to be persuaded of *their* errors. The last great frontier of aviation is about to be tackled.

But how?

To see the pitfalls, it is helpful to glance back to aviation's older sister, the sea. Seamen and airmen operate exclusively in their own individual elements. Seamen are by far the senior and have had far more experience. And nobody – least of all the British government – did more for aviation in the early days than the seamen. They gave the airmen their charts, their navigation, their instruments, their rules, their knowledge of the elements, their communication codes, their lights, their radios, their procedures. When I took my 'B' pilot licence, I still had to pass an oral examination in tides and lights, conducted by a bearded master mariner. And as aviation spread all over the world, all the time, unconscious of the future ahead, the seamen had been saving the lives of their most deadly competitors when they flopped into the drink with engine trouble.

In November 1990 a unique conference was held at the Royal Aeronautical Society on 'Safety at Sea and in the Air'. It illuminated particularly the difficulties and dangers the marine side had experienced, most of which, under severe competition, appeared to derive from deregulation and going for the cheapest option.

The story is a cautionary tale for aviation.

Ship safety has always been dominated by the freedom of the seas. Two hundred miles off-shore, the master is 'under God alone'. Ship quality was originally controlled two hundred years ago by Lloyds of London. Now there are fifty Classification Societies competing with each other. None of their governing bodies appear to have representation of seafarers, passengers or the public, and most of them are reported to concentrate more on the safety of property at sea than on safety of life.

The lives of sailors (always rated cheaply) are not usually covered by insurance, nor are the victims of oil-spillage accidents. Companies scour the world for the cheapest crews, and often bring together a motley one indeed, and as few of those as is possible. Ships can be owned by one company, operated by another, with a crew from a third, and sail under a flag of convenience (FOC). Standards of safety are controlled by the registering state while safety regulations are administered by the Classification Societies, all competing for business. Inevitably, companies are tempted to register with a cheap FOC with lax safety regulations. For cost, not Britannia, rules the waves. Now this country has sunk to a position of having to charter (at enormous cost) ships from other countries in national emergencies.

The sinking of a ship does not make the headlines that an aircraft accident does. Most ships carry cargo, so the public do not readily identify with the accident as they would if the ships carried passengers. The Inquiry into the loss of *Derbyshire* showed that losses of bulk-carriers since 1960 have been appalling. Six were lost in a month off Japan, four reporting taking on water forward (there is a contention that hatch covers weren't strong enough), five disappeared after sending SOS. Only one incident was investigated.

Ships are not required to have a seaworthiness certificate to match an aircraft's essential airworthiness certificate, and ship-owners, unlike airlines, are not required to have an operating certificate. Once the master and other officers have passed their qualifying examinations, that is it. No six-monthly checks and medicals for them. Until recently, they had their qualifications for life. Career structures for officers and crew are mostly a thing of the past. During the war, survivors from torpedoed ships went into the Pool, from which crews would be assembled. The Pool still operates, so crews change ship regularly and are often self-employed, and so there is little esprit-de-corps or loyalty.

There are no regulations regarding hours of work, and captains can be on duty for days. Fatigue is endemic, and particularly dangerous in that there may be no one to monitor it. Single bridge-manning by officers of the watch is normal by day and common practice by night. Most ships operate from 17.00 to 08.00 on Unmanned Machinery Space (UMS).

Thus the seas are made more threatening by rotten craft, inadequately crewed by men and in some cases women who may not speak the same language and may know little about seamanship or the ships they sail; who are a danger to other mariners, to themselves and to the environment; whose captains may be answerable to God but whose owners answer only to the bottom line.

Statistics on safety are hard to come by, and unreliable. After an accident, the proceedings can last for years. 'Crew negligence' is the easiest way of settling a claim.

The International Marine Organisation, the equivalent of the International Civil Aviation Organisation, also has trouble with its bottom line, because 30 per cent of its members have not paid their subscriptions. It has allowed trials to take place for ships fitted for one-man bridge operations.

Automation is being promoted as a safety measure. Its protagonists argue that by reducing crew you reduce the chance of human error, for accidents due to human error are estimated to be at about 70 per cent – much the same as in aviation. Cost, however, appears to be a considerably stronger driving force than the pursuit of safety. Yet even if the merchant-service develops a fully automatic ship (Japan is considering such a one), the human factor in shipping will need to be addressed, and in this they are woefully behind their younger-sister service.

As with aviation, the sea should have learned by its disasters, but it is in the interests of ship-owners and countries of origin alike to keep these quiet. Ships lost in the China seas or the Pacific Ocean make little impact on the rest of the world. At the end of 1988, three ferries sank in the Philippines within a six-week period, killing 1,300 people. There have been terrible accidents involving ro-ro ferries, but these mostly happen abroad and are rarely reported in the British press. Information about them is scarce, held to be politically or commercially confidential.

In 1854, Brunel saw that everyone on board the *Great Britain* had a seat in a lifeboat. Yet on 15 April 1912, when the *Titanic* struck an iceberg while attempting a fast Atlantic crossing, only a third of its passengers could be accommodated in lifeboats, and 1,513 of the 2,224 souls on board perished.

On 31 January 1953 the ferry *Princess Victoria* went down in the Irish Sea. Of 176 souls on board, only 45 were saved. According to one of the cew at the inquest, the guillotine doors above the stern gates were never closed. A heavy wave hit the ship and burst them open. The water swept on to the car deck uncontrollably, causing the ship to list.

On 6 March 1987, the *Herald of Free Enterprise* set sail from Zeebrugge at 19.20 local time – twenty minutes late due to loading delays. The captain would have been well aware that an important criterion among shipping companies in evaluating a captain's performance is his ability to keep to schedule.

The *Herald* began to gather speed and had reached 18 knots, when suddenly sea was reported pouring into the hull. The assistant bosun responsible for closing the bow doors was asleep in his cabin, and they had been left open. The ship became waterlogged, listed 90 degrees to port and settled on her side on a sandbank. 192 people died.

In the subsequent Sheen Inquiry, it was disclosed that

throughout the company complacency and sloppiness were the order of the day. 'The Board of Directors', the report stated, 'did not have any comprehension of what their duties were.'

At the inquest, a verdict of 'unlawfully killed' was brought in for all the victims. The master, assistant bosun and top managers were prosecuted for negligence and breach of duty. The case was dropped.

There is a danger, in view of the same problems of deregulation, costs and competition, with the added complications of the recession and the aftermath of the Gulf War, that the fliers may follow the same primrose path that the mariners have trod before them.

'We must expand,' say the aviation money men. Getting bigger is bound to be better. Early in the twenty-first century air travel will have doubled, so instead of building more astronomically expensive airports, let's have ever bigger aircraft, manned by ever fewer crew. The further strain on air traffic controllers will be enormous, as will be the danger of collisions. To counteract these, the authorities are putting their money on ever more complicated machines, both airborne and on the ground, to combat such possibilities rather than on the study of and training in human factors.

Already, twin-engined aircraft with a crew of two pilots fly long transoceanic routes like the Atlantic. From both a human and a mechanical point of view, is that wise? As an Inspector pointed out at the Kegworth inquest, 'Three heads are better than two.' Would such a simple error as happened then have been a factor if there had been a three-man crew? The debate continues.

Many businesses these days appear to concentrate on the bottom line and to be led by accountants, not by the people who have 'been through the business'. However, there has been one small step forward: the public is now becoming slightly more informed, is beginning to question whether 'they', the faceless ones in airlines and government, have their best interests at heart. In various countries, including America, airlines have been prosecuted on charges of falsifying aircraft documents to avoid expensive delays. Indian aviation officials are being charged with receiving kickbacks during the purchase of airliners.

How can the traveller be protected from this lethal corruption? By making it public, and by making personnel resistant to the pressures to conform. Conformity, as has been shown, has contributed to many aircraft accidents. Inexorably, all roads lead to human factors. Not only is the proper study of mankind Man – it is also the most important one for his survival. And it is a strange fact that the veritable explosion of Man's technological advance in the air has been the most important single factor in forcing him to study himself.

Mankind has looked up to the heavens for enlightenment since he began. For he did indeed come from the stars. The chemicals that make his physical being were themselves born billions of years ago by a burst of a supernova far out in the galaxy. Made of the stars, the secret lay inside himself all the time. His inventiveness, his intelligence, his weakness all lie within the machine he has created. But these machines are so fast, so powerful, so unforgiving of human error that the operating of them has forced him to look into himself.

Now human factor study should spread from aviation to all other forms of transport, to other trades, professions and ways of life. What is discovered in the aviation context has value and meaning for anything mankind undertakes.

So how can the process be helped forward?

Firstly, there should be an acknowledgement that if and when the pilot makes a mistake, his will probably be the final enabling one at the apex of a whole pyramid of errors down below. This will, in turn, take the heat off investigations – the 'we intend to find and punish the culprit' syndrome. Only then can the pilots come forward and admit to mistakes they made or nearly made, and the reasons why be coolly analysed and lessons learned. Reporting of such episodes should be mandatory, so that a huge data bank can be built up for study.

Central to the study of accidents should be a stronger AAIB. And central to the AAIB should be accident prevention as well as accident investigation. This is as vital as preventive medicine to health.

The AAIB are now turning their attention to management and latent areas that might cause an accident. Although they liaise with experts in survivability, pathology, human factors and others, they would be stronger in having experts on their staff, particularly in ergonomics. The design of instruments, switches and levers and their position in the cockpit should be thoroughly tested for ease of reading and operating. It should not be possible for such instruments as the three-pointer altimeter that has been a factor in a number of fatal accidents (see photograph 4a) and the Kegworth 737-400 engine-instrument arrangement (see photograph 7a and diagram on page 183) to be fitted on aircraft.

In addition, the AAIB needs the powers to implement its own recommendations quickly without having to consider commercial considerations, thus ensuring the faster production of reports. It also needs a capacity to chase up the implementation of those recommendations.

At present it is helping the newly formed Marine Accident Investigation Branch, who are so far behind, particularly on the human factor side. It also has much to offer various other accident investigation branches, such as those for road and rail. There are a number of such organisations independently concerned with safety and accidents which have little intercommunication with each other.

Yet safety is a unity and anomalies are manifold. While the AAIB look after safety in the air, the safety of people at airports on the ground is looked after by the Health and Safety Executive. Yet it is clear that the same sort of errors cause similar human factor accidents in all forms of transport.

Unfortunately, the AAIB operate in a retro-active area. They are brought in when the horse has already bolted. They should have a pro-active role in probing weaknesses, examining doubtful procedures, and the authority to secure the stable door while the horse is still inside.

It was proposed by Doctor Corlett at the November 1990 Conference of Safety at Sea and in the Air that there should be an independent International Safety Bureau for shipping, funded by and reporting to a United Nations agency, working with IMO. But should there not also be an international safety bureau, which could be more easily set up than a marine one, for worldwide aviation, free of the dread hand of politics, headed by people who have had direct experience of what they are administering, not political nominees, nor friends in high places. Such an organisation could then be extended to all forms of transport and eventually to safety in other organisations. At the moment, the axiom of politicians, management and commerce appears to be the less the public know the better.

I don't take the dim view of the public that the airlines and government take. The public is, after all, ourselves. They only want the cheapest fare, airlines say. The public don't care about anything else. But don't they?

The public don't make a fuss because they don't know all the horrors they should make a fuss about. They should be told about tired pilots, cost-cutting airlines, over-worked controllers, ageing aircraft and marginal airports. Amid the coloured umbrellas, the blue skies and the golden sands of the holiday brochures, there should be printed the rating of the airport they will be landing at, the safety record of the airline, the aircraft that will be carrying them and the number of seats that will have been crammed in.

Most passengers would surely prefer to know if their crews are adequately rested, and that the stewardesses are part of the crew concept, that they are strong enough, trained enough, to haul them to safety, not girls with very little experience, as had happened in the British Airtours Ringway disaster.

In the Ontario crash (Chapter 18) the cabin staff should have felt able to point out the accretions of ice on the wings. Similarly, in the M1 crash, the cabin crew should have felt able to tell the pilots that the smoke was coming out of the left engine. The public should insist that the stewards and stewardesses are part of the safety envelope. It is a step in the right direction that now some airlines' cabin and operating crew train together on emergency drills. After all, if it were brought sufficiently to the public's notice, they would certainly prefer a well trained crew member alert to possible problems and able to deal with emergencies to a well made-up face and a smart inflammable uniform.

The FAA was concerned about uniform material that quickly burned or melted, but surveys of flight-attendant union members found that most were not willing to 'sacrifice style, comfort and cleanability to obtain uniforms of higher flame resistance'.

In *The Aircraft Cabin*, Elwyn and Mary Edwards pointed out that these uniforms are particularly dangerous when they are long-skirted national costumes. In one accident in Honolulu, during an emergency evacuation, all the flight attendants sustained extensive friction burns on their buttocks where their loose-fitting skirts slipped over their hips, exposing their skin as they escaped down the slide. Other airlines, like Qantas, prescribe sensible shoes and the stewardesses can wear slacks. Some airlines now forbid smoking on board, a vital safety precaution which the public should applaud.

A further part the public can play is that they can decline to purchase duty-free alcohol unless a system is operated whereby they can collect it at the end of their journey and not take it on board. It was postulated that some of the very swift fires within the cabin at Manchester were because of duty-free liquor. And 'duty-frees' appear to exert a kind of hypnotism on passengers – judging by the number of times they insist on taking their loot down the slide with them after an emergency.

Of course, it is worth it for some. British Airports Authority derive nearly one-fifth of their £642 million annual income from duty- and tax-free sales. This should come to an end with the advent of the single European market. But will it?

Predictably, airport operators, airlines, ferry companies, distillers and tobacco companies have formed a pressure group to fight their corner, under the flag of 'preserving the consumer's liberty'. Not only is the consumer captive, he is also psychologically impressionable. It has been suggested that passengers over-indulge in airport shopping to combat the stress of flying. One only has to go into duty-free shops and watch people compulsively cramming potentially lethal goodies into cabin baggage to see the stress and fear that underlie these sprees. It would be nice if even at this late stage the airport operators could plough back some of these profits from exploiting human factor weakness into human factor study to make flying even safer and lessen that fear. But would it be economical?

For, particularly now, when because of economic pressures aviation is being forced to restructure, it must resolve the opposing pulls of commercialism and safety. Unfortunately, airlines are suffering from sharply falling profits at a time when they need to re-equip with new and more efficient aircraft. This problem will be exacerbated with de-regulation. Politicians may announce that it will benefit the public because airlines will compete with lower fares. But will they also compete with lower standards of safety?

The American experience leads us to expect that it may, and also that it won't necessarily make the fares lower, although some of the gross price-fixing which has so far pertained in Europe may go. The American experience of aviation clotting into large oligopolies has been mentioned; that the larger an organisation becomes, the more it feels that it can lean on government, regulating agencies and employees; that less is being spent on maintenance at a time when the aircraft are ageing; and that cost-cutting with fuel and the employment of less experienced pilots is widespread. It is also noticeable that, when commercialism is rampant, advertising and the image take precedence over anything as mundane as safety, with enormous budgets for media coverage and for trivia.

It should be reiterated that the profit/safety interface is as dangerous as the next interface that has to be tackled – that of the man/machine. Its human error perils have been touched upon in

Chapter 11, The Clockwork Pilot. Man has invented a machine that, though not the monster of science fiction, is on occasion just a bit beyond his human limitations to deal with speedily. And therein inevitably lies danger.

The need for new control facilities, and a Europe-wide flow-management system is urgent. An *en route* radar programme and a new approach control at Heathrow airport are underway. ICAO's future Air Navigation Systems (FANS), which propose far-reaching improvements to the present control, navigation and surveillance systems will take years to implement fully.

There is further improvement in that all large aircraft landing in the US will eventually have to be fitted with an airborne collision avoidance system. There is also a ground anti-collision system being introduced – unfortunately too late for the two Northwest aircraft that collided at Detroit on 3 December 1990.

But, as with the pilot, what of the human being at the centre of that complex Air Traffic Control system? Controllers have gone through the same struggle as pilots went through in the 1950s. The resistance of the authorities is amazing. The number of air-misses over Britain in 1988 increased to seventy-three, and fifteen of these were considered to be 'risk-bearing' – i.e. there was the possibility of a collision. And in that year overworked controllers handled 11 per cent more flights. In the last two years the number of flights handled has increased 20 per cent. Hardly an equation that reinforces safety.

The CAA is spending £600 million, increasing the capacity to control British airspace by at least 30 per cent in the next five years by means of a new flow-control management computer in the West Drayton Centre.

European air-traffic-delay problems are generated by having twenty-two separate authorities, each with their own incompatible control systems. To reduce delay, hotlines have been established between Britain and the main European air traffic control centres. There is evidence now of an international approach to the European organisation of air traffic control, which is already producing results in improving the traffic flow.

America already has a Central Control Facility – the largest and most complicated computer system in the world, integrated with the centres of twenty regional traffic control centres. It scans an exact air situation anywhere in the States and has complete power in respect of all take-offs and landings. So now controllers are benefiting from the hard work, research and persuasion that went on over the decades into human factor study of pilots.

At a recent International Symposium on Air Safety Captain Caesar of Lufthansa spoke eloquently about the 'ghost fleet that belongs to the insurers' of 392 Western-built heavy passenger jets lost through accidents in the last thirty years (twenty of them in 1988), which have left a legacy of tragedy to men and women, airlines and states. And this figure does not include the ones lost through terrorism and sabotage.

He warned that we are 'facing a situation in which we are sharing the overcrowded and insufficiently supervised and controlled airspace with more and more companies, with increasingly old aircraft, manned by sometimes inexperienced, hastily recruited and minimally trained crews, causing more stress, fatigue and motivation problems for all in the system'.

In other words, an exacerbation of the human factors already present in the man and in the system – those human factors, *not* 'pilot error', which at present cause over 70 per cent of the accidents. Captain Caesar pointed out that economic pressure is 'forcing companies and states to reduce spending in prophylactic tactics and to invest only the absolute minimum they are required to by regulatory bodies'.

This then is where governments can play a decisive and positive role. Aviation is trans-world and trans-frontier. The profit motive cannot be accepted as the be-all and end-all. The passengers who go so blithely and blindly, we are told, for the cheapest fare, must demand the safest. They must pressurise their governments to establish international safety minima, and information must be freely exchanged. Most importantly, they must press for human factors to be examined at significant depth

– not in a paper-thin package, not only in the pilot, but in the system where latent error lies.

We have two choices, Captain Caesar warned. We can 'accept the present loss rate, deny moral responsibility, calculate the cost with the insurers', or we can 'regard any loss as too high . . . encourage independent thinking . . . and fight collective mistakes by recognising that man is faulty and to err is human, that a breakthrough towards better safety can best be achieved by improving the performance of cockpit crews. The more severe an accident, the more predominant is the human factor.'

Yes, but this is the human factor throughout the whole aviation structure, not only in pilots. From tackling that will come the breakthrough that will enable us at last to conquer 'the last great frontier in aviation'.

Appendix

CAA
Human Performance and Limitations

Syllabus

This syllabus is divided into four main topic areas;
  1 Basic Aviation Physiology and Health Maintenance
  2 Basic Aviation Psychology
  3 Stress, Fatigue, and Their Management
  4 The Social Psychology and Ergonomics of the Flight Deck

1 Basic Aviation Physiology and Health Maintenance

1a Basic Physiology and Effects of Flight

- Anatomy and physiology of the eye, ear, vestibular, circulatory, and respiratory systems.
- Composition of the atmosphere, gas laws, and the nature of the human requirement for oxygen.
- Effects of reduced ambient pressure and of sudden decompression; times of useful consciousness.
- Recognising and coping with hypoxia and hyperventilation.
- Entrapped gases and barotrauma.
- Diving and flying.
- Effects of acceleration $(+/-G)$ on circulatory system, vision, and consciousness.
- Mechanism, effects, and management of motion sickness.

1b Flying and Health

- Noise- and age-induced hearing loss.
- Visual defects and their correction.

- ECG, blood pressure, stroke, arterial disease, and coronary risk factors.
- Diet, exercise, and obesity.
- Fits, faints, and the EEG.
- Psychiatric diseases; drug dependence, and alcoholism.
- Tropical diseases and their prophylaxis; hepatitis, and sexually transmitted diseases.
- Common ailments and fitness to fly; gastro-enteritis, colds, use of common drugs and their side effects.
- Toxic hazards.
- Causes and management of in-flight incapacitation.

2 Basic Aviation Psychology

2a Human Information Processing

- Basic plan of human information processing, including the concepts of sensation, attention, memory, central decision-making, and the creation of mental models.
- Limitations of central decision channel and mental workload.
- Function of attention in selecting information sources, attention-getting stimuli.
- Types of memory; peripheral or sensory memory, long term (semantic and episodic) memory, short term or working memory, motor memory (skills).
- Memory limitations and failures.
- Perception, the integration of sensory information to form a mental model.
- Effects of experience and expectation on perception.

2b Cognition in Aviation

- Erroneous mental models; visual, vestibular, and other illusions.
- Recognising and managing spatial disorientation.
- Use of visual cues in landing.
- Eye movements, visual search techniques, mid-air collisions.
- Skill, rule-, and knowledge-based behaviour.
- The nature of skill acquisition, the exercise of skill, conscious and automatic behaviour, errors of skill.
- Rule-based behaviour, procedures, simulator training, failures of rule-based behaviour.

- Knowledge-based behaviour, problem solving and decision making, inference formation, failures in knowledge-based behaviour.
- Maintaining accurate mental models, situational awareness, confirmation bias.

3 Stress and Stress Management

3a Models and effects of stress

- Definitions, concepts, and models of stress.
- Arousal; concepts of over- and under-arousal.
- Environmental stresses and their effects; heat, noise, vibration, low humidity.
- Domestic stress, home relationships, bereavement, financial and time commitments.
- Work stress, relationships with colleagues and management.
- Effects of stress on attention, motivation, and performance.
- Life stress and health, other clinical effects of stress.
- Coping strategies, identifying stress, and stress management.

3b Sleep and Fatigue

- Biological clocks and circadian rhythms, sleep/wakefulness and temperature rhythms, 'zeitgebers'.
- Sleep stages, sleep at abnormal times of day, required quantity of sleep.
- Work-induced fatigue.
- Shift work.
- Time zone crossing, circadian disrhythmia, resynchronisation.
- Rostering problems, sleep management, and naps.
- Sleep hygiene.
- Management of sleep with drugs.

4 Social Psychology and Ergonomics of the Flight Deck

4a Individual Differences, Social Psychology, and Flight Deck Management

- Individual differences, definitions of intelligence and personality.
- Assessing personality.
- Main dimensions of personality: extraversion and anxiety. Other important traits: warmth and sociability, impulsivity, toughmindedness, dominance, stability, and boldness.

- Goal-directed, person-directed types of behaviour.
- Autocratic and democratic leadership styles.
- Individual personality-related problems of flying, especially risk-taking.
- Personality interaction on the flight deck, and the interaction of personality with status or seniority, role (eg handling/non-handling), and perceived ability of crew members.
- Concepts of conformity, compliance, and risky shift. Implication of these concepts for the flight deck with regard to effects of crew size (especially 2 v 3 crew).
- Methods of maximising crew effectiveness and improving flight deck (cockpit resource) management.
- Verbal and non-verbal communication, different communication styles.
- Interacting with cabin crew, air traffic services, maintenance personnel, and passengers.
- Making decisions and assessing risk.

4b Design of Flight Decks, Documentation, and Procedures

- Basic principles of control, display, and workspace design.
- Eye datum, anthropometry, and workspace constraints. External vision requirements, reach, comfort and posture.
- Display size, legibility, scale design, colour, and illumination. Common errors in display interpretation.
- Control size, loading, location and compatibility of controls with displays.
- The presentation of warning information and misinterpretation of warnings.
- The design and appropriate use of checklists and manuals.
- Effects of automation and the 'glass cockpit'. Integration of information from many data sources on one display, and automatic selection of displayed information. Mode and status representation.
- Machine intelligence and relationship between aircraft decisions and pilot decisions.
- The avoidance of complacency and boredom, and maintaining situational awareness. Maintaining basic flying skills.

Glossary

AAIB	Air Accidents Investigation Branch
ADF	Automatic Direction Finder
ALPA	Airline Pilots Association (USA)
ATC	Air Traffic Control
BALPA	British Airline Pilots Association
CAA	Civil Aviation Authority (UK)
CHIRP	Confidential Human Factors Incident Reporting Programme
CRM	Cockpit Resource Management
CVR	Cockpit Voice Recorder
DME	Distance Measuring Equipment
EAI	Engine Anti-Ice
EIS	Engine Instrument System
EPR	Engine Pressure Ratio; a measure of engine thrust which can be displayed to the pilot.
FAA	Federal Aviation Agency (USA)
FOC	Flag of Convenience
FMS	Flight Management System
GPWS	Ground Proximity Warning System
HF	High Frequency (radio communications)
IAM	RAF Institute of Aviation Medicine
IATA	International Air Transport Association
ICAO	International Civil Aviation Organisation
IFR	Instrument Flight Rules
ILS	Instrument Landing System
IMO	International Marine Organisation
INS	Inertial Navigation System
LOFT	Line Orientated Flying Training
MAS	Management of the Automatic System
MEL	Minimum Equipment List

MOR	Mandatory Occurrence Report
NASA	National Aeronautics and Space Administration
NTSB	National Transportation Safety Board (USA)
QFE	Barometric pressure setting for altimeter causing it to read zero on landing
QNH	Barometric pressure setting for altimeter causing it to read height above mean sea level on landing
RVR	Runway Visual Range
STICK-SHAKER	An artificial stall-warning device that causes both control columns to vibrate when the airspeed falls within not less than 7 per cent of the actual stall speed
V1	Decision speed in the event of an engine failure on take-off; at which the take-off may be either abandoned or continued.
V2	Take-off safety speed; the lowest speed at which the aircraft can be flown after take-off following an engine failure.
VASI	Visual Approach Slope Indicator; a system of coloured light beams defining the safe approach angle to a runway.
VFR	Visual Flight Rules
VHF	Very High Frequency (radio communications)
VOR	VHF Omnidirectional Range

Select Bibliography

Barlay, Stephen, *The Final Call* (Sinclair-Stevenson, 1990)
Beaty, David, *The Heart of the Storm* (Secker and Warburg, 1954)
—— *Cone of Silence* (Secker and Warburg, 1960)
—— *The Wind off the Sea* (Secker and Warburg, 1962)
—— *The Human Factor in Aircraft Accidents* (Secker and Warburg, 1969)
—— *The Water Jump* (Secker and Warburg, 1976)
—— *Errors made on the Flight Deck; how far fatigue can be considered a factor* (MPhil Thesis, University College, London, 1977)
—— *Strange Encounters* (Methuen, 1984)
—— *The Complete Skytraveller* (Methuen, 1986)
Brodrick, A. H., *Man and his Ancestry* (Methuen, 1960)
Bunning, E., *The Physiological Clock* (Academic Press, 1964)
Brent, Peter, *Charles Darwin* (Hamlyn, 1981)
Carroll, J. B., *Language of Thought* (Prentice Hall, 1964)
Corkindale, K. G. G., *Behavioural Aspects of Aircraft Accidents* (AGARD Conference Proceedings, 1985)
Dember, William, *The Psychology of Perception* (Holt, Reinhart and Winston, 1964)
Dixon, Norman, *On the Psychology of Military Incompetence* (Cape, 1976)
Dixon, Norman, *Our Own Worst Enemy* (Cape, 1987)
Duffy, Elizabeth, *Activation of Behaviour* (Wiley, 1962)
Edwards, B., *Drawings on the Right Side of the Brain* (Souvenir Press, 1981)
Edwards, Mary and Elwyn, *The Aircraft Cabin* (Gower, 1990)
Ersting, J. and King, P., *Aviation Medicine* (Butterworth, 1988)
Foley, R. (ed.), *Hominid Evolution and Community Ecology* (Academic Press, 1984)

Freud S., *The Psychopathology of Everyday Life* (Benn, 1954)
Gerhardt, Rolf, *The Human Factor in Aviation* (Armed Forces Publication, 1959)
Ginsberg, M., *The Psychology of Society* (Methuen, 1969)
Haining, P., *The Compleat Birdman* (Hale, 1976)
Hawkins, F. H., *Human Factors in Flight* (Gower, 1987)
Hoffer, W. and M., *Freefall* (St Martin's Press, 1989)
Harris, S., *The First to Fly* (Methuen, 1970)
Isaacs, H., *Idols of the Tribe* (Harvard University Press, 1989)
Janis, I. L., *Victims of Groupthink* (Houghton, Mifflin, 1972)
Leakey, Richard, *The Making of Mankind* (Michael Joseph, 1981)
Lorenz, Konrad *Aggression* (Methuen, 1966)
Lowell, Vernon, *Airline Safety is a Myth* (Bartholomew House, 1967)
Maerth, O. K., *The Beginning was the End* (Michael Joseph, 1981)
Minski, Marvin, *The Society of the Mind* (Heinemann, 1987)
Milgram, S., *Obedience to Authority* (Tavistock, 1974)
Norman, D. A., *The Psychology of Everyday Things* (Basic Books, 1988)
Norris, W., *The Unsafe Sky* (Arrow, 1981)
Oparin, A. I., *The Origin of Life on Earth* (Oliver and Boyd, 1957)
Ornstein, R. J. and Ehrlich, P., *New World New Mind* (Doubleday 1989)
Pilbeam, D., *The Ascent of Man* (Macmillan, 1972)
Perrow, C., *Normal Accidents: Living with High-risk Technologies* (Basic Books, 1984)
Prince, M., *Crash Course* (Grafton, 1990)
Ramsden, J. M., *The Safe Airline* (MacDonald and Jane, 1976)
Rasmusson, Duncan, LePlat (ed.), *New Technology and Human Error* (Wiley, 1987)
Rohmer, R., *Massacre 007* (Coronet, 1984)
Reason, J. and Mycielska, K., *Absent-Minded? the Psychology of Mental Lapses and Everyday Errors* (Academic Press, 1984)
Reason, J., *Human Error* (Cambridge University Press, 1990)
Robinson, D., *The Dangerous Sky* (Foulis, 1973)
Roscoe, S. (ed.) *Aviation Psychology* (Iowa State University Press, 1980)
Shakley, M., *Wild Men* (Thames and Hudson, 1983)
Smith, J. M., *The Theory of Evolution* (Pelican, 1958)
Stewart, Stanley, *Air Disasters* (Ian Allen, 1986)
St Exupéry, Anton, *Wind, Sand and Stars* (Cape, 1941)
Taylor, Laurie, *Air Travel – How Safe Is It?* (BSP Professional Books, 1988)

Tebbit, Norman, *Upwardly Mobile* (Weidenfeld and Nicolson, 1988)
Tench, William, *Safety is No Accident* (Collins, 1985)
Vette, S. and Macdonald, T., *Impact Erebus* (Hodder and Stoughton, 1983)
Weston, Richard, *Zagreb One Four* (Bartholomew House, 1967)
Wiener, Earl and Nagel, D. (ed.), *Human Factors in Aviation* (Academic Press, 1988)
X, Captain, *Safety Last* (Pinnacle Books, 1975)
Yates, A. J. (ed.), *Frustration and Conflict* (Van Nostrand, 1965)

Papers and Publications
Toronto Star, Independent, Sunday Times, Daily Mail
Thirty years of Jet Losses – Did we draw the right conclusions?, Captain Heino Caesar (International Air Safety Seminar, Athens, 1989)
A tachiscopic method for differential diagnosis of dyslexia, R. Gerhardt
Survey of accidents to Australian civil aircraft 1987 (Australian Government Publishing Service)
Aerospace
Flight International
The BALPA Log
British Airways News
CHIRP
Touchdown
Canadian, British, American and Australian Aircraft Accident Reports
ICAO Aircraft Accident Digests
Papers delivered at the 'Safety at Sea and in the Air – Taking Stock Together Conference, at the Royal Aeronautical Society (13–15 November 1990)
Text of *Coded Hostile* by Brian Phelan, Granada Television

Index

Absent-mindedness 131, 132–43, 246
Accident-proneness 146
Accident recommendations 263
Accidents and incidents
  Alaska, Constellation 160
  Anchorage, DC-8 202
  Athens, DC-8 258
  Bangalore, A320 129
  Bay of Naples, Comet 259
  Beaufort Sea, Twin Otter 88
  Beauvais, R101 Airship 163, 246–53
  Brazil, 133
  Chicago, DC-8 164–7
  Dallas, Tristar 24
  Dryden, Ontario, F-28 254, 255, 256, 287
  Elba, Comet 259
  Ermenonville, DC-10 33, 234
  Gander, DC-8 194, 227, 228, 243
  Gimli, B-767 115–18
  Grand Canyon, DC-10 and Constellation 160, 161
  Great Bear Lake, Twin Otter 86–9
  Habsheim airshow, A320 129
  Heathrow, Dove 175, 176; B-707 206
  Hollywood, light aircraft 69
  Jangipara, Comet 259
  Karachi, Comet 152–5
  Kegworth (M1), B-737 180–5, 240, 263, 287
  Kerrville, DC-3 191
  Knox County, 235–8
  Kuala Lumpur, Airbus 300 109–11
  Lagos, VC-10 191

Lockerbie, B-747 228, 274–9
Los Angeles, Nord 62 126, 177; DC-9 and Piper 53
Madrid, B-747 178
Manchester, B-737 240–3, 263
Medicine Bow, C-54 200
Miami, Tristar 235
Minneapolis, DC-6 69
Mount Erebus, DC-10 162–3
Mount Ogusa, B-747 226
Mount Oiz, B-727 128
Munich, Elizabethan 32, 260
New Orleans, B-727 24
New York, DC-10 119–22
Orlando, DC-8 56, 57
Pago Pago, B-707 72
Paris, DC-10 33, 242
Portland, DC-8 59–67, 158
Riyadh, Tristar 38, 95–101
Samos, Short 330 74
San Diego, B-727 and Cessna 45–7, 50, 51
San Francisco Bay, DC-6 71
Singapore, Constellation 187
Snowdon, Gazelle 91
Spokane, Beechcraft 33, 197–200
Springfield, Convair 72
Staines, Trident 127, 134, 240
Taipei, B-727 258
Tenerife, B-747s 37, 41, 75, 78–86, 157, 193, 201, 259
Tenerife, B-727 34–7, 41, 43, 108–9 127, 259
Washington Bridge, B-737 33, 101–5, 201
Washington 57, 58

Zagreb, Trident 42
Adam and Eve 11
Adrenalin 9, 17, 94, 188, 189
Advertisers, airline 13, 289
Advertising 20, 29, 207
Aeroflot 139, 269
Aeromexico 53
Affirmative action 158
Air Accident Investigation Branch
   (AAIB) 182, 184, 262, 286
Air Canada 115, 253
Air Florida 101–5, 243
Air India 129
Air New York 102
Air New Zealand 161–3
Air Ontario 254–6
Air Traffic Control 34, 41, 42, 43, 45,
   46, 47, 80–3, 103, 108, 161, 168,
   175, 176, 177, 179, 195–6, 199,
   254, 290
Air Transport Auxiliary (ATA) 14
Airbus Industrie 129, 130
Aircraft
   Airbus Industrie A300 53, 109, 110,
      111, 114, 270, 273
   Airbus Industrie A320 21, 128, 129
   Auster 113
   Avro Elizabethan 32, 260
   Avro Vulcan 115
   Avro York 153, 154
   BAe Concorde 53
   BAC VC-10 191
   Beechcraft 197, 199
   Boeing 377 114
   Boeing 707 72, 112, 138, 139, 159,
      160, 206, 242, 269
   Boeing 727 24, 34, 35, 37, 42, 43,
      44, 45, 78, 108, 128, 243, 258
   Boeing 737 33, 78, 101, 103, 105,
      180, 181, 182, 184, 235, 240,
      286
   Boeing 747 (Jumbo) 15, 37, 39, 41,
      43, 53, 74, 75, 78, 79, 81, 84,
      108, 138, 139, 142, 146, 157,
      178, 194, 218, 219, 226, 228,
      259, 268, 269, 274
   Boeing 757 240
   Boeing 767 115, 116, 117, 118, 253
   British Aerospace 748 235

Cessna 44, 45, 46, 47, 50, 51, 53, 55,
   56
Convair 72
Curtis C-54 114, 200
De Havilland Comet 112, 129, 148,
   149, 151, 152, 153, 155, 259
De Havilland Dove 175
De Havilland Twin Otter 86, 87
Douglas DC-3 73, 114, 115, 157,
   191
Douglas DC-4 112, 115, 190
Douglas DC-6 69, 71, 73
Douglas DC-7 160
Douglas DC-8 58, 59, 78, 164, 165,
   194, 201, 227, 258
Douglas DC-9 42, 102, 126, 274
Douglas DC-10 33, 119, 134, 147,
   161, 162, 163, 228, 232, 233,
   234
Falcon 53
Fokker F-28 254, 255
Gazelle 91
Hawker Siddeley Trident 42, 127
Jaguar 91
Lockheed Constellation 113, 114,
   115, 160, 174, 175
Lockheed Tristar 24, 38, 67, 95, 98,
   99, 195
Martin 114
McDonnell Douglas MD-80 267
Nord 262 177
Short 330 74
Supermarine Spitfire 14
SU-15 (Soviet) 144, 145
Tornado 91, 125
Tripacer 113
Vickers Viscount 112, 113
Aircraft Cabin, The 288
Aircraft Proximity Hazard Reporting
   System 225
Aircrew Resource Management (ARM)
   211
Airline Pilots Association (ALPA) 227,
   239
Airships
   R100 247, 248, 249, 250
   R101 163, 246, 247, 248, 249, 250,
      251, 252, 259
Alarms, flight deck 193
Alaska, bush pilot syndrome 89

Alcohol 17, 201–3
Alitalia 53
Aloha Airlines 235
Altimeter settings 43, 177
Altimeter, three-pointed 71
Altitude pre-select 124
Ambiguity 56
American Airlines 228–33
Anchor sleep 195
Ancient man 8
Ansett 217
Antarctic Treaty Conference 162
Anxiety 90
Apes 17, 38
Applegate, Dan 234
Arousal 60, 94, 95, 133, 156, 180, 199
Arrow Air 227
Artificial Intelligence (AI) 219–20
Asch, conformity experiment 155
Assertiveness 37, 158, 169
Attention 107, 109
Attitude, aircraft 26, 70, 71, 72, 155
Australopithecus afarensis 21
Authoritarianism 29, 75, 81, 157
Authority 10, 75, 85, 86, 148, 150, 157, 208
Autofeathering 126, 177, 185
Automation 119–31, 132, 133, 134, 218, 219, 282, 283
Autopilot 67, 147, 162, 167
Autothrottle 119, 120, 134
Avianca 43, 108, 128, 178
Aviation Safety Reporting System (ASRS) 33, 193, 194
Aviation medicine 25

Bader, Group Captain Douglas 191–2
Ballanchey 156
Barthol and Hu 111
Bartlett, Professor 41, 186
Beekeeper's Journal 22
Bennett, Air Vice-Marshal 130
Billings and Reynard 28
Biological clock 188
Bird strikes 125
Birdmen 21, 22
BKA (German Federal Office for Criminal Investigation) 276
Black-hole effect 72
Bladud, King 22

Blood pressure 188
Body temperature 188
Book, the 149
Booth, Squadron Leader Ralph 249, 250
Boredom 13, 29, 131, 132–43, 195
Brain 9, 10, 11, 17, 49, 55, 57, 94, 133, 172, 188, 193
Brancker, Sir Sefton 249
Bressey, Captain Peter 192
British Airline Pilots Association (BALPA) 153, 187, 191–2, 260
British Airports Authority (BAA) 288
British Airtours 240–2
British Airways (BA) 53, 107, 195
British European Airways (BEA) 32, 260
British Midland 107, 180
British Overseas Airline Corporation (BOAC) 107, 148, 151, 152, 153, 154, 167, 186, 187, 189, 190, 259
British South American Airlines 130
Bureau of Air Safety Investigation 263
Bush pilot syndrome 89
Butler, Captain Roy 210, 220

Caesar, Captain Heino 33, 38, 291, 292
Cambridge Cockpit experiments 186
Canadian Air Safety Board (CASB) 255
Canadian Pacific Airlines 152
Cannibalism 9
Capnobates 21
Cardiovascular disease 13, 18
Cave man 8–10, 18
Cayley, Sir George 22
Central Control Facility (US ATC) 291
Central Intelligence Agency (CIA) 138, 276
Cephalisation, Index of 11
Channon, Paul 275
Check flights 14, 86
Checklists 95, 102, 166, 206
Chronobiology 189
Churchill, Winston 259
Circadian rhythms 188
Civil Aviation Authority (CAA) 33, 71,

191, 192, 193, 206, 224, 225, 242, 261, 263, 265, 266, 280, 290
Classification Societies 281
Clearances (ATC) 35, 42, 43, 82, 83, 199
Cobra Ball 139, 143
Cockpit Resource Management (CRM) 209
Cocquyt effect 71
Cody, Samuel 23, 24
Cognitive dissonance 128
Cognitive load 107
Collisions (mid-air) 51, 52, 53, 55, 91, 125, 160, 284, 290
Colmore, Wing Commander 249
Colombia 90
Commission on Aviation Security 278
Communication 31, 32–44, 81, 98, 106, 129, 180, 212
Complacency 108
Concentration 13, 98
Concorde 53
Conditioned reflex 93
Conditioned response 106
Conference on Safety at Sea and in the Air 287
Confidence 88
Confidential Human Factors Reporting Programme (CHIRP) 33, 127, 168, 194, 216, 225
Conflict 156
Conformity 29, 78, 116, 148–9, 212, 285
Confusion 36, 111
Congress (US) 39
Conscious awareness 58
Consciousness 11
Controlled Flight into Terrain (CFT) 74
Conversation, task-related 40
Corlett, Doctor 287
Courses, human factors 208–20
Cragh, Professor 77
Cranfield 206
Crew complement 116, 267–8, 284
Crew concept training 210
Crew co-operation 39, 236
Crew error 220
'Crew negligence' 282, 284
Cripps, Sir Stafford 252

Crutchfield 156
Cultural evolution 12
Curiosity 29

Daedalus 21
Daily Mail 22
Dan Air 34, 41, 43, 107, 108, 127, 214, 259
Darwin, Charles 21
Darwinian theory 7
Davenport, Captain 214
Davis, Russell 50
Day-dreaming 137
De Havilland 148, 151, 152, 259
Decision-making 13, 38, 39, 57, 88, 93–105
Decision theory 93
Defence mechanisms 156, 197, 212
Defence mechanism test 77, 107
Denial 98, 100, 224
Derbyshire, loss of 281
Deregulation 219, 226, 227, 228, 239, 266–8, 281, 284
Desire to please 78, 86, 148, 159, 160, 166
Director of Flight Safety 265, 266
Disorders, psychiatric 13
Distance Measuring Equipment (DME) 33, 199
Diurnal rhythm 31
Dixon, Professor Norman 58, 77, 174, 246
Dowding, Air Vice-Marshal 249
Downeast Airlines 235–8
Drugs 18, 202
Duncker 55
Duty time 187, 190, 191
Dyslexia 95, 172

Earhart, Amelia 14
Eastleigh, railway collision 145
Ecuador 73
Education 14, 204–20
Ego 29, 74, 75–92, 207, 246
Egotism 29, 75, 86
Egypt 90
Enders, John H. 75, 257
Engine anti-icing (EAI) 243, 244
Engine Instrument System (EIS) 182
EPR limitations 243, 244

Evolution 12, 21, 34
Examinations 14, 207, 214, 280, 282,
    Appendix
Exercise 195
Extrovert 13
Eye movements 50
Eye position 51
Eysenck, Hans 13

Familiarity 40
Family life 13
Farmer 76
Fatigue 30, 39, 49, 60, 79, 81, 86, 95,
    109, 142, 161, 186–203, 235,
    282
Fear 91, 161
Fear of failure 86
Federal Aviation Agency (FAA) 51, 52,
    53, 93, 158, 226, 229, 234, 237,
    261, 266, 275, 288
Feedback 225
Fire-fighters 99
Fire in the air 94, 95–9
Fixation 86
Flack test 25, 26
Fleming, Ian 170
Flight engineers 83, 84
Flight Operations Resource
    Management (FORM) 209–11
Flight safety 223–4
Flight Safety Foundation 75, 227
Flight-time limitations 30, 82, 187,
    191–3, 227
Florida 67, 101
Flow control (ATC) 290
'Fly by wire' 128
Flying Barons 76
Flynn, Errol 74
Follow-my-leader syndrome 60
Foote, Captain Harry 148–55
Forster, E. M. 31
Freud, Sigmund 19, 75, 224
Frustration 60, 79, 86
Fry and Reinhardt 76
Fuel, contamination 88
    lack of 43, 60–7, 108, 115–18,
    158, 208, 253–4
Functional fixity 55, 57

Gaddafi, Colonel 277

Gann, Ernest 173
George V, King 23
Gerhardt, Rolf 171, 174
Gestalt psychologists 69
Glass cockpit 219
Government 23
Great War 23, 25
Green, Doctor Roger 33
Ground Proximity Warning System
    (GPWS) 36, 37, 74, 127, 128,
    134, 162, 178, 179, 181
Group pressure 156, 159
Groupthink 212, 258, 259
Guild of Air Traffic Controllers 196

Habit 137, 138
Hallucination 133
Hartwick, Sonia 257
Harvey 157
Health and Safety Executive 286
Heart rate 60
Heartbeat 9, 94
Herald of Free Enterprise 240, 264,
    265, 283–4
Hierarchy 38, 157
High and the Mighty, The 173
Holland International Travel Group 78
Hominid 8, 9
Hubel, D. H. 57
Human error 27, 28, 92, 118, 134,
    185, 238, 270, 274
Human Error (1990) 221
Human factors 28, 47, 52, 78, 86, 89,
    100, 108, 127, 158, 204–45, 265,
    270, 280, 283, 284, 285, 286,
    291, 292
*Human Factor in Aircraft Accidents,
    The* 225, 261
Huxley, T. H. 8
Hypothalamus 189

Icarus 21
Id 75
Identify Friend or Foe (IFF) 144
Ice 33, 88, 101–5, 243, 254–7, 287
Illusions 68–73
Imprecision 41
Inattention 29, 70, 138, 139
Inertial Navigation System (INS) 138–
    42, 146, 161, 162

Instinct 24
Institute of Aviation Medicine (IAM)
  33, 76, 107, 182, 189
Instrument Flight Rules (IFR) 46, 57,
  73, 74, 159, 200
Instrument Landing System (ILS) 34,
  110, 127, 178, 179, 258
Instruments, 70, 71, 132, 182–4, 286
International Air Transport Association
  (IATA) 206, 224
International Civil Aviation
  Organisation (ICAO) 42, 139,
  206, 224, 237, 282, 290
International Federation of Airline
  Pilots
  Association (IFALPA) 18, 139,
  154, 206, 258, 260
International Marine Organisation 282,
  287
Interruptions 204
Involvement, crew 39
IQ 8
Iran Airbus shootdown 270–4
Irwin, Flt Lt 'Bird' 248–52

Jacksonville 114
James, Henry 19, 137
Janis 259
Japan Airlines 146, 202–3, 226
Jet-lag 187, 189, 202
Joint Air-Miss Working Group 225
Judgement 15, 93, 165, 196, 213
Jung 19

Kinshelwood, James 172
KLM 32, 37, 78–86, 108, 157, 217,
  260
Köhler 55
Korean Airlines 138, 269–70
Korlins, Professor 212
Krech 156

Lack of moral fibre 186
Landing gear 56, 57–67
Lane, Doctor John 70
Lane, Geoffrey, Lord Chief Justice 261
Language 9, 41, 42, 81
Laterality 30, 43, 95, 170–85
Law Lords 164
Learning 106–18

Le Mans, Wilbur Wright demonstration
  22
Leakey, Richard 155
Leonardo da Vinci 22
Life expectancy 18
Lighting 72
Lilienthal, Otto 22
Line-Oriented Flight Training (LOFT)
  209–11
London 74, 127
Loop, the 123, 125, 129, 131
Losing face 38, 84, 142
Luchin's jar-filling test 190
Lufthansa 15, 38, 39
'Luggage' 16, 197, 218
Lund University 77

MacDonald, Ramsay 248
Machoism 13, 29, 75, 76, 90, 91, 128,
  138, 143, 239
Maclean, J. 128
Maintenance 225, 226, 227, 229, 230,
  231, 235, 256, 289
Malaysian Airline System 109
Man 7–20, 21, 57, 124, 285
Management factors 207, 208, 221–45,
  262, 286
Manchester United 260
Mandatory Occurrence Reporting 33,
  224
Marchioness 240, 261
Marine Accident Investigation Branch
  264, 286
Maritime safety 280–4
Mearth, Oscar 9
Medical checks 14, 86
Memory store 101, 106, 136, 137, 138
Mental capacity 11
Miami International Flight Academy
  209
Microbursts 24, 25
Milgram, Professor, 'electric chair'
  experiment 150
Military pilots 90
Minimum Descent Altitude (MDA) 199
Minimum Equipment List (MEL) 116,
  227
Misinterpretation 41
Montgolfier brothers 22, 227
Ministry of Civil Aviation 151

Misinterpretation 41
Monan, Captain 94
Monitoring 38, 122, 124, 126, 157, 158, 218
Moore-Brabazon, Colonel 252, 253
Moorgate train disaster 125, 142
NASA 33, 194, 257
Nahanni 88
National Transportation Safety Board (NTSB) 47, 53, 66, 105, 124, 158, 233, 237, 238, 261
Nature 9
Neanderthal man 8, 10
Near misses 53, 290
New Zealand Airline Pilots' Association 163
Nicholl, Captain Jack 107
Noise 199
Noradrenalin 10, 189
Norwegian Air Force 171
Northwest Airlines 203

Obedience 150, 151
Occurrence Digest 224
Oedipus complex 77
Origin of Species 8
Olympic Airways 74
Onassis, Alexander 177
Osipovich, Colonel 145
Overlearning 93, 108, 116, 171
Overload 86
Oxford Flying School 107
Oxygen 24, 25

Pacific Southwest Airlines 44, 45
Pair-bonding 17
Pan Am 37, 41, 78–86, 209, 210, 220, 259
Panic 38
Parachutes 24
Passengers 16, 79, 96, 134
PD factor 244
Pearson, Captain Robert 117
Pecking order 10
Peer pressure 213
Pentland, Captain Charles 152–5
Perception 30, 48, 49, 106, 144
Perkins, Sir Robert 154
Perrow, Charles 233
Personality 13

Piano stool test 25
'Pilot error' 20, 26, 27, 30, 91, 92, 129, 155, 203, 221, 260, 291
Pleistocene era 9
Politicians 145, 246–68
Popular Front for the Liberation of Palestine 276, 277
Practice 93
Presidential Task Force on Aircraft Crew Complement 268
Prestige 86
Primate 9
Princess Victoria disaster 283
Privy Council 164
Profumo, John 154, 187
Proneness to error 28
Psyche 75
Psychological profile 107
Public Inquiries 262
Public transport 135
Purley rail accident 240

Qantas 211–12, 214, 244
QFE 43
QNH 43

Radar-assisted collisions 265
Reagan Administration 267–8
Reason, Professor 135, 146, 220, 223
Redding, Gordon 244
Regression 30, 109–18
Reticular formation 49
Retrospect 214
Retribution 239
Reversed numbers 171, 177
Rezaian, Captain Mohsen 270
Richmond, Colonel 249
Risk perception 107, 218
Risk-taking 9, 77, 86, 90, 92, 246
Road Research Laboratory 265
Rogers, Captain Will 271, 272
Role-playing 216
Rome (Comet) accident 148–55
Roscoe, Professor Stanley 15, 107, 221
Rotating lights 69
Rote learning 106
Roth, Senator 226
Royal Aeronautical Society 280
Royal Air Force 14, 18, 23, 25, 28, 40,

77, 90, 91, 92, 107, 115, 125,
148, 186, 249, 261, 264
Royal Army Medical Corps 25
Royal Flying Corps 23
Royal Naval Air Service 23

Safety is No Accident 240
Saint-Exupéry, Antoine 173
Santos-Dumont 22
Scandinavian Airlines System (SAS)
119, 126
Scanning 55
Scapegoat 11, 27, 130, 258
Scientific Methods Inc. 211
Scott, Major 249, 250, 251
Seaworthiness certificate 281
Seeing 45–54
Selection, pilots, 25, 107
Self-censorship 213
Self-confidence 90
Self-image 14, 134, 135
Sensory acuity 188
Serial ordering 106
Service Bulletin (SB) 233
'Set' 47, 55–67, 190
Sex urge 18, 28
Sexual activity 17, 86
Sexual symbols 18
Sheen Inquiry 283, 284
Shun, Emperor 21
Shute, Neville 248
Sidestick 128
Sightseeing flights 162
Silverback 17, 38
Simon, Sir John 247, 251
Simulators 27, 107, 108, 115, 213
Simulator checks 14, 39, 86
Singapore Airlines 211–12
Skill rhythm 93
Skill sequence 93, 94
Sleep 17, 18, 188, 189, 190, 193, 194,
195
Slips 129, 146–7, 180, 207, 208, 238
Slush 32
Smithsonian Institution 11
Social group 10
South America 90
Spanish Civil Aviation Authority 85
Speed error 120–3

Spontaneity 16
Spooner, Captain Tony 187
Stabiliser trim 167
Stall Warning System 126, 127, 134,
154
Stalling 147, 153, 155, 182, 230, 243
Standardisation 42
Startle reaction 137
Stickshaker 103, 181, 230, 243
Stimulation 132, 133
Strangers 34
Stress 16, 18, 19, 49, 58, 86, 88, 89,
93, 94, 95, 102, 107, 110, 112,
114, 126, 129, 171, 174, 180,
185, 186–203, 218
Stroop test 190
Stultz, Wilmer 14
Superego 75
Supervising 125
Surgeons 157
Surinam Airways 201
Survival Studies Group 262
Swedish Air Force Defence Mechanism
Test 77
Swift Aire Lines 177
Swissair 217, 258
Synergy 211

Tait, Air Vice-Marshal Victor 153
Taylor, Captain Laurie 192
Teacher/learner concept 208
Teamwork 37
Tebbit, Norman 167
Technology 19
Tench, Bill 240, 264, 265
Terceira (Azores) accident, turned
wrong way 174, 175
Terminal Control Area (TCA) 52, 53
Terminal Control Radar Service Area
(TCRSA) 45, 52, 53
Test pilots 130
Thain, Captain James 259–61
Theory of Evolution 21
Thernhem, Captain 126
Thomson, Rt Hon. Lord 247, 249–52
Thought transference 9
Time of day 189
Time pressure 16, 78, 79, 86, 102, 110,
200–1, 213, 255
Time zones 13, 31, 142, 188, 189, 194

Times, The 22, 23
Tiredness 49, 188
Tool-making 9
Training 19, 20, 56, 59, 184, 206, 222, 254, 255, 256
Transposition error 177
Transworld Airlines 42
Trial-and-error learning 106
Trippe, Juan 279
Turkey 90

Unanimity 39, 213
Uncertainty 79
Undercarriage 56, 57, 58, 59, 60
United Airlines 59, 108, 158, 164, 208, 230
United States Air Force (USAF) 18, 90, 91, 92, 160
Unmanned Machinery Space (UMS) 282

Varig 242
Vertigo 69
Vibration 180, 235, 236
Vibration Indicators 180, 182–5

Vincennes 271–4
VIPs 79
Visibility, cockpit 50, 51
Vision, mental 94
   physical 29, 45–53, 55
Visual Flight Rules (VFR) 45, 46, 49, 71, 73, 74, 87, 162, 200
Volcanic dust 15

War 19
Warburton, Adrian 86
Weather 87, 254
Wertheimer 55
Whiteout 161
Wiener, Professor E. 130
Wilberforce, Bishop 8
Wind, Sand and Stars 173
Windscreen reflection 72
Windshear 24, 257
Women pilots 14, 76, 77
Woodworth 74
Word-blindness 172
Wolfe, Tom 13
Workload 125, 128, 129, 186, 196
Wright brothers 21, 22, 23, 81

Zeigarnik effect 88, 201, 218